THE FIRST WACO HORROR

Number 101:

Centennial Series of the Association of Former Students

Texas A&M University

DATE DUE

THE FIRST
WACO
HORROR

The Lynching of
Jesse Washington and
the Rise of the NAACP

PATRICIA BERNSTEIN

TEXAS A&M UNIVERSITY PRESS
College Station

Library of Congress Cataloging-in-Publication Data

Bernstein, Patricia, 1944–
The first Waco Horror : the lynching of Jesse Washington and
the rise of the NAACP / Patricia Bernstein—1st ed.
p. cm. — (Centennial series of the Association of Former
Students, Texas A&M University ; no. 101.)
Includes bibliographic references (p.   ) and index.
ISBN–10: 1-58544-416-2 (cloth : alk. paper)
ISBN–13: 978-1-58544-544-8 (pbk.)
ISBN–10: 1-58544-544-4 (pbk.)
1. Washington, Jesse.   2. Lynching—Texas—Waco—History—20th century.
3. Murder—Texas—Waco—History—20th century.   4. National Association for the
Advancement of Colored People—History—20th century.   5. United States—Race
relations.   I. Title.   II. Series.
HV6465.T4B47 2005
364.152'3'09764284—dc22
2004016120

To Leo J. Hoffman, my darling dad,
who first tried to convince me that Texas
history was actually interesting.

Doing history [is] an act of responsibility to the future.

—James Carroll, *Constantine's Sword: The Church and the Jews, A History*

CONTENTS

ACKNOWLEDGMENTS

This book would have been impossible without the help of many, beginning with the good people of Waco. Their generosity and kindness in sharing information and time with a stranger was a continuing source of delight and has immeasurably enriched this book. I mention in particular, and with much gratitude, Nona Baker, "Lucy Bee" Wollitz Kirkland, Lawrence Johnson, Nannette Booker Hutchison, John and Kenneth Frazier, Mildred Richter, Martha Kettler, Bill Wuebker, Thomas Hague, John McNamara Jr., Mary Kemendo Sendon, J. B. Smith (reporter for the *Waco Tribune Herald*), and James SoRelle, chairman of the history department at Baylor University. It was Professor SoRelle's insightful article, "The 'Waco Horror,'" that first alerted me to the facts and ramifications of the Jesse Washington story.

My thanks to the residents of Waco would be incomplete without a special thank-you to Bruce and Dorothy Dyer, hosts at the Judge Baylor House Bed & Breakfast, who became almost my second family while I was researching the lynching of Jesse Washington and who offered their help with Waco contacts. It was through them that I met ninety-nine-year-old Mary Kemendo Sendon.

Many librarians were extremely generous with their time. The staff at the marvelous Texas Collection at Baylor University was particularly excellent, especially Kent Keeth, the director, who went out of his way to offer me very useful unpublished material and to find and reproduce a 1913 map of Waco for me.

Other remarkably helpful librarians include the very patient Roxanne Dolen at Houston Public Library; Ann McGuffin Barton at the Woman's Collection, Texas Woman's University Library; Jim Moske at the Manuscripts and Archives Division of the New York Public Library; Doris Popoff and Winnie Ragsdale at the Altadena Library District in California, who actually visited a cemetery in Altadena on my behalf to look for the grave of Elisabeth Freeman; Ellen Shea, reference librarian at the Schlesinger Library, Radcliffe Institute for Advanced Study, Harvard University, who pointed out important sources of information on Elisabeth Freeman; Stephanie Malmros, registrar, Center for American History, University of Texas at Austin; William Kopplin, assistant head of reference at the Perry-Castañeda Library, University of Texas at Austin; Wendy Thomas, humanities librarian at the Women's Library in the United

Kingdom; Susan Halpert, reference librarian, and her staff at the Houghton Library, Harvard University; Mike Kelsey at the Temple, Texas, Public Library, who tracked down information on the 1915 lynching of Will Stanley; Liz Triplett, reference librarian at the Richmond, Virginia, Public Library; Jerry Smith and Charles Browne at the Broome County Library in Binghamton, New York; Bill Buckner at the Waco–McLennan County Library, who traced clues that helped me finally discover what became of Sheriff Sam Fleming; Janice E. Ruth, women's history specialist at the Library of Congress, who identified important materials pertaining to Elisabeth Freeman; Sheridan Harvey, women's studies specialist in the Humanities and Social Sciences Division of the Library of Congress; and Cristel Schmidt, of the Motion Picture, Broadcasting and Recorded Sound Division of the Library of Congress, who kindly obtained a copy of the Edison Kinetoscope "Votes for Women" for me. Thanks also to Kathleen Sabogal, Carnegie Hall archivist.

I want to particularly thank Julie Buckner Armstrong, professor of English at the University of South Florida–St. Petersburg, with whom I spent the better part of an afternoon and an evening talking about lynchings and especially the painfully tragic tale of Mary Turner. Julie was very generous in allowing me to use material from her paper on Mary Turner.

Many thanks also go to Rogers Melton Smith, who recorded priceless interviews with Wacoans now long dead in his Master's thesis at Baylor University. Thanks also to Katherine Walters, who generously shared invaluable information on George Fryer's libel suits against various defendants associated with the *Paul Quinn Weekly*, which reprinted the *Chicago Defender* story claiming that Fryer had been arrested for killing his wife. Walters's Master's thesis on race relations in Waco and the battle against the white primary contains much information that was extremely helpful.

My office staff — Marie Wright, Mary Polnau, Christy Penders, and Therese Paul — are amazing. My research trips and many aspects of putting this book together would have been impossible without their wonderfully reliable assistance.

And, of course, above and beyond all, my family — Alan, Jessica, and Rebecca — who were so patient with and understanding of all the inconveniences caused by this long-term effort and who, with Katherine, make it all worthwhile.

THE FIRST WACO HORROR

INTRODUCTION

In April 1995, Lawrence Johnson, black city councilman from Waco, Texas, visited Memphis to attend the National Conference of Black Mayors. While he was there, he took the time to see the National Civil Rights Museum. Built around the remains of the Lorraine Motel, where Dr. Martin Luther King Jr. was shot in 1968, the museum is designed, like the Holocaust Museum in Washington, D.C., to take the visitor on a journey. The museum leads visitors through the history of the abuse heaped on black Americans over more than three hundred years and the long, grinding struggle to win equal treatment. Visitors see the tarnished hulk of a burned Freedom Riders bus from the 1960s and a complete re-creation of a Woolworth's lunch counter where young black students protested segregation by "sitting in" while they were beaten, taunted, and splattered with ketchup and mustard. One can even step into an actual Montgomery, Alabama, city bus and hear a recording of a bus driver angrily ordering black riders to "move to the rear."

But in one corner of the museum, in a display about the lynching of almost five thousand Americans, most of them black, between 1880 and 1930, Lawrence Johnson spotted a photograph that sears the sight of the viewer. The picture Lawrence Johnson saw is infamous among historians who study early-twentieth-century America. It has appeared in many books about lynching and in at least one history of Waco. This photo is still not well known to most Americans, though it should be as familiar as the flag raising on Iwo Jima in 1945, the image of the *Hindenburg* airship bursting into flame over Lakehurst, New Jersey, in 1937, or the Pulitzer Prize–winning photograph of a naked, weeping Vietnamese girl fleeing a napalm bomb in 1972. The picture Lawrence Johnson saw, taken by Waco commercial photographer Fred Gildersleeve, is one of the few extant photographs of a lynching caught in progress rather than after the fact.[1]

At first, the picture appears to be nothing more than a group of hundreds of men crowded into a city square, almost all of them wearing the flat-crowned straw "boater" hats that were popular in the summer of 1916. This ocean of flat-brimmed white hats is lapping against a scraggly little tree in the center of the square.

Only when you look closer do you see a fuzzy area in the center of the picture, below the tree, like a ribbon of smoke. And then, through the smoke, you can just make out . . . a leg, a foot, an elbow. A naked human being lies collapsed at the bottom of the tree on top of a smoldering pile of slats and kindling. Around his neck is a chain, which stretches up over a branch of the tree.

A man in a white shirt with a dark fedora mashed down on his head stands by the folded-up body, yanking on one end of the chain. He is wearing a heavy glove on the hand that holds the chain because it has been heated by the fire and is hot. This self-appointed executioner may have been caught in the act of jerking the blistered creature below the tree upright against the tree trunk in order to display him to the mob. Or perhaps he has just lowered his victim back into the fire. In the meantime, another man in white shirt and light-colored hat is poking and prodding the dying man with a stick or rod of some kind, almost as if he is trying to turn the body on the fire. The onlookers watch intently. Some appear to be smiling or shouting encouragement to the torturers.

After standing transfixed for a moment before the picture, Lawrence Johnson read the caption and learned to his amazement that this particular lynching had taken place in Waco, Texas, his hometown, on May 15, 1916. The caption also explains that the mayor of Waco, who watched the entire episode from an excellent vantage point on the second floor of City Hall, was concerned that the lynchers might damage the tree but expressed no concern for the human being who was stabbed, beaten, mutilated, hanged, and burned to death before his eyes.[2]

Lawrence Johnson had lived in Waco all of his life but had never heard of the lynching of Jesse Washington. When he returned home, he went to the library and found the whole story on microfilm as it was reported in Waco's newspapers of the day. He also found the tale of Jesse Washington, entitled "The Waco Horror," described in detail in a July 1916 supplement to *The Crisis*, a monthly magazine published by the National Association for the Advancement of Colored People (NAACP).

In May 1998, Johnson shocked the city of Waco and other city council members by reading the story of the lynching of Jesse Washington, as described at the time in unblinking detail in the *Waco Times Herald*, during his swearing-in for a fifth term as city councilman. He further stunned his audience by demanding that city officials formally denounce the 1916 lynching and commission some kind of monument or memorial that would describe and disavow what had happened. The lynching was a city-condoned event, Johnson said; the mayor and police chief watched and did nothing. It was up to the city to make amends.[3]

To date, however, although Central Texas is sprinkled with historical markers of all kinds, although Texas history has enshrined the stories of other episodes of cruelty (the Alamo, for example, the sacred monument to the massacre of at least 189 "Texians" by Santa Anna's army, is visited by about three million people annually),[4] there is no monument, plaque, or marker anywhere commemorating or apologizing for the 1916 torture-murder of seventeen-year-old Jesse Washington before a crowd of ten thousand to fifteen thousand cheering Wacoans.

The sadistic nature of the crime and the enthusiastic participation of thousands of spectators are plain in the photograph described above and in others taken by commercial photographer Fred Gildersleeve that day. Even in the vast bloodbath of lynchings that washed across the South and the Midwest during the late 1800s and the early 1900s, the Waco lynching stands out. There were so-called race riots in other cities, large and small, in which dozens of black people were injured or killed and whole black neighborhoods destroyed.[5] There were also other supremely hideous lynchings of individuals and small groups of people, but most of these took place in small towns, rural areas, or out in the woods. The Waco Horror — public torture treated as a thrilling spectacle by thousands in a well-established modern city with some pretensions to culture and enlightenment — was unique.

Yet the story behind the killing of Jesse Washington has up to now been largely unexplored beyond periodic brief mentions in histories chronicling the mistreatment of blacks in America, a few scholarly articles, and the eight-page discussion in the July 1916 issue of *The Crisis*. How could such a medieval barbarity possibly have taken place in our own nation *within the memory of persons still living*, in front of many educated, middle-class people who enjoyed all the comforts of the modern age, including automobiles, ready-made clothing, telephones, and public libraries?

The true story of the lynching of Jesse Washington, told here at length for the first time, is not a simple one. Villains appear in this tale, as do unsung heroes, although, unfortunately, no heroes stepped forward in Waco on May 15, 1916. One heroine, in particular, plays a major role in the story and undeniably risked her own safety to make sure that Jesse Washington's tragic end and the circumstances around it were recorded and spread abroad. And there were genuine American heroes in the young NAACP — "cranks," as Clarence Darrow styled them, mostly white, who simply would not sit down and shut up anymore and allow the abuse of black Americans to continue without raising carefully orchestrated hell about it.[6]

In the summer of 1916, these three disparate forces — a vibrant, growing city bursting with optimism on the blackland prairie of Central Texas; a young woman already tempered in the front-line battles for women's suffrage; and a very small organization of grimly determined "progressives" in New York City — collided, with consequences no one could have foreseen. They were brought irrevocably together by the public murder following prolonged torture of a black Waco teenager named Jesse Washington — the atrocity that became known as the Waco Horror.

CHAPTER I

"ALERT, PUSHING, AND RICH"

The Setting of the Waco Horror

In other words, Waco is a typical
southern town, alert, pushing, and rich.

—*The Crisis*

THE setting for the Waco Horror was no dusty little dump of a town, no
Tumbleweed Junction sprung up at an isolated crossroads. Waco's first
city block was laid out in March 1849 at the confluence of the Bosque
and the Brazos rivers, in good farming country on the blackland prairie, about
halfway between Dallas and Austin. The land thereabouts was so fertile that the
Huaco Indians, for whom Waco Village was named, cultivated corn and peach
trees at the site before they were driven out in the 1820s by the Cherokee.[1]

By 1916, however, Waco was no longer a mere village. It was a prosperous
city of over thirty thousand souls.[2] In the previous year, McLennan County,
the countryside surrounding Waco, had produced the second-highest number
of cotton bales in the entire state: 24,017 against the Hill County's 26,191.[3] But
this local cotton production was only a small portion of the cotton that passed
through Waco. In 1916, the town, neatly situated at the vertex of seven railroad
lines, claimed to be the largest inland, or "wagon," cotton market in the country, producing over one million bales annually.[4]

Map of Waco, Texas, and Suburbs, 1913. Waco, McCall-Moore Engineering Co., 1913.

MAP OF
WACO, TEXAS
AND SUBURBS
Compiled from County Records and Private Surveys
by
McCALL-MOORE ENGINEERING CO.
CIVIL AND CONTRACTING ENGINEERS
WACO, TEXAS.
Aug. 1, 1913.

REFERENCES

CITY LIMITS
RAIL ROAD
STREET CAR
INTERURBAN
1-46 FARM LOTS
½ HALF-MILE CIRCLES
WITH 8TH & AUSTIN
ST. AS CENTER

Copyright 1913 by H.S. McCALL, BART MOORE, JR.

More notably, even in the age of King Cotton and in the heart of Texas cotton country, the Waco economy was no one-trick pony. In 1916, over two hundred manufacturing operations produced cottonseed oil[5] — yes — but also sashes and doors, bank and store fixtures, clothing, welding machinery, mattresses, structural iron, boilers, and iceless refrigerators, among other items, including Dr Pepper soda, which was invented and first mass-produced in Waco.

The town boasted sixty-three churches, seven railways, nine banks with assets of over seven million dollars, seventy-five miles of paved streets, ten parks with a total of 255 acres, seventeen public schools (thirteen white and four "colored"), and several institutions of higher learning, including two "colored" colleges and Baylor University, which, with two thousand students, was one of the largest universities in the state.[6]

In addition to numerous businessmen's clubs, country clubs, and lodges, Waco had several genteel ladies' clubs, including chapters of the Daughters of the American Revolution, Daughters of the Confederacy, and Daughters of the Republic of Texas, a Humane Society, the Waco Shakespeare Club, the Woman's Club of Waco (dedicated to self-improvement under the motto: "If I rest, I rust"), and the Waco Federation of Women's Clubs — plus more sternly activist organizations like a chapter of the Woman's Christian Temperance Union, and a group working for women's suffrage.[7]

Waco even had the beginnings of a modern skyline in the first skyscraper in the state, the twenty-two-story Amicable Life Insurance Building, completed in 1911. The Amicable was originally planned to be twenty stories high, but the Adolphus Hotel in Dallas was being built at the same time and, when the builders of the Amicable heard that the Adolphus was also to be twenty stories high, they immediately added an additional floor to the Amicable. When the Adolphus Hotel then added a twenty-first story, the height of the Amicable was raised to twenty-two stories. At that point, the developers of the Adolphus threw in the towel. Waco and Waco alone would boast the distinction of having the tallest building in the state of Texas.[8]

To celebrate the completion of the Amicable, the Young Men's Business League held a Prosperity Banquet on April 10, 1911, in the middle of South Fifth Street between Austin and Franklin. Hundreds of guests sat at four long tables and enjoyed such delicacies as "oyster cocktail à la prosperity" and "consommé à la Amicable," ending with "mints, cigars and Dr Pepper," while they listened to speakers. The program featured Mayor J. H. Mackey enthusing on the theme "Watch Waco Grow." "Waco boosters," said a much-later newspaper account, "knew the old town was going to be the center of the universe in a few more years."[9]

The Amicable Life Insurance Building (now called the Alico) still stands in downtown Waco, having withstood the 1953 tornado. The only skyscraper ever built in the city, it is a relic of an age when anything seemed possible and the future seemed to beckon Waco like the opening of a golden door.

In 1916, Waco had many complimentary names for itself, including the "Wonder City" and the "Convention City."[10] One of the most commonly used, however, was the "Athens of Texas," because of Waco's many educational institutions.[11]

Wacoans' notion, however, that the city was widely regarded as a center of culture and refinement was no empty delusion. The *Houston Chronicle*, published in a city three times the size of Waco — even in a scathing editorial about the lynching of Jesse Washington — referred to Waco, without any irony intended, as "the cultured, reputable City of Waco."[12]

The heart of early-twentieth-century Waco was the tree-studded central square around City Hall, an imposing two-story building with an elaborate cupola featuring large clocks facing all four sides of the square. In 1916, automobiles were beginning to replace horse and buggy rigs in the streets of Waco, but farmers still came to the square in horse-drawn wagons to market their fruit, vegetables, hay, and cotton.

On the first Monday of the month, for many years, anyone with a mind to dicker could bring a horse or mule to sell or trade on the north side of the square. On the south side were iron benches where elderly men congregated to discuss the Bible and other weighty subjects. One of the trees under which they held their discussions came to be known as "the Tree of Knowledge" because of their endless disputations. In one of these trees was a small box containing a Bible, which the debaters referred to in the course of their arguments.[13]

In the spirit of the rampant boosterism of the time, as early as 1912, representatives of Waco were trying to stimulate interest in trade with the city by visiting and distributing information as far away as Toronto.[14] In a 1910 article, the secretary of the Waco Business Men's Club bragged that "the 1910 census will show Waco to be a city of at least 34,000 inhabitants, all of whom are making money as fast as is good for the ordinary mortal."[15]

All of this sounds homey and comfortable and jam-packed with the naïve optimism and absolute faith in the positive benefits of commerce that characterized many a growing American town in the early part of the twentieth

Waco City Hall, circa 1912. *Courtesy* Archives Division of The Texas Collection, Baylor University, Waco, Texas.

century. But the town that bragged in the 1916 telephone directory about having "the cleanest and best-sprinkled streets of any city in the state" also had a long history of violence,[16] which had earned it, some say, in addition to nicknames like "the City with a Soul" (because of its many churches),[17] the older and less-flattering sobriquet of "Six-Shooter Junction."[18]

Whether the name Six-Shooter Junction was in actual use or not, the violence of Waco's past is undeniable. In the beginning there was fierce fighting periodically between Anglo settlers and Native Americans; during the 1860s and the 1870s, the area south of Waco was called the "Dead Line" because it was so rife with outlaws and robbers that no one dared go that way if he or she was likely to be suspected of carrying money.[19] The entire region was infamous for decades. Historian Richard Maxwell Brown once commented that "no region [in the United States] . . . has surpassed the acute, long-term violence of central Texas."[20]

The famous cattle drive route, the Chisholm Trail, or southern extensions of it, and another cattle drive route called the Shawnee Trail ran through or close to Waco.[21] Maybe it was partly the city's desire to accommodate the cow-boys that contributed to the decision of Waco authorities in 1889 to establish Texas' first legally licensed red-light district. The "Reservation," as it was called, was only the second prostitution district allowed to operate legally in the entire United States, following in the footsteps of—of all places, Omaha, Nebraska. Houston, Dallas, Fort Worth, Galveston, Austin, and El Paso all followed Waco's example and established districts of legalized prostitution for a time during the early 1900s.[22]

Before 1889, prostitutes were identified as "actresses" in the Waco city directory. Afterwards, they were simply identified as female residents of North Second Street, which locals, with a wink, called "Two Street." For more than twenty-five years, the venerable, high-minded, and very Baptist Baylor University was located on one side of the central business district while the prostitutes freely practiced their trade on the other side.[23] The shameless hypocrisy of the social setup is illustrated by the fact that prominent Waco men did not dare drive their own buggy rigs and park them in front of houses on Two Street, for fear they would be recognized. So they parked their conveyances elsewhere and rented rigs from a livery stable to go to the Reservation and back.[24]

In 1916, at the time that the Jesse Washington lynching took place, the Reservation was still going strong. Legalized prostitution was not ended until the following year, when the U.S. Army let Waco know that no military base would be established there as long as the innocence of young soldiers was endangered by the Reservation.

In addition to a designated area for legalized prostitution, in pre-Prohibition 1916, Waco had sixty-nine saloons to counterbalance the sixty-three churches. C. T. Caldwell, longtime pastor of Waco's First Presbyterian Church (who will make a brief appearance later in this book as a rare voice of conscience in Waco), once commented that when he came to Waco in 1903, "saloons were on nearly every corner. City politics was of a brand that was dangerous to engage in."[25]

Certainly there was no shortage of whiskey in Waco, despite the local power and influence of the Baptists. In fact, one of the most notorious outlaws of Texas song and story enjoyed an evening at one of Waco's saloons a matter of days before he died. Sam Bass, outlaw and train robber, visited Waco on a July evening in 1878 and paid for a round of drinks at the Ranch Saloon for himself and one of his pals with an 1877 gold double eagle, the last of three thousand he and his gang had seized in the Union Pacific train robbery in Big Springs, Nebraska.[26] A few days later, on July 21, Bass's short, bad life ended in Round Rock, Texas, in a shootout with Texas Rangers. It was his twenty-seventh birthday.[27]

Well into the early part of the twentieth century, it was accepted conduct in Waco for men to carry guns. "Where all men are armed, conflicts among them are inevitable and the violent death of some is certain," said one of Texas' most famous historians, Walter Prescott Webb.[28] Life in turn-of-the-century Waco confirmed that axiom. Public shoot-outs of the gunfight-at-the-OK-Corral variety occurred on the streets of Waco. County Judge George "Big Sandy" Gerald, a colonel in the Civil War who had led a regiment at Gettysburg, was known for absolute integrity along with a powerful streak of untamed irascibility. Of all his notable antics, Judge Gerald is most famous for fighting a gun battle on the streets of downtown Waco in the middle of the day against two younger opponents and killing them both.

The quarrel began with Gerald's attempt to publish a letter in the *Waco Times Herald* defending the intensely controversial editor William Cowper Brann (of whom, more in a moment). Jim Harris, editor of the *Times Herald*, refused to publish the letter or to return it to Gerald. In response, Gerald circulated a handbill accusing Harris of all manner of misdeeds. Thereupon, Harris and his brother William ambushed Gerald at the intersection of Fourth and Austin on the edge of the main square.

Although Gerald was much older than the two brothers and was wounded so badly in the initial attack that his left arm had to be amputated, he succeeded in killing both Harrises. He was charged with murder but was acquitted by a jury nine months later. It was *after* this episode that he was elected to his second term as county judge.[29]

Dramatic though it was, the Gerald/Harris war was merely a satellite of the primary conflagration engrossing Waco at the time: the battle between William Cowper Brann and Baylor University. Brann, a highly eccentric journalist who had been fired from other newspapers because of his rabidly independent, quarrelsome nature, settled in Waco and, after a brief tenure on the staff of the *Waco Daily News*, made a second attempt to publish his own "journal of personal protest" called *The Iconoclast*. *The Iconoclast* specialized in unrestrained literary assault on anyone Brann did not like.

In Waco, Brann experienced the only real success he ever knew. *The Iconoclast* caught on and eventually reached an audience of close to 100,000 per issue, selling far beyond Waco. In an era in which sources of public entertainment were limited, reading *The Iconoclast* was sort of a literary version of watching the World Wrestling Federation today. It was thrilling for spectators to open up a new issue and find out whom Brann had chosen to pound on this time and how he would go about doing it.

Brann's overheated sarcasm is evident in a description of Waco: "Her streets are so smooth that a mountain goat can traverse them with comparative ease, and so clean that it is seldom a mule gets lost in the mud. The tax rate is so low that if your property be well located you can usually persuade the collector to accept it as partial payment . . . that we are making rapid progress is evidenced by the fact that a tree on which only 37 men have been hanged, is now regarded with a species of awe by the younger natives."[30]

Brann targeted people and institutions that seemed to him to be particularly fraudulent, pretentious, or hypocritical. His favorite target during his short career as perpetrator of The Iconoclast was Baylor University, an institution that he considered to be the very apex of hypocrisy. The battle between Baylor and Brann reached a climax when Brann began to apply his special brand of public ridicule to a scandal involving a young Brazilian girl who came to Baylor University, stayed in the home of the august president, Dr. Rufus Burleson, and ended up unwed and pregnant. She publicly accused the brother of Burleson's son-in-law of having raped her.[31] In the process of attempting to peel back the layers of sanctimony covering the corruption at the heart of the institution, as he saw it, Brann went as far as to imply that sexual immorality was a general problem at Baylor.

This time Brann had gone too far. In October 1897, he was abducted by a group of Baylor students who threatened to hang him; a few days later, he was violently caned by the father and brother of a female teacher at Baylor. But Brann was unbowed. He bragged about the assaults he had endured and continued to deride his assailants and Baylor in print, daring them to attack him again. The Gerald/Harris duel in November of that same year only intensified the controversy.

Finally, on April 1, 1898, one infuriated Wacoan decided, once and for all, to rid the world of William Cowper Brann. Tom Davis, a local real estate man and son of one of Waco's pioneers, could have been motivated by any of several possible complaints when he made his decision to go gunning for Brann. His sister was a teacher at Baylor. In addition, Brann had dredged up and printed in The Iconoclast an old accusation that Davis, in his wild younger days, might have been involved in a stage holdup at Lampasas, Texas. Davis was also interested in going into local politics and may have thought that killing Brann would earn him a lot of Baptist votes.

The moment of truth arrived when Brann and a friend passed Davis standing outside of his real estate office on South Fourth Street on the afternoon of April 1, and Brann may (eyewitness accounts vary) have cursed Davis under his breath as he passed. Davis proceeded to pull his gun and shoot Brann in the back, right where his suspenders crossed. Brann whirled, drew his own gun, and began to fire bullets into Davis. Before Davis fell, he got off another shot. Stray bullets wounded a streetcar motorman and a black passerby.

When the police chief arrived, Davis was on the ground and Brann was still standing. The police chief seized Brann and began to march him to City Hall, but by the time they arrived, blood from Brann's wounds had filled up his shoes. Brann was taken to his home and died there in the middle of the night. Davis died the following afternoon.

A huge crowd attended Brann's funeral, but, even after his death, a Wacoan who was apparently still angry at him took a potshot at the bas-relief profile of the editor on his monument in Oakwood Cemetery.[32]

The Brann/Davis duel and the Gerald/Harris gunfight were only two of the more spectacular killings in Waco around the turn of the twentieth century. There were even shootings in the courtroom during trials. As late as 1922, in fact, a complaining witness shot a defendant to death during a trial in Waco's 54th District Court. Seventeen-year-old Marcie Matthews was about to take the witness stand in a trial for criminal assault when she pulled out a revolver and shot defendant J. S. Crosslin three times. "He disgraced me, ruined my health and deprived me of an education," she told a reporter afterward, "but he will never ruin another girl."[33]

Beyond the comic-opera feuds and courtroom shootouts, there was also a vicious tradition of mob violence in the country around Waco. East Texas lay right on the fault line where the casual violence of the frontier met the mad-dog racism of the Deep South. Between 1880 and 1930, approximately 4,697 lynchings took place in the United States. About 3,344 of those lynched were black. Nearly 500 of these lynchings took place in Texas.[34] Lynchings and attempted lynchings of black people were common, and some of the most hideous lynchings on record took place in the East-Central Texas area.

There is explicit evidence in print that illustrates precisely how Waco's whites felt about their darker-skinned neighbors. The *City Directory for Waco* published in 1876 expresses the general sentiment clearly, if a bit indirectly: "Our population is made up of immigrants from every State in the Union . . . Nor will you come among ignorant and debased people; for general intelligence, industry, sobriety and enterprise, the citizenship of our county (*barring, of course, those recently held in bondage*) will not suffer in comparison with the citizenship of any inland community of the same size in America."[35]

Waco's newspapers, like those of many other towns during this period, kept up a daily drumbeat of articles that depicted black people as either criminals or fools. Typical headlines from two Waco newspapers during the two months preceding the Waco Horror include the following: "Negro Suspect Is Caught by Falls County Officers"; "Negro Has Small Chance of Get-Away"; "Negro Arrested and $385 in Gold Found under Barn"; "Negro Woman Wanted in Marlin Arrested Here"; "Cow Killed, Hide Sold and Negroes Arrested"; "Negroes Break Jail at Longview and Escape"; "Negro Lad Entices Newsie and Robs Him"; "Quick Work Made of Oklahoma Negro"; "Riot Narrowly Averted When Negro Kills Sailor and Marine at Norfolk"; "Negro Is Scheduled to Be Hanged Here within Sixty Days"; "'Too Much Noise' Says Negro, and Begins Shooting"; and "This Negro's Middle Name Is Trouble."[36]

Anyone who was a regular reader of these papers would conclude that black people were mostly idle, conscienceless, natural-born criminals who could barely manage to stay out of trouble for five minutes at a stretch. And, if they were not criminals, they were idiots whose primary function in life was providing comic relief for white folks. Even supposedly respectable black professionals and businessmen were slicked up only for company; their true nature, the headlines implied, would inevitably out, as in "Bag of Yellow Gold Proved Too Much for Negro Banker."[37]

Of course, one can legitimately question whether newspaper coverage of black people stimulated and intensified racism or merely expressed the racism that was already there. One of the issues to be examined in more detail later in this book is the degree to which the more intelligent, more educated, more powerful members of the Waco community, including the newspapermen, were responsible for the Waco Horror.

Positive items on the black community did appear in the newspapers here and there — a story about graduation exercises at Paul Quinn College, for example — but they were infrequent compared with the incessantly negative coverage.[38] A favorable article such as "Aged Negro Saves Nearly Hundred Lives on Train" or "Negro Pays Bill and Joke Is Not on Dick Smith" is, in fact, so rare (and usually so condescending) that it seems to shimmer for an instant and then vanish, leaving no lasting impression, like a silver coin thrown into a pool of muddy water.[39]

Probably no one in the history of the city ever expressed himself in print quite as forcefully on the subject of black people as the aforementioned William Cowper Brann. Brann, the same Brann who defended Jews, who took up the cause of Catholics in an age of anti-Catholic fervor, whose sympathies were often with the despised and the downtrodden, could not find it in his heart to defend the former slaves. In fact, the very first issue of *The Iconoclast* in Waco featured a venomous spew of overwrought racist rhetoric:

> I once severely shocked the pseudo-philanthropists by suggesting that if the South is ever to rid herself of the Negro rape-fiend she must take a day off and kill every member of the accursed race that declines to leave the country . . . We have tried the restraining influence of religion and the elevating forces of education without avail . . . but the despoilment of white women by these brutal imps of darkness and the devil is still of daily occurrence . . . The Negro is, for a verity, the Bete Noire of the South, a millstone about her neck, tending ever to drag her down into the depths of social and political degradation . . . The Negro will remain right where he is, wear the cast off clothes of the white man, steal his fowls, black his boots, rape his daughters, while the syphilitic "yaller" gal corrupts his sons. Yes, the Negro will stay, stay until he is faded out by fornication — until he is absorbed by the stronger race, as it has absorbed many a foul thing heretofore.[40]

Brann's verbal rhapsodies of hatred did not disturb his readers; they may even have helped sell his papers. For his attacks on blacks, Brann's readers applauded him. For his attacks on Baylor and Baptists, they kidnapped him, assaulted him, and finally killed him.

That fact, though it outrages modern sensibilities, should not be surprising, given the times. All across the country in the early part of the twentieth century, racism and bigotry directed at various ethnic groups, and particularly at blacks, were common and interwoven with every day's events and conversations at the most trivial and the most sublime levels.

In the South, in the aftermath of emancipation and Reconstruction, and in parts of the Midwest, where blacks were sometimes viewed as an economic threat to white laborers, the hatred of black people was simply more naked and more unrestrained than elsewhere, close to the bone and continually close to the razor edge of violence. If the genteel classes disdained black people, the lower classes regarded lynchings of alleged black malefactors as a morally defensible form of free entertainment, available at a moment's notice.

But Waco was supposed to be different. Waco was supposed to be more refined than other towns. Oscar Emil Hessdoerfer, a Waco grocer for over forty years, expressed Waco's sense of itself with a certain mischievous glee: "Waco was a kind of a — oh, I think it was a little bit more societylike than a lot of small towns and they had a lot of people that thought highly and acted mannerly and everything."[41] Waco was supposed to behave itself better than surrounding communities; Waco had a different image of itself.

In fact, Waco's exaggerated sense of class distinctions, which accompanied the drive toward gentrification, expressed itself in insults and ostracism directed at anyone who was different, not just at blacks. Mary Kemendo Sendon, born in Waco in 1901, was the daughter of an Italian immigrant and grew up in a neighborhood of immigrants. The Kemendos had neighbors who were Mexican, Jewish, Irish, German, Italian, and Czech.

As Sendon approached school age, she grew more and more excited at the prospect of meeting new children to play with, but when she finally arrived at her primary school, she was rejected by the children of native-born families because her father was an immigrant. The only children who would associate with her in elementary school were two other girls from immigrant families, one German and one Irish. Mary was taunted with the epithet "Dago." The Irish girl was called a "Mick," and the German girl was addressed as "Sauerkraut."

The discrimination continued through high school. In those days, said Sendon, the senior prom was an elaborate party held at the private home of a wealthy member of the graduating class. But when invitations were sent out to the prom, Mary and five other girls, one German, one Irish and three Mexican, were not invited. When Sendon told her family what had happened, her mother promptly invited all five girls to the Kemendo home for a special dinner on the night of the prom. After dinner each girl was given $1.00 to ride downtown on the streetcar, go to a movie, and finish the evening with a visit to the Palace of Sweets. "And that," said Sendon, "was our prom."[42]

But there is no need to depend on a few isolated stories or hints or on fragments of local writing to get a feeling for what Wacoans thought about immigrants, black people, mob violence, or much of anything else. Few towns have had their local mores, customs, and foibles more thoroughly and mercilessly recorded than Waco with the appearance in 1952 of what was at the time of its publication the longest novel ever published in book form, the 1,731-page *Sironia, Texas*, by Waco native son Madison Cooper Jr.[43] Cooper, a lifelong resident of Waco, with the exception of his college years at the University of Texas and his service during World War I, claimed all his life that "Sironia" was not Waco.[44] But since Waco was all he knew, it is unlikely that *Sironia, Texas*, was inspired by Peoria, Grovers Corners, or Xanadu.

With all due deference to historian and journalist A. C. Greene, who included *Sironia, Texas*, in his list of the fifty best books on Texas, *Sironia* is not a good book.[45] It is not even a good read in the spirit of, say, *Gone with the Wind*. It is spectacularly overwritten, in terms of both length and style. Plot turns in *Sironia* are so improbable and abrupt as to be either hilarious or surreal. Yet, in its own way, *Sironia, Texas*, is unforgettable. Reading it is like living through an endless, fevered nightmare about a town. Whatever its limitations as a work of fiction, *Sironia* is fascinating and without peer as a sociological record. Above all, *Sironia*, an account of events in a Texas town from 1900 to 1921, is permeated, infected, with the issue of race.

Cooper and those characters presented as most honorable in the novel seem to be aware that there is something about black/white relations in Sironia that is not quite right. But they are convinced that, well, that is just the way things are, a fact of life that cannot be helped.

After graduating from the University of Texas in Austin in 1915, Cooper returned to Waco and worked at his father's wholesale grocery company until he entered officers' training camp in 1917.[46] He would have been almost twenty-two when the lynching of Jesse Washington took place on the town square in 1916. He might well have been one of the young men on the square wearing a straw boater in Fred Gildersleeve's photographs of the Waco Horror.

In fact, the climactic incident in the novel *Sironia* is the lynching of a black man. Bennie Henderson, a visiting entertainer who was raised in Sironia, is brutally lynched on the town square because he has had consensual sex with a drunken white woman in his dressing room. Some of the details of Cooper's fictional lynching are clearly inspired by the Waco Horror: the lynching takes place on the main town square by City Hall; the victim is stripped, battered, and sliced up before he is burned; there is even a brief reference to a lynching "long ago" after which the body was dragged "all over town."[47] Dragging was, as will be seen, part of the Waco Horror.

The main character in *Sironia*, Tammas Lipscomb, who seems to be in some ways an alter ego for Madison Cooper, risks his own life trying to prevent the lynching. Unfortunately, in the case of the real-life 1916 Waco Horror, no hero like Tam Lipscomb stepped forward to put his life on the line to save a black man. If the young Madison Cooper Jr. was present at the real lynching, there is no record that he, or anyone else, made any attempt to help the victim.

The story of what happened to the fictional Bennie Henderson may have been inspired by more than one Waco lynching, however. On August 8, 1905, a young black man named Sank Majors was hanged from the new bridge across the Brazos in Waco by a mob of about two hundred men. In August 1905, Madison Cooper Jr. would have been eleven years old, certainly old

"Bird's-eye view" of Waco City Hall and the town square about 1917. Note suspension bridge, ca. 1870, in the center of the photo, and, to the left, the "iron bridge," built in 1902, where Sank Majors was hanged. *Courtesy* Archives Division of The Texas Collection, Baylor University, Waco, Texas.

enough to remember the incident. The Majors lynching was something of a landmark in Waco history. It was the only lynching in the city between 1889 and 1916, despite nearly constant mob violence throughout East Texas.[48]

The events that propelled Sank Majors to his death began at dusk on July 11, 1905, near the small town of Golinda at the southern end of McLennan County close to the Falls County line. A young woman named Clinnie Mackey Robert, only seventeen or eighteen years old and married a matter of weeks to Ben Robert, was sitting on the back step of her home near Golinda. Her husband had gone into town. She saw Sank Majors, twenty-year-old son of a woman who had worked for the Mackey family, passing through her yard—a fact which puzzled her because her husband had ordered Majors, she said afterward, to stop walking through their yard.[49] According to the newspapers, there was some kind of quarrel between Majors and Ben Robert; the reason for the bad feeling was never clarified.

The next thing Clinnie Robert knew, someone attacked her from behind, grabbing her by the back of the neck and forcing her head between his knees. Her unknown attacker immediately began beating her and cutting her with a knife. She was pushed backward onto the floor and soon lost consciousness.

During the struggle she never saw the man's face but did catch a glimpse of a scar on his hand. Later she had a vague sense that she heard someone run off through the weeds. She knew nothing more until her husband came in and found her lying on the bed with a pan of bloody water containing a handkerchief by the side of the bed. When she was revived, she, as the newspaper daintily puts it, "in mortal terror and sickening anguish, examined herself and found that the negro had accomplished his purpose" — in other words, she had been raped.[50]

As soon as the assault on Clinnie Robert was reported to the authorities, a general hysteria ensued. Day after day, from July 12 until July 21, when Sank Majors was finally caught, the newspapers described a wild, bumbling Keystone Kops hunt for the man who everyone assumed was the guilty party.

According to one newspaper story, officers of the law, trying to go about their business in a professional way, were hindered by "a big mob of excited men, chiefly young hot-blooded fellows" who followed them about, hoping to grab the alleged assailant and lynch him as soon as he was found.[51] The story speculates that these amateur trackers probably created so much confusion, they enabled Clinnie's attacker to get away.

On July 21, Sank Majors was finally located and arrested at the home of his brother Polk Majors, a few miles outside of the town of Lockhart, over one hundred miles south of McLennan County. The sheriffs of Caldwell and Hays counties located him, primarily, it seems, by finding out where he had family who might be hiding him.[52] As soon as he was seized by authorities, Majors began to protest his innocence consistently and vigorously, telling a *Times Herald* reporter who traveled to Austin expressly to interview him in jail, "Ise the one they lay it on . . . but I did not do it."[53]

Sheriff George Tilley of McLennan County also went to Austin to interview Majors in the Travis County jail but did not take him back to Waco until local residents assured him that they would allow Majors to be tried if the trial and punishment proceeded quickly. Although the Waco newspapers dutifully reported Majors's continued declarations of innocence, the stories continually undercut these passages with phrases like "Sank Majors, who assaulted Mrs. Ben Robert near Waco . . ."[54]

Sank Majors was permitted to testify at his trial, after Clinnie Robert gave a heart-wrenching account of the assault and identified the scar on his hand as the scar she had seen on the hand of her assailant. According to the reporter covering the trial, "[Majors] . . . gave a rambling and disconnected account of himself on the day of the assault."[55] Further, according to the *Times Herald* story, Majors confessed to the crime before the trial, and the specifics of his confession tallied perfectly with the known details of the crime.

Once he was on the witness stand, however, Majors recanted and insisted that he had confessed only because he was scared. Despite the recantation, his confession was admitted into evidence. The jury required a full three minutes to determine that Sank Majors was guilty of the assault on Clinnie Robert and to sentence him to death.

At this point the train of events designed to carry Sank Majors smoothly to his ugly end hit an obstacle which some feared might derail — or excessively prolong — the whole process. On August 5, the trial judge, Marshall Surratt, granted Majors a new trial, agreeing with the defense attorney, George Barcus, that he, the judge, had failed to charge the jury correctly. The judge was apparently concerned that, if he did not grant a new trial, the conviction would be overturned on appeal. There would be as little delay as possible in prodding Majors toward his appointed death: the judge's announcement was made on Saturday, August 5, and the new trial was scheduled for the following Wednesday, August 9. The newspaper story announcing the new trial, however, ends with the provocative supposition that Majors, "if he thought he could save his neck, or gain time in the execution of the law," was going to draw things out as long as he could and would continue to appeal to higher courts.[56]

Feeling apparently ran so high in the city at this news that the *Times Herald* felt obligated to run a follow-up editorial the next day explaining that no one should blame defense attorney Barcus for representing his client to the best of his ability.[57] Who knows what kind of retribution was visited on George Barcus, who made the mistake of trying to do his job, and how that might have affected the legal representation of Jesse Washington eleven years later?

Despite the unrest, however, Sheriff Tilley did not anticipate any trouble. He still trusted the assurances given him before the first trial that there would be no mob action. He either did not hear or did not heed the grumblings, particularly by men from the Golinda area, about the fact that Clinnie Robert would be forced to testify again.

Near midnight on the evening of Monday, August 7, 1905, a crowd of about two hundred men gathered on the circus grounds and then proceeded quietly to the jail yard. They filled both the jail yard and the courthouse yard so quickly and silently that the jailers did not realize what was happening until it was too late. The *Times Herald* reporter observes with obvious admiration that "it was as carefully planned as an attack made upon an army."[58]

The mob demanded that the jailer release Sank Majors to them. The jailer refused to give up his prisoner and sent an officer running for Sheriff Tilley. In the meantime, the mob got to work on the task of forcing their way into the jail, first by attacking the outer doors with a crowbar and then, when that failed, with a sledgehammer. Tilley arrived and begged the mob to let the second trial proceed and allow the law to take its course.

"We are here for Majors," said one of the men, "and we are going to get him." Some of the mob leaders placed an armful of dynamite by the jail door to force the officers to stand out of the way so they could get at the door more easily.

Eventually, the outer doors to the jail gave way to the sledgehammer. The inside doors were breached much more quickly. By this time city police under the authority of Chief John Dollins (who will reappear in the Jesse Washington story), including the two mounted police who usually patrolled the central town square, had also arrived. But at that point some of the mob members were already inside the jail, and the situation was out of control. The jailers feared that if the mob was allowed to break the lock to the door leading to the cells, every prisoner in the jail would escape, so they simply opened Majors's cell door and allowed the men to extract him.

Majors had already been told that the mob was coming after him. He tried to climb into the flue leading out of his cell but was pulled loose and dragged away. One man in the mob was heard to say, "New trial granted and change of venue from Waco to hell."

At first, the mob proposed to burn Majors. They took him to a post in the middle of the town square and began to pile boxes and other combustibles around him. But someone announced that Clinnie Robert had asked that he be hanged, not burned. Sank Majors was thereupon dragged to the new bridge across the Brazos and forced to climb on a horse. One of the men climbed up on the crossbeam of the bridge right under the first electric light on the east side. A rope was put around Majors's neck.

At that point someone decided it would be a good idea to try to get Sank Majors to admit his guilt before he was hanged — or perhaps members of the mob simply announced after the lynching that Majors had "confessed," whether he had or not. The vague paragraph in the newspaper story describing Majors's supposed "death bed" confession is unconvincing in both language and tone: "He was asked if he wanted to make a statement. He replied that he did not. He was then asked if he was not the negro who outraged Mrs. B. Robert. He replied in the affirmative. 'Was any one with you?' was asked. 'Nobody,' said Majors. 'I did the deed myself and am the guilty party.' Someone asked him if he did not think he should be hanged and he replied in the affirmative." If Majors actually uttered any semblance of a confession, it was undoubtedly forced from him by the mob.

The rope around Majors's neck was tossed up to the man on the bridge, who pulled it over the crossbeam. The men below led the horse away, and Sank Majors fell to his death. As soon as he was dead, the mob rushed to the body to slice away fingers, pieces of his shirt, pieces of the rope, anything that would serve as a grisly memento. "Nearly every man took some souvenir with him," says the *Times Herald* article.[59]

Almost one hundred years later, it is hard to assess the likelihood of Majors's guilt. Was the scar on his hand the same as the scar on the hand of Clinnie Robert's rapist? Did Robert accuse Major simply because she had seen him shortly before she was attacked? The guilt of the lynch mob that murdered Sank Majors, however, is not in question.

Another perspective on the story of Sank Majors is available, beyond the customary sensationalized newspaper reports of the day. His great-niece Nona Baker, a teacher's assistant at the Texas Youth Commission in Marlin, still lives in Waco and heard the whole story from her grandmother Mary Majors Green, Sank Majors's older sister. "I was ten when Grandmother died," Nona Baker said. "I remember her telling us [the story] when we were little kids . . . She had just gotten married in 1904 . . . My grandmother was pregnant with her first child at the time . . . they searched all their houses. [She] told me how terrified she was."[60] Baker explained how her grandmother carried the pain of what had happened to her little brother to her grave: "It still hurt her. It would hurt her to talk about it, but she knew it was probably the only way we were going to know about it. She wanted us to know he was innocent." The entire Majors family was certain that Sank was innocent. "If it was dusk," said Nona Baker, "and Sank was very dark-skinned, how could she see a scar on his hand?"[61]

The most poignant part of Baker's account is her description of how Sank's mother (Nona Baker's great-grandmother) was called to come to the lynching and was present when her son was killed: "Someone came and got his mother, and she came to Waco down to where the jail was . . . He was calling for his mother and she wanted him to know she was there . . . It wasn't something she ever got over. Now they would call it depression but back then they didn't have that name." Sank Majors was his mother's youngest child, the baby of the family.

Baker said that her grandparents both told her that the tornado that hit Waco in 1953, killing 114 people, injuring 145 others, and destroying most of the downtown area, traveled the downtown streets along the precise route the mob followed in dragging Sank Majors from the jail to the bridge. This story, repeated in various forms to this day and associated with various lynchings by other members of Waco's black community, reflects an irresistible conviction among African American Wacoans that the ferocious tornado was God's long-delayed retribution for the lynchings that took place in the early years of the twentieth century.[62]

There was certainly no retribution at the time. One brief newspaper story published the day after the lynching blandly announces, "Majors had a sister residing in this city [probably Mary Majors Green], and relatives living near Gurley. They came in the morning a short time before noon and asked to be permitted to take charge of the remains. This request was granted and the remains will be shipped to Gurley via Sap this afternoon."[63] Sank Majors was buried in the Majors Chapel cemetery outside of Golinda. One can hardly bear to imagine the feelings of a family confronted with the spectacle of what was left of Sank after the mob got through with him.

Blacks who spoke out against the Majors lynching were severely punished. McLennan County authorities made a heavy-handed effort to keep restless "negroes" in line, both by offering assurances of safety to blacks who kept quiet and by allowing vigilante attacks on any black man who proclaimed his disgust publicly.

Only two days after the lynching, a story in the *Waco Times Herald* described an incident in Eddy, a small town near Waco: "Eighteen or twenty men" had bestowed 150 lashes on a black man referred to only as "Lawyer" — obviously, a derisive nickname — because he had dared to "censure" the people of Golinda for the lynching. The story implies that Lawyer had also been ordered to get out of town and then concludes, with tongue-in-cheek delight, "No one has any idea who constituted the committee of chastisement."[64]

In response to rumors of unrest, the authorities must have made a decision that white folk needed to be calmed and reassured. Several articles were published soon after Lawyer's beating announcing that rumors of "secret meetings" of blacks since the lynching of Sank Majors were untrue, that some blacks had been fined as much as one hundred dollars or arrested for "incendiary language" because they had spoken out too freely about the Majors lynching, and that "a close watch [was] to be made at all places where there might be any congregation of negroes." Officers of the law, white Wacoans were told, were making sure that angry talk about the lynching was kept down.[65]

The whole operation represented the imposition of something like a police state on black people. Horrible outrages were perpetrated against them, but they were not allowed to express their righteous indignation in public — or, indeed, behind closed doors, if there was any chance of betrayal. The system was structured to punish the victims instead of the criminals who abused them. If anyone made the mistake of complaining out loud, he or she could be fined or jailed by the legal system or given up to the rough justice of extralegal vigilantes. The vicious beatings described so casually in the newspaper stories probably often resulted in lifelong mutilation or maiming — if not death. Yet a few individuals had the courage to raise their voices anyway, though they knew they faced the threat of pain and suffering and the possibility of being driven from their homes forever.

On August 18, another incident took place that illustrates how lynchings could be prevented (and periodically *were* prevented) by the courage of just one person who had the strength to face down a mob. A black man named Andrew Dinwiddie was arrested and accused of attempted criminal assault in Paris, Texas, a town located near the Texas/Oklahoma border. A particularly horrible public lynching had taken place there only three years earlier.[66] As Sheriff M. S. Carpenter was questioning Dinwiddie in his office at the courthouse, a mob gathered outside, then swept up the stairs, broke the lock on the door of the room where Dinwiddie was being kept, and seized the terrified man. The mob ignored Carpenter's declarations that he was not even sure Dinwiddie was the man who had committed the crime.

The mob dragged Dinwiddie down the staircase, all the while beating him and even trying to "gouge his eyes out" and stab him with pocketknives. He was hauled off to the town square and taken up to the bandstand, where the mob intended to lynch him. County Judge John W. Love arrived, climbed up on a wagon, and addressed the mob. He promised the mob that Dinwiddie would have a speedy trial and begged them "to desist for the good name of the county, telling them they would receive the commendation of good people all over the United States if they would stand out for law and order and let the law take its course."[67] In a tone of amazement, the reporter telling the story continues: "His address acted like magic on the mob, which at once weakened and carried the prisoner back to the court house and turned him over to the sheriff."

In the meantime, the mayor pro tem quietly closed the saloons for the rest of the day. At ten o'clock that same night, a mob gathered again at the jail and demanded the prisoner once more, but this time Sheriff Carpenter, who had discovered his backbone, declared he would defend with his life any attack on the jail, and the mob dispersed.

The entire ugly history of lynchings in the South and the Midwest is punc-
tuated by instances of this kind, where one brave man (or even, on occasion, a
woman), usually the rare public official who took his job seriously, faced down
a mob and simply by declaring, "You will do this only over my dead body,"
stopped the mob in its tracks and sent it home. Lynch mobs, which appeared
to boil up and surge forward with all the irresistibility of a lava flow, were pre-
ponderantly made up of drunks, bullies, and cowards. When confronted with
determined resistance by one person armed with moral certainty, the mob's
volcanic anger seemed to melt away, the raging fires instantaneously snuffed.
None of the flotsam and jetsam that made up a mob wanted to face the consequences of killing a white man.[68]

It turned out that Andrew Dinwiddie, in fact, was not the man who had
committed the crime. A few days later he was "released quietly," though "severely beaten and bruised."[69] Lynchings could be stopped, but there was no
one as determined and effective as Judge Love on hand to stop the lynching of
Sank Majors in Waco in 1905.

This then was Waco in the early years of the twentieth century — a proud
little city that had acquired many of the surface trappings of social refinement
and felt itself poised on the brink of a great, gleaming future. It was also a nasty
town where, in the very recent past, men had routinely settled disagreements
with bullets, and sporadic mob violence was still considered a form of popular
entertainment. Under a thin veneer of "sprinkled" streets, public parks, and
handsome homes, Waco was still at heart a frontier burg, raw and dangerous.
Black people, in particular, could never feel entirely safe and secure in this
"pushing" town. There was always the possibility of violence, always the threat
of the mob.

CHAPTER 2

"ACTIVE FOR GOOD"

The Beginnings of the NAACP

[Every citizen] must be active
for good or he will be counted for evil.

—Moorfield Storey

AS the deluge of blood from lynchings and pogroms against blacks washed across the South during the early twentieth century, with occasional broad streams flowing up into the Midwest, most people not directly involved were content to sit back and watch, some with tacit approval, others with a muttered "tsk-tsk" or a quickly forgotten pang of disgust over the morning newspaper.

There were a few individuals, however, who viewed the mistreatment of blacks with a rising sense of outrage and who had already come to believe that moral revulsion should be followed by action.[1] The key actors in this chapter of the story had been observing the ebb and flow of lynchings, in particular, with growing disquiet. But the single event that finally stirred them to organize was an ugly race riot which occurred, shockingly, in Springfield, Illinois, the birthplace of the Great Emancipator, Abraham Lincoln, just a few months before the centennial celebration of his birthday. The Springfield riot was sparked by two incidents — the murder of a white mining engineer by a black man on the night of July 4, 1908, and the alleged rape of a white woman by a black man on the following August 13.[2]

On the night of July 4, a sixteen-year-old girl named Blanche Ballard woke up suddenly about 1:00 A.M. and realized that a man was sitting or lying at the foot of her bed. The girl screamed and the man fled, but Blanche's father, Clergy Ballard, caught up with the intruder in the front yard and the two men struggled. The family found Clergy collapsed and bleeding from stab wounds. Before he lost consciousness, he whispered that his attacker had been a black man. Clergy Ballard died the next day. In the other case, Mabel Hallam claimed that she had been raped in her home on the night of August 13 by a black man while her husband, a streetcar conductor, was working the late shift. On the basis of the flimsiest of evidence, two black men, Joe James and George Richardson, were accused of committing these respective crimes and jailed.

On August 14, a mob began to gather at the local jail, threatening to lynch both men. The sheriff decided to move the two prisoners out of town until the populace settled down. He called on a wealthy local citizen Harry Loper, proprietor of Springfield's "largest and most popular restaurant" and owner of one of Springfield's first automobiles, to provide a car for the getaway.[3]

The plan succeeded. The prisoners were taken in Loper's car to a waiting train and carried to the jail in Bloomington, Illinois, sixty-seven miles from Springfield. The infuriated mob, however, learning that the prisoners were gone and that Loper had helped them escape, burned Loper's car and then destroyed his restaurant. From there the mob proceeded to the black business district and advanced from building to building, destroying, pillaging, and burning as they went. When that project was completed, they continued into a residential area, where they committed their worst crimes.

Scott Burton, a middle-aged black barber who had sent his family away and stayed behind to defend his home, was captured, beaten, and hanged from a dead tree near a saloon. After he was dead, the mob stripped and mutilated his corpse and riddled it with bullets. The following evening, the mob attacked the home of William Donnegan, an eighty-year-old, well-to-do black man who was severely crippled by rheumatism. The mob dragged Donnegan out of his house, beat him with bricks, cut his throat with a razor, and tried to hang him from a small tree in front of the school across the street. He died the next day.

Both Burton and Donnegan were comparatively well off and lived in largely white neighborhoods. Donnegan had a white wife. The mob seemed to single them out because they were doing well and represented to whites tangible evidence that Negroes were getting too "uppity." A number of white citizens later put the motivation of the mob into words: "Why, the niggers came to think they were as good as we are!"[4]

By the time the militia arrived and was deployed in enough force to reestablish order, two blacks and four whites were dead. At least $120,000 worth of property had been destroyed or stolen. Over forty black families had lost their homes, and many blacks had fled the city. Attacks on individual blacks and instances of fire setting continued into early September. A number of the rioters were indicted, but in most cases, either the charges were eventually dismissed or the culprits pleaded guilty to minor charges and were given very light sentences. The few who were actually tried were acquitted, despite substantial evidence against them.[5]

Joe James was convicted of the murder of Clergy Ballard and hanged, even though he may have been no older than seventeen and there was little proof that he was the culprit.[6] George Richardson, by a kind of miracle, met a different fate. Mabel Hallam dropped all charges against him, claiming that a different black man had raped her, and then finally admitted to a grand jury that she had not been raped by a black man; in fact, she had not been raped at all. She had fabricated the entire story to cover up the fact that she had a white lover who had given her a venereal disease.[7]

While the city's newspapers — the same papers that had printed inflammatory editorials about the "hellish assault" on Mabel Hallam by a "negro fiend" and the "righteous indignation" of the mob during the riots[8] — were busy backpedaling and blaming the entire riot debacle on "the riff raff, the scum of the community,"[9] an outside journalist named William English Walling arrived on the scene the morning after the lynching of William Donnegan, with a clear eye and a different perspective.

Lanky, handsome Walling was born a privileged Kentucky aristocrat, but became a socialist and a radical journalist and activist. Walling's radicalization probably began in earnest when, in the fall of 1898, he left Harvard Law School and returned to the University of Chicago, where he had been an undergraduate, to study economics and sociology at the graduate level. That year, the Chicago School of Sociology was getting underway, guided by Albion Small, who had founded the *American Journal of Sociology* in 1895; and Thorstein Veblen, the reigning nonconformist luminary in economics, was just about to publish *The Theory of the Leisure Class*.

Following a year in graduate school at the University of Chicago, Walling went to live in a tenement near Jane Addams's Hull House and got a job as a factory inspector.[10] Not long afterward, he moved to the University Settlement on the Lower East Side of Manhattan. As a consequence of his up-close view of how the poor lived, worked, and struggled, Walling drifted into socialism and magazine journalism. In 1903, he helped organize an American version of Britain's Women's Trade Union League.[11]

In August 1908, Walling happened to be visiting family in Chicago with Anna, his Russian-Jewish immigrant wife, when he heard reports of the riots in Springfield. Anna and "English," as Walling was known, decided to get on a train to Springfield and investigate the riots for themselves. Walling had relatives in Springfield, although the gap between him and his Springfield cousins is evidenced by the fact that one cousin commented to Walling's wife, "Cousin Anna, I just heard Cousin English call himself a socialist. I can't understand it. I always thought that people were *called* socialists. I never knew that anyone called *himself* one!"[12]

The Wallings had just returned from a stint in Russia reporting on events following the Russian Revolution of 1905. Anna had visited the Russian town of Homel, in what is now Belarus, a few days after a pogrom in which over one hundred Jewish stores and dwellings were burned and more than a dozen people killed.[13] A local general named Orlov had ordered Anna to report to the outside world that the Jews had burned their own city so that they could make claims on their fire insurance policies.

The parallels between Springfield and Homel were startling to English and Anna. "The Wallings, leaving czarist Russia, had felt deep happiness on entering free America, but in the state of Illinois they saw a disregard for law and a venting of hatred of the Negro which they decided was worse than the Russian's hatred of the Jew," reported Walling's soon-to-be associate at the NAACP, Mary White Ovington.[14] Just as General Orlov in Russia had blamed the Jews, the Wallings noted, the Springfield newspapers were busy blaming the city's black citizens for what had been done to them: "It was not the fact of the whites' hatred toward the negroes," says one newspaper article, "but of the negroes' own misconduct, general inferiority or unfitness for free institutions that were at fault."[15]

English and Anna visited the mayor, the militia headquarters, the newspaper, the hospital . . . and the burned-out black neighborhoods. Walling's powerful indignation at what he saw was transmitted directly to the story he wrote for *The Independent*. "Race War in the North" almost seems to burn a hole in the pages of the magazine and transcends entirely the usual cant of the time: "The rioters proceeded hour after hour and on two days in succession to make deadly assaults on every negro they could lay their hands on, to sack and plunder their houses and stores, and to burn and murder on favorable occasion . . . We at once discovered, to our amazement, that Springfield had no shame. She stood for the actions of the mob."[16]

Walling did something extremely unusual for 1908. He did not rationalize and excuse the actions of the mob; he refused to make any allowance for what he disdainfully referred to as "mitigating circumstances." He would not blame the victims. He looked at what he saw before him and called it what it was — an outrageous and indiscriminate assault on an unprotected people. Walling also saw the larger implications, the threat to the whole structure of American democracy if one segment of the population were allowed to unleash violence on another segment unhindered: "Either the spirit of the abolitionists, of Lincoln and of [Elijah] Lovejoy must be revived and we must come to treat the negro on a plane of absolute political and social equality, or Vardaman and Tillman will soon have transferred the race war to the North[17] . . . The day these methods become general in the North every hope of political democracy will be dead, other weaker races and classes will be persecuted in the North as in the South, public education will undergo an eclipse, and American civilization will await either a rapid degeneration or another profounder and more revolutionary civil war, which shall obliterate not only the remains of slavery but all the other obstacles to a free democratic evolution that have grown up in its wake."[18] Walling ends his passionate diatribe with a plea for action: "Yet who realizes the seriousness of the situation, and what large and powerful body of citizens is ready to come to their aid?"[19]

Mary White Ovington, a white journalist and social worker who had lived for several months as the only white person in a tenement in the San Juan Hill section of Manhattan, was so moved by "Race War in the North" that she sat down and wrote a letter to Walling immediately after reading his article. "Drums beat in my heart," she said.[20]

On September 12, 1908, English and Anna appeared at Cooper Union in New York (the same place where in 1860 Lincoln delivered his famous speech against the spread of slavery) to give a presentation on European socialism. But the Wallings veered away from their prepared remarks to talk about what they had seen in Springfield, comparing the riot to the pogrom at Homel. Ovington was in the audience. Afterward, she came up to speak to Walling and later urged him in a letter to take it on himself to be the one to organize the "large and powerful body of citizens" he referred to in his article.[21]

The National Association for the Advancement of Colored People actually began in January 1909 with a meeting of three people in the Wallings' small New York apartment on West 38th Street:[22] William English Walling, Mary White Ovington, and Henry Moskowitz, a New York social worker of Romanian birth who was Walling's friend and had traveled with him in Europe.[23] No black person was present at that first meeting, but Ovington was already a friend and admirer of William Edward Burghardt Du Bois, sociologist, educator, and preeminent black writer. She had participated in Du Bois's efforts to start a black organization with similar aims, the Niagara Movement, but it had foundered because of inadequate funding and internal dissension. Ovington immediately consulted Du Bois and made plans to pull him into the new organization.

According to Ovington, it was Walling who declared that the critical element in a successful organization to demand civil rights for black people would be publicity. He proposed that a strong statement be issued on the centennial of Lincoln's birth, February 12, 1909, a "call" for a meeting of citizens to work on improving the lot of blacks in America. The Call was to touch not only on lynching and race riots but also on the whole range of monstrous indignities to which blacks were subjected in early-twentieth-century America. To draft "The Call," Walling enlisted Oswald Garrison Villard, who could legitimately have claimed the title of "crown prince" of the abolitionist tradition. Villard was the grandson of William Lloyd Garrison, the abolitionist leader, and was, like his renowned grandfather, a newspaper editor and a gifted writer.

"The Call," as developed by Villard, enumerates the wrongs visited on black people. It moves from a gentle beginning to an increasingly impassioned recital of abuses and mistreatment. He describes the disenfranchisement of black voters by the state of Georgia, the failure of the Supreme Court to protect black people against discrimination, the encroaching segregation being forced on southern blacks, "for whose freedom a hundred thousand of soldiers gave their lives," and the brutality and violence visited on black people "North, South and West." In the final paragraph Villard arrives at a trumpet fanfare of rhetoric that echoes the words of Lincoln. He declares that "this government cannot exist half slave and half free any better to-day than it could in 1861." He concludes by demanding "a national conference for the discussion of present evils, the voicing of protests, and the renewal of the struggle for civil and political liberty."[24]

"The Call" was signed by sixty prominent blacks and whites, including — besides Du Bois, Ovington, Walling, Moskowitz, and Villard — social worker Jane Addams; muckraking journalists Lincoln Steffens and Ray Stannard

Baker; antilynching crusader Ida B. Wells-Barnett; Prof. John Dewey; writer William Dean Howells; well-known socialist and writer Charles Edward Russell; suffragist leader and daughter of Elizabeth Cady Stanton, Harriot Stanton Blatch; Rabbis Emil G. Hirsch of Chicago and Stephen S. Wise of New York; Pres. Mary E. Wooley of Mount Holyoke College; Bishop Alexander Walters of the African Methodist Episcopal Zion Church; and Oberlin graduate, writer, and lecturer Mary Church Terrell.

The initial response to "The Call" was so tepid that Villard questioned whether the proposed conference should actually be held. But Walling pressed forward and the National Negro Conference took place as proposed on May 31 and June 1, 1909, at the Charity Organization Hall and at Cooper Union in New York. Fifteen hundred people, black and white, attended one of the evening meetings.

Despite the discord and distrust expressed in the final meeting of the conference at which the new group was formally organized — and the defection or ousting of two powerful, outspoken black figures, antilynching activist Ida B. Wells-Barnett and Monroe Trotter, editor of the *Boston Guardian* — resolutions were passed demanding equal civil and educational rights for blacks, the right to work, and "protection against violence, murder and intimidation." The conference also provided for the incorporation of what was at first called "the Committee for the Advancement of the Negro Race."[25]

The most important figures in the very early years of what soon became the National Association for the Advancement of Colored People were almost all linked to the abolitionist tradition, almost all white, and deeply entrenched in the many other "progressive" reform movements of the time, from women's suffrage to labor battles to assistance for poor people. Many, though not all, had independent incomes, to one degree or another, which allowed them some freedom to ignore what other people thought of them.

The great exception among the NAACP founders was W. E. B. Du Bois, who was black and had no independent wealth. Du Bois became the eloquent voice of the NAACP as editor of *The Crisis*, the organization's journal. Yet, in terms of prickliness of temperament and obsessive efforts to expand his own power within the organization, Du Bois was much like many of his white colleagues.

Almost all of these early leaders could be said to be eccentrics in terms of the ordinary mores and values of the time — classic "cranks," as defined by Clarence Darrow. Darrow was a featured speaker at the second annual National Negro Conference, held in May 1910, at the same Charity Organization

Hall in New York City. In his customary way, Darrow spoke directly and without evasion about the nature of people who would have the nerve to stand up for blacks in the current climate: "Why, to stand here fifty years ago and plead for the rights of the negro in this building would make a man a hero. Standing here now makes him a crank — and if he wasn't a crank he wouldn't be here . . . I have no doubt that it is because of this modern god that we have adopted the god of wealth which compels all people, except a few cranks to conform to the society in which they live."[26] Albert Jay Nock, writing about a lynching in Pennsylvania in 1911, described the early NAACP a little differently, but the gist of the message is the same: "These people have given themselves to the most unpopular cause in the world."[27]

Given that single-minded reformers are seldom comfortable people to be around, the particular bunch of reformers who started the NAACP may have been, of necessity, even thornier and more doggedly individualistic than most, because they were challenging head-on generally accepted opinions and behavior related to the single most difficult, intractable, and emotional issue in American life.

William English Walling made a few very important additional contributions to the NAACP in the early days. He managed the complex maneuvers involved in the hiring of W. E. B. Du Bois as director of publicity and research, and he hit on a name for the organization's magazine, taken from James Russell Lowell's poem "The Present Crisis." ("Once to every man and nation comes the moment to decide, In the strife of Truth with Falsehood for the good or evil side.")[28]

But the glamorous and dashing English soon had to end his role as a spokesman for the NAACP because of a scandal that would scarcely stir public interest today, but was a monumental public relations disaster in his own day. In February 1911, he was sued for breach of promise in a New York court by Anna Berthe Grunspan, a young woman from Russian Poland with whom he had had an affair in Paris before he fell in love with and married his wife.[29] Even though Grunspan lost her case against Walling because she could not convince the jury that Walling had ever actually promised to marry her, Walling knew that he was finished as a public spokesman for the NAACP. He continued to serve on the board of directors for some time afterward and was active behind the scenes, but was no longer one of the primary voices speaking out for the rights of black people.

In contrast to Walling, the most respectable of the whole colorful lot of early NAACP leaders was Moorfield Storey, the fledgling organization's elder statesman and the closest link, in terms of personal experience, between the NAACP and America's abolitionist tradition. Storey was also the NAACP's first expert on constitutional law. He was already sixty-five when he became the first president of the organization in 1910. He served until his death in 1929 at the age of eighty-four, just a few days before the great stock market crash.[30]

Moorfield Storey was raised in Roxbury and Boston and attended Harvard with the son of Ralph Waldo Emerson, whom he occasionally joined at the Emerson home in Concord for dinner. Storey's mother was an abolitionist and his father a "Sumner Republican," but Storey may have been even more influenced by his service, from November 1867 to May 1869, as private secretary to Sen. Charles Sumner. Sumner had been one of the most outspoken opponents of slavery and continued to be a vigorous advocate for freed blacks after the Civil War. Storey's time as Sumner's secretary included the critical period of the nearly successful effort by the Radical Republicans to force Pres. Andrew Johnson out of office.[31] From his New England upbringing and his close observation of Sumner, Storey derived his sense that life must be lived and wrongs righted in terms of inflexible moral principles.

A highly successful corporate lawyer and former president of the American Bar Association, Moorfield Storey was respected and admired all of his life, even by those who opposed him or did not share his views. He was a man known for his capacity for gentle self-irony and lack of exaggerated ego, but when he had to choose between courtesy and principles, principles won. Mary White Ovington described an incident that she vividly remembered. In 1915, Storey and Ovington were both testifying before Boston mayor James Curley on behalf of the NAACP during a hearing on the issue of whether D. W. Griffith's inflammatory, racist movie *The Birth of a Nation* should be shown in Boston. The NAACP had been fighting against the exhibition of the movie for some months. Ovington describes the episode as follows: "Griffith, the producer, spoke pleasantly of freedom of speech as represented by Boston, and of his pleasure at being at the cradle of liberty. The Mayor said he could censor but had no power to stop the production. With this announcement the hearing was over. Moorfield Storey had spoken for a few moments and as he moved to leave the platform, Griffith turned to him saying, 'I am glad to have the opportunity of meeting you, Mr. Storey,' and held out his hand. Storey said quietly, 'I do not see why I should shake hands with you, Mr. Griffith.'"[32]

Storey's personal activism in connection with the downtrodden of the world really began, not with American blacks, but with the people of the Philippines. He was viscerally horrified by the U.S. acquisition of the islands in 1901 and the subsequent brutal suppression of a Filipino nationalist movement. In 1905, Storey became president of the Anti-Imperialist League, which used the arguments of the American Revolution to support the desire and right of all peoples for freedom. From then until his death, he fought for the self-determination of nations, opposing American intervention in Panama, Haiti, and Mexico, as well as the Philippines. His activism consisted of highly intelligent, analytical opposition and advocacy.

In the early 1900s, Storey began to see and point out parallels between the mistreatment of people of color abroad and the mistreatment of blacks at home. At that point he began to fight the injustices he saw close at hand, particularly instances of discrimination at Harvard and in the American Bar Association. He soon understood, however, that he needed to do more than fight individual episodes of unfairness. He pursued efforts to help blacks, despite the fact that his own Virginia-born wife "could never bring herself to meet with Negroes on social terms and . . . impeded his personal contact with them for forty years," according to one biographer.[33]

The secret to bettering the condition of blacks, as Storey saw it, was to apply the lessons of the abolitionist campaign — publicize individual atrocities to awaken the public conscience and illustrate the inevitable evils of an evil system, and then demand enforcement of the law at the highest level.[34] At first, Storey opposed a federal antilynching law as unconstitutional, but eventually he came to see federal enforcement as the only path out of the lynching jungle. "The process of education is necessarily slow," he wrote in a 1919 letter, "and I do not think this evil will await its results. Toleration of lynching by men and women all through the south is itself an educational force which is constantly setting a bad example."[35]

The greatest service that Storey rendered to the NAACP, however, was to lead the way to three great courtroom victories that set the pattern for the organization's long tradition of using publicity in an effort to change the hearts of Americans while pursuing courtroom battles to change the laws, whether hearts were changed or not. In June 1915, partly as a result of Storey's friend-of-the-court brief and argument before the court in *Guinn v. United States*, the Supreme Court struck down the "grandfather clause" of Oklahoma (and other states), which declared that no one could vote unless he was able to read and write, pay certain taxes, meet property ownership qualifications, etc., *or* was able to vote on January 1, 1866, or was the *descendant* of someone able to vote on January 1, 1866. Of course, this tactic eliminated many blacks from the voter rolls while allowing impoverished and illiterate whites to vote.[36] In November 1917, the Supreme Court granted Storey another victory in *Buchanan v. Warley*, otherwise known as the Louisville segregation case, by striking down a city ordinance in Louisville, Kentucky, which made it illegal for blacks to buy or move into any house on a block in which the majority of residents were white.[37] Finally, in February 1923, in *Moore v. Dempsey*, the Supreme Court declared invalid the conviction in Phillips County, Arkansas, of six blacks accused of murder and insurrection — because the trial was conducted in a mob-dominated atmosphere and therefore did not constitute due process. Moorfield Storey argued the case before the Supreme Court and won the victory for the NAACP.[38]

Moorfield Storey gave the NAACP the gift of his chief skill, an ability to sway judges with statements of the issues and arguments that were so elegant, so intelligently conceived, and so plainly stated that they were almost unanswerable. He established the principle that in the courtroom the NAACP was a force to be reckoned with. But Storey also bestowed on the organization the cachet of his highly regarded name and reputation. While William English Walling was forced to minimize his public connection with the NAACP to prevent besmirchment by association, the mere use of Moorfield Storey's name at the top of a sheet of letterhead was a preemptive strike against those who might seek to belittle the group as nothing but a collection of fringe misfits and agitators.

Another great force in the early years of the NAACP, and one much more intimately involved, for better or worse, in the daily workings of the organization was the monumental Oswald Garrison Villard, wealthy editor of the *New York Evening Post*. Had it not been for Villard's power, position, money, and stern fidelity to the cause, the NAACP would probably never have gotten off the ground. Villard (and Storey, to some degree) gave the NAACP in the beginning what Du Bois's Niagara Movement had lacked: financial support and a reliable conduit to positive publicity.

But if Villard had been allowed to run the NAACP entirely as he saw fit, the organization probably would have foundered and disappeared in a few years. Villard, with all his gifts, energy and genuine ability, seems also to have been afflicted with a talent for antagonizing people. He was always absolutely positive that he was right and suspected the motives of anyone who dared think otherwise than he.

Villard died in 1949, nine years after he severed all connections with the *Nation*, the magazine he founded, because of his anger at the abandonment of the pacifist cause by many of his associates in the face of Hitler's aggression.

After his death, *Nation* editor Freda Kirchwey wrote about Villard: "He would never have disputed another man's right to disagree with him about peace or racial equality or free trade; but it was hard to persuade him that such contrary views were sincerely held or honestly advocated. To him they were simply wrong, and to harbor wrong opinions was at least circumstantial evidence of evil motives."[39] Villard was much in the mold of his famous grandfather, whose motto on the masthead of the *Liberator*, which Villard frequently quoted, was, "I am in earnest — I will not equivocate — I will not excuse — I will not retreat a single inch — and I will be heard!"[40]

Oswald Garrison Villard was raised as a kind of American princeling. His German-born father, Henry Villard, began life as a revolutionary in Germany but became a railroad magnate in the United States. The climax of Villard's childhood was the 1883 ceremony at which a so-called golden spike (actually iron) was driven into a railroad tie at Gold Creek, Montana, symbolizing the completion of the first railroad in the American Northwest, a span of track linking St. Paul, Minnesota, to Portland, Oregon. Henry Villard was president of the Northern Pacific Railroad at the time, and Oswald, at age eleven, was an honored guest.[41]

In 1900, when he was twenty-eight and had only three years of newspaper experience, Villard inherited ownership and control of the newspaper his father had purchased in 1881, the *New York Evening Post*. For eighteen years, Villard developed and nurtured the *Post* as the influential voice of liberalism among intellectual easterners.[42] To justify the *Post's* limited circulation, Villard was fond of quoting New York governor David Hill, who had once remarked, "I don't care anything about the handful of mugwumps who read it [the *Evening Post*] in New York. The trouble with the damned sheet is that every *editor* in New York State reads it."[43]

Villard also inherited shares of the Northern Pacific Railroad and the Edison General Electric Company, which later became General Electric. (Henry Villard was an early and much-appreciated backer of Thomas Edison.) Villard expanded the family fortune by involving himself in real estate and banking. He was also active in the management of numerous elite clubs and societies, including the New York City Club and the Philharmonic Society.[44]

Villard might easily have become a typical self-satisfied plutocrat, but his upbringing and background led him to concern himself throughout his life with the great social wrongs he felt he had a responsibility to right. Rather than view himself as a tycoon, Villard was, in his own mind, a knight riding forth to slay the dragons bedeviling humanity. He was particularly affronted by what he perceived as the great wrongs visited on blacks in America. Part of this concern derived from his pride in his own family's heritage. But part of Villard's motivation for helping blacks was also earnest empathy for the sufferings of others.

In April 1902, he visited the South. After spending three days in Kowaliga, Alabama, which he described as "a lynching community," Villard wrote to his mother, Fannie (the daughter of William Lloyd Garrison), "I feel as if I had emerged from darkest America and the sense of the wrongs of the people of color is strong upon me."[45] His response at first was to publicize and support Booker T. Washington's activities at Tuskegee Institute and elsewhere.[46] But over time, he became disillusioned with Booker T. Washington's temporizing; he had already begun to think about forming an organization to advance the cause of black Americans when the invitation came from Ovington and Walling to draft "The Call."[47]

Villard strongly supported the activist spirit of the new group, saying later that, from the beginning, he believed the organization "should be aggressive, that it should be the watchdog of Negro liberties, and that it should allow no wrong to take place without its protesting and bringing all the pressure to bear that it possibly could."[48] He subsequently offered the NAACP office space in the *New York Evening Post* building at 20 Vesey Street, continued to play a major role in guiding the organization, and gave its activities generous and positive publicity in the newspaper's pages.[49] The NAACP stayed in the *Evening Post* offices until early 1914, when the organization relocated to a larger — and more independent — space at 70 Fifth Avenue.[50]

For his pains in supporting black civil rights, Villard was reviled by Sen. Carter Glass of Virginia as "the rankest negrophile in America."[51] Undoubtedly, Villard was pleased by this intended insult, rather than otherwise. In 1911, he was one of only eighty-four men who walked in the first joint parade of men and women in support of women's suffrage in New York City. Despite being "booed, hissed and ridiculed without a moment's cessation" and plagued with such cries as, "Who's doing the cooking while you're out?" Villard wrote afterward, "I have felt perfectly elated ever since . . . I do not know when I have enjoyed a day more and wish I could do it over again tomorrow."[52] Being morally correct was exhilarating for Villard, whatever the cost.

Under Villard's early leadership, however, dissension plagued the management of the NAACP. In the beginning, Villard couldn't get along with Walling. As Ovington's biographer describes it, "Villard found Walling erratic and impossible to work with . . . Villard raged at Walling and repeatedly threatened to resign. Walling had 'a damnably acute intelligence' but acted like a baby."[53]

More persistently, Villard could not get along with W. E. B. Du Bois, who had left his academic position at Atlanta University and joined the NAACP in 1910 as director of publicity and research. Villard did not want Du Bois to be part of the NAACP in the first place. The two men had already had a furious clash over the fact that Villard, author of a forthcoming biography of John Brown, had savagely criticized Du Bois's new book on John Brown in an unsigned review in the *Nation* on October 28, 1909. The *Nation* was, at the time, a weekly supplement to the *New York Evening Post*.[54] The review was reprinted the same week in the *Post*.[55]

It was undeniably tactless and self-serving for Villard to review unfavorably a book that was in direct competition with his own, whatever flaws he thought he had spotted in Du Bois's work. Du Bois reacted with fury to the Villard review, which may have hurt sales of his book. Du Bois was especially enraged because Villard would not even give him the courtesy of publishing his rebuttal to the review in the *Nation*. Villard then used Du Bois's anger as an excuse to oppose giving him an official position in the NAACP.[56]

When the NAACP executive committee met without Villard and offered Du Bois the position anyway, Villard accepted the decision. The two men finally met face to face and, as Mary Ovington later said, "shook hands across the chasm."[57]

In the years that followed, Villard continued to feud with Du Bois. "They circled each other like lions," says Ovington's biographer, who identifies the all-too-similar personalities of the two men as the central problem dooming their working relationship.[58] Du Bois also later expressed his strong resentment that, because Villard, like Moorfield Storey, had a southern wife, "I could never step foot in his house as a guest nor could any other of his colored associates. Indeed," said Du Bois, "I doubt if any of his Jewish co-workers were ever invited."[59]

In January 1914, Villard stepped down as chairman of the NAACP and became instead treasurer and chairman of the finance committee. The transition was eased by the gentle maneuvering of Mary White Ovington, who somehow managed over the years to keep these intense personalities in balance and hold the NAACP together.

William Edward Burghardt Du Bois was, like Villard, both gifted and difficult. He was also the outstanding black writer of his generation and the first black leader to successfully challenge Booker T. Washington's position as the ascendant spokesman for black Americans. Born and raised in Great Barring-ton, Massachusetts, Du Bois soon became aware of the "veil" of color, as he described it later, that separated him from his white classmates: "In a wee wooden schoolhouse, something put it into the boys' and girls' heads to buy gorgeous visiting-cards — ten cents a package — and exchange. The exchange was merry, till one girl, a tall newcomer, refused my card — refused it peremp-torily, with a glance. Then it dawned upon me with a certain suddenness that I was different from the others; or like, mayhap, in heart and life and longing, but shut out from their world by a vast veil . . . the Negro is a sort of seventh son, born with a veil, and gifted with second-sight in this American world — a world which yields him no true self-consciousness, but only lets him see him-self through the revelation of the other world."[60]

Given the place and time, Du Bois's achievements as a young black man without money are spectacular. He studied at Fisk University in Nashville, at Harvard, and at the University of Berlin, and in 1895 became the first African American to earn a PhD from Harvard. By 1903, at the age of thirty-five, Du Bois had already published *The Souls of Black Folk*, still considered a classic of American literature. The book is a collection of essays relating to various as-pects of Du Bois's experience as an African American in the United States.

Lifelong humiliation based solely on his color plagued Du Bois despite his achievements. Of all his white associates in the NAACP, only writer and re-former Charles Edward Russell seems to have fully understood the misery Du Bois experienced as a highly superior man doomed to be treated as an inferior by those who were in actuality far beneath him in terms of intellect and skills. In his autobiography Russell describes listening to a series of outstanding speakers holding forth at a luncheon forum and then hearing one, Du Bois, who was better than all the rest, who "astonished and charmed all that heard him."[61] Russell then goes on to detail the daily great and petty insults Du Bois suffered as a black man in America, beginning as follows: "And yet in no part of the country in which he was born would he, this man, be secure against daily and gratuitous insult and indignity; in no part would his great and un-usual attainments have either the recognition to which they were entitled or the opportunity for exercise from which society might profit. In no part of the United States would his status among his fellowmen be essentially above that of the criminal, the gangster and the moral leper. In no part of the United States could he pass freely without the unprovoked hostility, without the scornful or hateful gaze of most of the persons he might encounter."[62] The wonder is not that W. E. B. Du Bois was later accused of being thin-skinned, arrogant, and territorial, jealously guarding every hard-won prerogative and perquisite. The wonder is that he was able to function at all. The wonder is that he did not go mad.

Du Bois first pursued an academic career, teaching history and economics at Atlanta University from 1897 to 1910. He was determined to become a trailblazing American sociologist and to study his own people scientifically. For years, he persisted in his belief that right, reason, and education would in time change the views of whites toward blacks until, in April 1899, a transforming experience, directly connected to the barbaric lynching of Sam Hose, overtook him.

Sam Hose was a black farm laborer who worked for a white man named Alfred Cranford in Palmetto, Georgia, a town a few miles southwest of Atlanta. Hose could read and write and was the sole support of an invalid mother and a mentally retarded brother.

In early April 1899, Hose asked Cranford for an advance in pay (according to some accounts, it was actually back pay) and permission to visit his mother. Cranford refused and the two quarreled. The next day, while Hose was chopping wood, Cranford started arguing with him again, drew a pistol, and threatened to kill him. Instinctively attempting to defend himself, Hose turned and flung the axe at Cranford. The axe struck Cranford in the head and killed him instantly. Hose hid in the woods until he could make his way to his mother's cabin. He was eventually captured nearby.[63]

This version of Hose's "crime" is based on the investigations of Chicago detective Louis Le Vin, who was hired by the Rev. Reverdy Ransom and "other wealthy negroes of Chicago" to go to Georgia and find out what really happened.[64] After Detective Le Vin presented his report before a mass meeting at Chicago's Bethel A.M.E. Church on June 4,[65] it was published in the *Richmond Planet* and reprinted verbatim in a pamphlet by Ida B. Wells-Barnett called *Lynch Law in Georgia*.[66]

Fantastically exaggerated accounts of Hose's alleged wicked deeds appeared in white newspapers. This particular re-creation of the precipitating events was published in the *Atlanta Constitution* after Hose's death: "An unassuming, industrious and hard working farmer [Alfred Cranford], after his day's toil, sat at his evening meal. Around him sat wife and children . . . At peace with the world, serving God and loyal to humanity, they looked forward to the coming day. Noiselessly the murderer with uplifted ax advanced from the rear and sank it to the hilt in the brain of the unsuspecting victim. Tearing the child from the mother's breast, he flung it into the pool of blood oozing from its father's wound. Then began the culmination which has dethroned the reason of the people of western Georgia during the past week . . . the wife was seized, choked, thrown upon the floor, where her clothing lay in the blood of her husband, and ravished . . . remember that shocking degradation which was inflicted by the black beast."[67] According to Le Vin's investigation, Mrs. Cranford never said that Sam Hose had assaulted her or even that he had entered the house.[68]

There may have been various versions of Hose's acts, but the stories about what happened to him were entirely consistent with one another. About two thousand people witnessed his lynching on April 23, 1899, near Newnan, Georgia. Hose was stripped and chained to a tree. His ears, fingers, and genitals were cut off and his face skinned. Then he was saturated with oil and burned. At one point, impelled by extreme agony, Hose managed to loosen the chains on the upper part of his body. The fire was put out while he was chained up again. The fire was lighted again, and this time Hose was burned until he was dead. Afterward, the crowd fought over pieces of his body, which they wished to retain as souvenirs. There was one story that a member of the mob planned to deliver a piece of Hose's heart to the governor of Georgia.[69]

When the story of Sam Hose's murder of Alfred Cranford first became known, Du Bois wrote out a carefully reasoned letter "concerning the evident facts" to the editor of the *Atlanta Constitution*. He picked up his cane and gloves and set off on foot to deliver his letter in person, also taking with him a letter of introduction to editorial writer Joel Chandler Harris. On his way downtown, Du Bois was told that Sam Hose had already been lynched and that Hose's burned knuckles were on display in the window of a grocery store farther down the street on which Du Bois was walking. "I turned back to the university," wrote Du Bois. "I began to turn aside from my work. I did not meet Joel Chandler Harris nor the editor of the *Constitution*."[70]

As Du Bois explained it himself, he had a stark realization that day that "one could not be a calm, cool, and detached scientist while Negroes were lynched, murdered and starved."[71] His faith in the scientific search for the truth and his belief that the truth would speak for itself were badly, permanently shaken.

One month later, Du Bois's firstborn child, his son Burghardt, died of diphtheria at the age of eighteen months. While Du Bois and his wife walked behind the horse-drawn cart carrying Burghardt's coffin to the Atlanta train station (the child was to be buried in Great Barrington), white people glanced at them and called them "niggers."[72]

Soon after, Du Bois and others began to struggle against the domination of the black community by Booker T. Washington and Washington's insistence on accommodation and ingratiation as the appropriate stance for blacks in a white world. In the meantime, Washington, increasingly annoyed by Du Bois, took steps to prevent him from getting the financial support he needed to pursue his sociological studies.[73]

After the failure of Du Bois's Niagara Movement, the dawning of the NAACP must have seemed like a good opportunity for him to escape Atlanta, the South, and the limitations of an underfunded academic career and to pursue his passionate desire to fight directly for the rights of blacks — to continue, in effect, his Niagara Movement under a different name, but this time with the support of the money and power of influential whites.

The Crisis, the NAACP's journal, was successful from the first issue, which appeared in November 1910. Without question, Du Bois's stirring writing helped kick-start the NAACP and make it a force to be reckoned with, even while funding for the organization was limited and the membership small. Mary White Ovington, always eager to give Du Bois full credit, describes the impact of The Crisis in her autobiography: "Before the year [1910] was out it [The Crisis] had a circulation of 12,000. In another year it was mailed into every state but one in the Union . . . the most avidly scanned section was the editorial page. Always scholarly in his effort to print the truth, in expressing an opinion Du Bois could vigorously voice approval or blame, sometimes with the passion of the poet who wrote the 'Litany of Atlanta.'"[74]

Within ten years, The Crisis had a circulation of 100,000. But Du Bois had also made a kind of devil's bargain and spent much of his time during his early years with the NAACP in a constant struggle for more power and independence. He wanted the NAACP to fund his magazine but let him run it precisely as he liked and say and do whatever he liked.

Fortunately, by the time of the Waco Horror, a new chairman, Joel Spingarn, was in place. He was another unique character, just as prickly and independent as Villard. Always independent and rather cold, Spingarn was described by his wife as having "in maturity, no close friends except *possibly* his brother Arthur."[75] But the new chairman was somehow more patient with Du Bois and more in tune with the latter's aims — so much so that Du Bois dedicated one of his autobiographical works, *Dusk of Dawn,* "To keep the memory of Joel Spingarn, Scholar and Knight."

The son of an Austrian Jewish immigrant who had made a fortune in the wholesale tobacco business, Joel Elias Spingarn had no family ties to the tradition of abolitionism.[76] His interest in black people may have been inspired in the beginning by his mentor at Columbia University, Prof. George E.

Woodberry, who was concerned with the fate of both American Indians and African Americans.[77]

By the time he became chairman of the NAACP, Spingarn had already given ample proof of his willingness to sacrifice everything to principle during his first career as an academic. He seems to have spent almost the entire ten years that he taught at Columbia University as a contrarian. He became the first scholar in America to try to introduce Italian philosopher Benedetto Croce's theories of literary criticism into American scholarship, and he pioneered what became the "New Criticism" — the concept that a work of art has an intrinsic value apart from its impact on the viewer, its moral influence, its place in history, or whether it follows certain rhetorical rules.[78]

Spingarn's views were considered highly controversial at the time, although they came to be adopted as the standard academic approach to literature long after his academic career was over.[79] But when Spingarn first broached his theories, other critics reacted violently with bigoted ad hominem attacks: Spingarn was a New Yorker and a Jew "seeking to conquer America for his children," said one critic.[80]

As if weathering blatantly anti-Semitic attacks was not difficult enough, Spingarn proceeded to run head-on into a collision with Columbia University president Nicholas Murray Butler and the university's trustees. The critical point for Spingarn at Columbia came in early 1911, when the trustees fired Harry Thurston Peck, a professor at Columbia for twenty-two years and an international authority on classical languages. Peck was the defendant (much like Walling that same year) in a scandalous breach-of-promise suit. Spingarn organized a group of professors to protest Peck's dismissal and the whole dismissal procedure. As a consequence, Spingarn was relieved of all duties on March 6, 1911. Although the debate raged for months and other professors, including John Dewey, vigorously supported Spingarn, he was never reinstated.[81]

Spingarn memorialized his exile by publishing a famously mocking poem entitled "Heloise sans Abelard," featuring the lines

> *O passionate Heloise,*
> *I too have lived under the ban,*
> *With seven hundred professors,*
> *And not a single man.*[82]

Joel Spingarn's interest in helping American blacks had already begun, at least in a small way, before he was ousted from Columbia. In 1910, he pur-

chased an estate called Troutbeck outside the town of Amenia, near the Con-
necticut border in New York's Dutchess County. He also bought the local
Heart of Hope Club, which had been established to provide free meals and
recreational facilities for Amenia's poor black families. Not having any idea
how to run the club, Spingarn wrote a letter to W. E. B. Du Bois asking for advice.[83] That initial contact was the beginning of a lifelong friendship.

Spingarn's wife, Amy, was also a different breed of female from either Ju-
lia Sandford Villard of Kentucky, daughter of a Confederate captain,[84] or
Gertrude Cutts Storey, whose mother was a descendant of the Randolphs of
Virginia.[85] Amy Einstein Spingarn was the daughter of a wealthy Jewish busi-
nessman. Her first American ancestor was said to have been a drummer boy
who came with Lafayette to America; therefore, she was a member of the
Daughters of the American Revolution (DAR). But she gave up her membership in 1939, when the DAR refused to allow Marion Anderson, a highly
acclaimed black singer, to perform at the DAR-owned Constitution Hall in
Washington, D.C.[86] The Spingarns hosted two major conferences of black
leaders at Troutbeck and received many black friends there.

As in the case of William English Walling, however, it was a single story of
injustice against blacks that roused Joel Spingarn to involve himself heart and
soul in the NAACP. In the fall of 1910, he read a newspaper account of the
misfortunes of an illiterate black laborer in Arkansas named Steve Greene. In
1910, Greene's white landlord told him he was planning to nearly double his
rent. Greene and the man's other tenants promptly moved out. As Greene was
leaving, his landlord threatened him, declaring that, if Greene left, he better
not try to work elsewhere in the same county.

Greene ignored the threats and began working for a neighbor. One day,
Greene's infuriated former landlord rode past him while he was working and
shot at him, hitting him in the neck, left arm, and right leg. Greene rushed
home, grabbed a rifle, and killed his attacker. Then Greene ran away, traveling
on foot and by train, and finally managed to reach Chicago. In Chicago, he was
betrayed to the police, who arrested him on a trumped-up minor charge and
held him without food or water for four days while he was questioned about the
killing in Arkansas. After he was released, pending correction of a defect in the
extradition papers from Arkansas, Greene was smuggled to safety in Canada.[87]

Spingarn said later that the moment he read the story about Steve Greene,
he told himself that the long-suffering Greene would never be extradited to
Arkansas to be burned by a mob if he, Spingarn, had anything to do with it. He

immediately sent a check for $100 to the NAACP for Greene's legal defense. Villard saw an opportunity to bring another prominent man into the organization and invited Spingarn to join. By November 1910, Spingarn was a member of the executive committee.[88]

One of the ongoing problems the NAACP faced was the difficulty of getting press releases published beyond the *New York Evening Post* and a handful of black newspapers. Even as late as 1914, according to Ovington, the NAACP was still just one among the many "insignificant" reform groups in New York.[89] To remedy this situation and to gain more attention for the organization, Spingarn took it on himself to embark on a series of speaking tours across the United States over the next three years. He talked to audiences about what he called the "New Abolition," as represented by the NAACP.[90]

For the most part, Spingarn spoke to black audiences, trying to arouse his black listeners to fight for their own rights. He took pleasure in later years in recounting how, when he did speak to white audiences, people often started leaving long before he was finished and he would end the evening talking to the black waiters leaning against the back walls of the room.[91] His focus became establishing branches of the NAACP in cities that had none and enlarging the membership of the branches that did exist. Spingarn estimated later that he had spoken before seventy thousand people during his three tours.[92]

Spingarn was soon in the forefront of every NAACP battle, struggling, cajoling, threatening, trying to engage more blacks in local civil rights efforts, and even involving a few influential white people who were kindly disposed toward the aims of the NAACP and had the means to help. In March 1913, he established the Spingarn Medal, a gold medal then valued at $100, to be awarded annually to an African American who had attained the highest level of achievement in any field.[93] The Spingarn Medal is still awarded annually by the NAACP.

Joel Spingarn was, therefore, the logical choice to take over the chairmanship of the NAACP when Ovington eased Villard into the treasurer's position in January 1914.[94] By the fall of 1914, however, Spingarn too was having his difficulties with the imperious Du Bois. At the November 4, 1914, board meeting, Spingarn and Du Bois confronted each other in an ugly scene. Ovington must have defended Du Bois and been accused by Spingarn afterward of excessive devotion to him. She answered the charge in a letter: "You think I idolize him [Du Bois] — and perhaps I do. To me, the rest of us on the Board are able journeymen doing one day's work to be forgotten tomorrow. But Du

Bois is the master builder, whose work will speak to men as long as there is an oppressed race on the earth."[95]

The quarrel between Spingarn and Du Bois was eventually patched up and the work continued. Two years later, when the Waco Horror took place, Spingarn was still chairman and Du Bois was still editor of *The Crisis*. In later years, Du Bois said of Spingarn: "I do not think that any other white man ever touched me emotionally so closely as Joel Spingarn . . . We fought each other continually in the councils of the Association, but always our admiration and basic faith in each other kept us going hand in hand."[96]

The 1914 exchange vividly illustrates how Mary White Ovington, an unassuming woman who never attempted to draw attention to herself, kept the NAACP moving forward when it must have seemed that the clashing of intense personalities and strong wills would inevitably bring it to ruin. She was born in Brooklyn, daughter of the owner of a china shop. She was a Unitarian, a socialist, a writer, and a social worker who was strongly influenced as a child by her passionately abolitionist grandmother. As a result, Ovington's youthful fantasies revolved around stories of the Underground Railroad and pictures of the characters in *Uncle Tom's Cabin*, rather than tales of princesses, goblins, and dragons.[97]

After attending several private schools, Ovington spent two years at Radcliffe, then called the Harvard Annex. A handsome blonde with pale blue eyes, the young Ovington was courted by many suitors but explained later that she never married because "the man who would marry her and the man she would marry were never the same."[98] In actuality, though she may not have been fully aware of it herself, the high-minded Ovington was looking for something more serious to occupy her life than the typical society marriage.

After college, during seven years as head of the Greenpoint Settlement House in Brooklyn, which she had helped found, Ovington learned firsthand about the problems of the poor — and about the senseless nature of prejudice. One day she took fifteen boys of different nationalities on an outing to Prospect Park. It was a hot day, and she and the boys were riding in an open trolley. As they passed by some black women sitting outside in front of their apartments, the boys all started yelling at once, "Nigger, nigger, nigger!" — for no reason, Ovington discovered, except that it was a "ritual that they had learned."[99]

In 1903, while she was still head of Greenpoint, Ovington attended a dinner for Booker T. Washington on behalf of the Social Reform Club. During the course of that evening, Ovington discovered what was to be her life's work.

Part of the evening's program was devoted to a presentation on the problems of blacks, not just in the South, but in New York, at Ovington's very doorstep. She could not get what she had heard about "ramshackle tenements, high infant mortality, and discrimination in employment" out of her mind.[100]

The following year Ovington left Greenpoint and went to Greenwich House in Greenwich Village to study "the Negro in New York City."[101] While she pursued her research, her increasing concern for the downtrodden led her to join the Socialist Party and to begin to write articles for the *Masses*, the *Call*, and Villard's *New York Evening Post*.

In 1904, Ovington first wrote to W. E. B. Du Bois in Atlanta to ask for his advice as she proceeded with her study of blacks in New York. Seven years later, she published the results of her sociological research as *Half a Man: The Status of the Negro in New York*. A major source of inspiration and guidance had been Du Bois's own 1899 *Philadelphia Negro: A Social Study*.

In May 1905, Ovington, invited to speak at one of Du Bois's conferences at Atlanta University, went south and met Du Bois face to face. She was as impressed by the man in person as she had been by his writings and later enthusiastically described the dapper Du Bois with his neatly trimmed, pointed beard: "His head [was] like Shakespeare's done in bronze."[102]

During the first decade of the twentieth century, Ovington made several trips to the South to gather information for a variety of journalistic pieces, including an article for the *Outlook* on the Atlanta riots. These visits also stimulated her to produce what was perhaps her most memorable written work, a story first published in *The Masses* in 1915 called "The White Brute." The title is, of course, an ironic play on the endless newspaper articles and political speeches of the time that referred to alleged black rapists as "*black* brutes."

"The White Brute" is only ten pages long, but, once read, it cannot be forgotten. Ovington included the story in her autobiography, probably in an effort to win a wider readership for it because she understood the explosive effect it might have by forcing on the reader a sudden, intense insight into the pain of black experience in America. Without offering much detail, Ovington claims in her autobiography that "The White Brute" was based on a true tale whispered to her by the wife of the Republican postmaster at Alexander City, Alabama — a man who had been severely beaten for printing material favorable to blacks in his little newspaper. The postmaster's wife was so fearful of the local whites that she pulled all the shades down before she told Ovington the story.[103]

In "The White Brute," Ovington manages to turn inside out the familiar southern imagery of "black brutes" violating chaste vessels of southern white womanhood by portraying an extreme example of the much more common despoiling of black women by southern white men. She tells the story of Sam, a hardworking field hand, and his new bride, Melinda, who are returning home on the train from their wedding in the depths of Mississippi. Forced to wait for several hours at a railroad junction in a small town, Sam and Melinda attract the unwanted attention of two disreputable-looking young white men hanging around the station. The men ultimately carry Melinda off for a few hours to have what they call "a good time." Sam, knowing the reputation of the place as a lynching town, can do nothing to stop them. The men return his bride as promised, but all the joy of their new marriage has left Sam and Melinda, probably for good.[104]

"The White Brute" vividly conveys Mary White Ovington's deep outrage at the injustices heaped on black Americans. For Ovington, this outrage was not a short-lived rocket flare of emotion, but a slow-burning fire that sustained her in a struggle that lasted her entire life.

In 1908, Ovington left Greenwich House and went to live at the Tuskegee, a brand-new, long-hoped-for settlement house for blacks at 233 West 63rd Street in the rough San Juan Hill section of Manhattan. During the months she spent at the Tuskegee, she was the only white person in the building and in the neighborhood. Despite her parents' fears, Ovington always insisted that no one ever bothered her or even questioned her right to be there.[105]

Instead, it was white racism that caused her trouble. One of the most embarrassing episodes of Ovington's life, which plainly exposed the bigotry of both northerners and southerners, as well as the slanted journalism of the time, was the newspaper coverage of the mixed-race Cosmopolitan Club dinner held at Peck's Restaurant on Fulton Street on April 27, 1908. The Cosmopolitan Club had been organized by a group of black and white New Yorkers to discuss race questions. The club's meetings were usually held in private homes, but Ovington had been looking for a venue for a larger gathering. She picked Peck's Restaurant because she had attended a socialist dinner there.

The April 27 meeting at Peck's featured very solemn speeches heard by an audience about equally divided between black and white, mostly middle-aged, middle-class people. Halfway through the session, a group of reporters came in. The newspaper coverage that followed depicted the very serious meeting—which had focused on a sober discussion of a Christ-like character in a play currently playing on Broadway called *The Servant in the House* — as a kind of wild interracial orgy with half-dressed white women draping themselves over black men. The papers heaped blame on the white participants in particular.

Poor Mary Ovington bore the brunt of the infamy, which was most melodramatically embroidered in an extended account published in the *Savannah News:* "Worst of all was the high priestess Miss Ovington whose father is rich and who affiliates five days every week with Negro men and dines with them at her home in Brooklyn, Sundays. She could have had a hundred thousand Negroes at the Bacchanal feast had she waved the bread-tray. But the horror of it is she could take white girls into that den. That is the feature that should arouse and alarm northern society."[106]

"For six weeks," Oswald Garrison Villard reported, "Mary White Ovington, in herself the personification of lovely and spiritual womanhood, was compelled to have her mail opened by male relatives."[107] Ovington herself laughingly admitted that she ran away to her sister's house to escape the flood of obscene letters. But in typically cheery fashion, she also said she had received one letter that made up for all the rest. A man wrote from Maryland, "I am a white man, but I glory in your spunk in standing up for what you believe to be right."[108]

This nasty episode occurred at a time when a woman could "lose her character" even for rather subtle infractions of the social code. If she did allow her reputation to become stained, she might thereafter no longer be received in polite society — a prospect that terrified most "well-bred" women. But Mary White Ovington had already crossed so many boundaries that were as imposing as barbed wire to most of her contemporaries that she would not be driven away from her reformist commitments by a few vicious paragraphs in the newspapers. Her gentle style cloaked a spine of steel. One year after the Cosmopolitan Club dinner at Peck's Restaurant, she would play a major role in starting the NAACP and would continue to guide the organization and to soothe and mediate disputes between its noisier, more troublesome leaders for most of her long life.

These, then, were the major figures in the group working out of the NAACP office at 70 Fifth Avenue, New York, in 1916, as the Waco Horror was looming on the horizon. Joel Spingarn was chairman, Oswald Garrison Villard was treasurer, W. E. B. Du Bois was director of publicity and research and editor of *The Crisis,* and Mary White Ovington was a very active member of the board of directors who had been secretary and would become chairwoman in 1919. Moorfield Storey was a kind of legal guardian angel overseeing the operation from his law office in Boston.

Lynching, of course, was one of the NAACP's major concerns from the very beginning. The first item in the NAACP general lynching file archived at the Library of Congress is a postcard or flyer showing a photograph of four black men hanging from a tree. It is captioned, "Scene in Sabine County, Texas, June 15, 1908." Below the picture is a poem of sorts:

> *This is only the branch of a Dogwood tree;*
> *An emblem of WHITE SUPREMACY.*
> *A lesson once taught in the Pioneer's school,*
> *That this is a land of WHITE MAN'S RULE.*
> *The Red Man once in an early day,*
> *Was told by the White's [sic], to mend his way.*
> *The negro, now, by eternal grace,*
> *Must learn to stay in the negro's place.*
> *In the Sunny South, the Land of the Free,*
> *Let the WHITE SUPREME forever be.*
> *Let this a warning to all negroes be,*
> *Or they'll suffer the fate of the DOGWOOD TREE.*

The verse is not signed. An attribution at the bottom says only, "Pub. by Harkrider Drug Co., Center, Texas."[109]

This bit of doggerel with its sample of the specialized field of lynching photography is a fitting emblem of the forces that were arrayed against the NAACP in its struggle to end lynching. Nevertheless, Du Bois began in the earliest issues of *The Crisis* to describe, with his special brand of razor-edged sarcasm, the horrors of specific lynchings and to dissect lynching episodes and the people and communities that perpetrated them. While he attacked lynching with his prose, officers of the NAACP like Villard and Spingarn wrote again and again to local residents asking for information and to public officials demanding that something be done. Eventually, the NAACP hoped to force authorities to prosecute lynch mob leaders and to give prosecutors more and stronger laws to use against lynchers. But passing new legislation and inspiring vigorous, effective prosecution would take time and would require a political will that was noticeably lacking.

In the meantime, leaders of the NAACP planned to pillory lynchers and

lynching communities, as Walling had suggested in the beginning, with relentless publicity. The NAACP would refuse to allow lynch mobs to slink away
into the darkness and lynching towns to go about their business as usual, pretending that nothing out of the ordinary had happened. The NAACP would
expose lynchings as the atrocities they were and shame towns that tolerated
them with the ferocious glare of national — sometimes even international —
publicity. As J. E. Spingarn said in his chairman's report at the NAACP annual
meeting on January 3, 1916, "The object of every great agitation is, as [the abo-
litionist] Wendell Phillips put it, 'To tear a question open and riddle it with
light.'"[110]

An especially disturbing lynching in the early days of the NAACP was the
murder of a black man accused of killing a white man in Livermore, Kentucky, on April 20, 1911. The local marshal arrested the black man, Will Potter,
and decided that, since the jail was flimsy, he would take his prisoner to the
more substantial opera house, bolt the doors, and hide him in the basement under the stairs. A lynch mob of fifty men showed up, broke into the opera house,
overpowered the marshal and his deputies, and eventually found Potter.

Potter was tied up on the stage, and the members of the mob stood around
the stage in the orchestra pit. When a signal was given, they all shot him at
once. Potter screamed one time and died. When they were finished, leaving
Potter "a limp and bloody bundle" on the stage, they lowered the curtain and
turned off the lights before they went out.[111]

The NAACP organized a group of Washington, D.C., citizens to present
a resolution to President Taft demanding that Congress take action. Taft replied
that he was helpless. Lynching, he said, was a matter for the states to handle —
the standard refuge for federal officials at the time.[112]

The writer of the *Times* editorial about the Livermore lynching appears to
be quite amused. He begins his piece by commenting that, "whatever else may
be said about the inhabitants of Livermore, Ky., it cannot be denied that in
them the dramatic sense is strongly developed. For, when they deemed it ex-
pedient to lynch a negro, they managed to do the familiar deed in a way not
only entirely new, but highly picturesque in the literal meaning of that much-
abused word."[113] His intent might have been to slyly ridicule the whites of Livermore, but his jocular approach seems today to be tasteless and callous. The
piece demonstrates how desperately Du Bois's stern exposés of lynchings in
The Crisis were needed — a forceful expression of outrage at every new murder, a sensibility that never became so jaded or wearied that it failed to respond
with anger and disgust.

The lynching event that stimulated the most vigorous NAACP action before the Waco Horror was the murder of Zachariah Walker in Coatesville, Pennsylvania, on August 12, 1911. Walker had fought and killed a private policeman who worked for the local steel mills. During the fight Walker was also injured. After he was arrested, he was taken to the hospital for treatment, but was chained to his iron bedstead so he could not escape.

A Coatesville mob surged into the hospital, tore apart the iron bed, and dragged Walker, still chained to the footboard, through the streets. They then threw him on a pile of wood, drenched him with oil, and burned him alive. At one point, when Walker, in excruciating pain, broke his chains and tried to escape, the mob drove him back into the fire with fence rails. The policeman assigned to guard Walker at the hospital did nothing to stop the lynching.[114] As in the case of the Springfield riots, NAACP activists were especially horrified because the lynching mania of the South had once more infected the North.

This time the NAACP sent Mary Dunlop Maclean to investigate the lynching personally. Maclean was a New York Times feature writer who had helped Du Bois with The Crisis since its inception, first as a volunteer and then as managing editor.

After several local men were tried as lynchers and acquitted, the NAACP, using funds supplied by Oswald Garrison Villard, hired the William J. Burns Detective Agency to find out more about the lynching. The detectives set up a restaurant in town as a front and were able to identify additional participants who had not been indicted, but no further prosecutions took place.[115] The Pennsylvania Supreme Court denied a motion for a change of venue, and Coatesville-area jurors, like those in Springfield, simply would not convict the lynchers. The local sheriff was reelected while under indictment for manslaughter in the Walker case.[116]

In the early years, NAACP officials often found that it was difficult to determine the facts surrounding a faraway lynching. NAACP representatives would find themselves writing to residents in the area where a lynching had taken place, begging for information from "some reliable person living in the neighborhood" or "anyone who lives near enough to the scene of this crime to be in a position to get . . . the details."[117] Newspaper accounts and reports by local residents were often unreliable and contradictory. The lynching of Marie Scott on March 31, 1914, in Wagoner, Oklahoma, was one case that was smudged and blurred by conflicting accounts.

Marie Scott had, according to the newspapers, stabbed a young white man named Lemuel Pearce to death. Pearce had visited the "negro section of the town" (other sources in the NAACP file refer to the neighborhood as a "restricted" or "red-light" district). As Pearce and his friends were leaving one house, Scott supposedly charged him and stabbed him in the heart.

Scott was arrested and jailed. Early the next morning, there came a knock on the jail door and a voice cried out to the sole jailer, a one-armed man, that an officer was bringing prisoners in. When the jailer opened the door, he "faced twelve revolvers in the hands of masked men." The jailer was tied up and his keys taken. Scott was dragged screaming from her cell. The masked men put a rope around her neck and pulled her a block away to a telephone pole, where she was hanged. The New York Times story adds, by way of explanation, that local residents were afraid that, had Scott been tried and given the death penalty, the governor might have commuted her sentence. He opposed capital punishment and had already commuted the sentences of other blacks condemned to death.[118]

The NAACP attorney at the time, J. Chapin Brinsmade, and NAACP secretary May Childs Nerney both wrote to various contacts in the area, asking for more information about the Scott lynching. After corresponding with the Muskogee, Oklahoma, branch of the NAACP, Brinsmade wrote to another contact that the NAACP would not pursue the case "because her [Marie Scott's] character was as bad as possible and because the circumstances of her crime were revolting and shocking." "I do not consider Oklahoma the best possible place for such an investigation," Brinsmade continued. "Reports of other lynchings in that State made to us at first hand by colored people, seem to show that it is as much a general spirit of lawlessness as race hatred which occasions such crimes there."[119]

Nevertheless, Du Bois published in The Crisis a letter from one James Harold Coleman, manager of Blackdom, New Mexico, "a Negro Colony, Founded by Francis M. Boyer in 1909, on Free Government Lands." Coleman would seem to have been quite removed from the Wagoner locale, but, nonetheless, he sent a letter which offered an entirely different version of the lynching. Coleman said that an innocent seventeen-year-old Marie Scott had been quietly combing her hair in her room when two white men caught sight of her through the window. They came into her house, locked themselves in the room with her, and raped her. According to this report, it was Marie's brother who, hearing her cries, rushed into the room, was beaten by the white men, and, returning with a knife, killed one of them and ran away. Marie,

Coleman's letter said, was arrested and lynched only because the authorities could not find her brother. Coleman claimed to know all these things because Marie's brother had escaped to New Mexico.[120]

Over time, NAACP officers seem to have concluded that the only reliable way to get the indisputable facts in the case of a particular lynching, so that they could be publicized far and wide, was to send a trusted NAACP investigator to the scene as soon as possible. This approach eventually became standard procedure, and a number of NAACP representatives literally risked their lives going into lynching communities while passions were still aflame and asking nosey questions. One of the first of these was the investigator of the Waco Horror.

While lynchings in the North still shocked and surprised the NAACP, certain areas of the South seemed to be well-known and chronic hotbeds of lynching fervor. The NAACP had reason to focus on Central Texas, particularly the area near Waco, before the Waco Horror took place. In the January 1916 edition of *The Crisis*, Du Bois reported on a lynching in Temple, Texas, in which a black man was burned alive. Temple is located just thirty miles south of Waco.

The story of the Temple lynching began about 9:00 A.M. on the morning of July 29, 1915, when a neighbor arrived at the home of the Grimes family, about two miles southeast of Temple. The neighbor discovered that Mr. and Mrs. Grimes had both been severely beaten and three of their six children, twins seven months old and an eight-year-old boy, had been killed. Officers later theorized that the adults and children had been attacked by someone using a rail cutter. Subsequent newspaper accounts reported that the mother had been raped and so badly beaten that her features had been reduced to "a raw pulp."[121]

As soon as the news of the terrible attack spread, the community was in an uproar. The following day, a rumor ran through the county that officers had arrested a black man named Will Stanley in the nearby town of Rogers. On the way to the jail in Belton, where they planned to hold Stanley temporarily, the officers and their prisoner were pursued by a caravan of about one hundred cars, each packed with people. The lawmen tried hiding with Stanley in a cave along the river bottoms to escape their pursuers, but they were found and ordered by the mob to proceed at once to Temple.

In the meantime, a crowd, anticipating an immediate lynching, had gathered in the public square at Temple. Once the lawmen arrived back in Temple, however, they rushed Will Stanley into a courtroom, and a standoff ensued for seven hours while deputies — and a group of citizens — questioned Stanley and two other black men. About midnight, the mob, now five thousand strong and tired of waiting, stormed the courtroom and seized Stanley, who was immediately hustled to the public square and burned to death. The other two black men in custody were released by officers and told to run for their lives, which they did.[122]

The *Temple Daily Telegram*, under the headline, "The Late Unpleasantness," ran an editorial which faintly criticized the lynchers, but also tried to justify what they had done: "Without expressing a single argument in defense of the action of the people who punished the criminal in a way that might be termed the slickest, quickest and best, we will say that the reproach that will fall upon Temple and the loss of prestige that we must suffer is offset, in a measure by the establishment in the consciousness of the wandering rapist that Temple is not a good place in which to operate. When the white mother lies down with her babies at night in the country home near Temple she knows that, whatever the power of the law, she may put her trust in a manhood whose vengeance is quick and terrible."[123]

Among the curiosities in this piece that are typical of lynching journalism in the South are the emphasis on the rape rather than on the three murders; the assumption that lynching was an indisputable expression of "manhood"; and the invocation of the fearsome image of the "wandering rapist," which seemed to justify any kind of frenzied response. This type of hypocritical pablum served only to reinforce the lynching mentality and reassure the lynchers that they were justified in their actions.

Du Bois carried a brief news story about the lynching plus excerpts from letters to *The Crisis* which reported that the governor of Texas was doing nothing in response to the lynching, and that two lynching photographs, reprinted in *The Crisis*, were selling for ten cents each on the streets of Waco.[124] One of the Temple photographs shows the mob washing up against the doors of the courthouse. The other picture displays the charred remains of Will Stanley hanging by a chain from what appears to be a telephone pole. His legs have been mostly burned away. His body is naked except for a towel or napkin that has been draped around his hips. His arms are upraised and bent at the elbow, drawn up either in agony or in rigor mortis. The usual crowd of slack-jawed yokels in hats is gathered below the suspended corpse.[125]

The Temple lynching was one more installment in what was becoming a regular feature in *The Crisis*, an ongoing Chamber of Horrors. But about the same time that the Temple story was published, just a few months before the Waco Horror, an event occurred that offered some hope to the NAACP reformers fighting the plague of lynchings.

By January 1916, according to Joel Spingarn's annual report to the board of directors, the NAACP had a membership of ten thousand in sixty-three branches across the country and *The Crisis* had a circulation of thirty thousand.[126] But money was in short supply. At the same meeting at which Spingarn's annual report was presented, Villard reported proudly that the NAACP had a grand total of $2,000 in the bank.[127]

One month after this meeting, in February 1916, Moorfield Storey received a letter from an acquaintance, Philip G. Peabody, offering the NAACP a gift of $10,000 in cash — but only if the organization could develop a plan which would convince Peabody that his money could be used effectively to reduce the number of lynchings. The man who made this generous offer was, by anyone's definition, a rather odd duck. A wealthy lawyer, he was also the son of a U.S. Supreme Court Justice and the brother of an insurance company president. Nevertheless, Peabody seems to have been a man whose intentions were good, but who was not overburdened with intelligence and did not know much about how the world wagged outside of his own social caste.[128]

Peabody begins his letter to Moorfield Storey by claiming that he is not wealthy (true, perhaps — by comparison with J. P. Morgan) but wants to help: "I am not a rich man, but I have ten thousand dollars which I would like to use, at once, for any course which commends itself to me as wise, hopeful, and reasonably likely to accomplish a part of the object, of preventing lynching, or even drawing attention to it, in a beneficial way. Can you suggest anything? . . . Lynching is rather too common for good taste!"[129] Peabody's letter set off a flurry of activity at the NAACP, as the acting secretary of the organization at the time, Royal Freeman Nash, tried to determine what everyone's thoughts were as to the best way to spend such a miraculous sum.

It is obvious that, from the beginning, Peabody was extremely pessimistic about the likelihood that his proposed gift would do any good. His follow-up letter to Nash contains this encouraging thought: "I did not see, and do not now see, how the expenditure of ten thousand dollars can do much good in this way; if, however, it attracts other sums; or, by itself, can be made to do an amount of good proportionate to its value; I shall be glad . . . I desire to be satisfied that some *definite* and *material* good will result, before I act."[130] Peabody then tells Nash that he is going to Europe for a month and will meet with representatives of the NAACP when he returns.

It is almost as if Peabody wrote the initial letter out of a sudden impulse, "in desperation at the thought that so few cared about this permanent crime,"[131] and then was somewhat taken aback when the NAACP took him seriously. William English Walling was chairman of the NAACP's Anti-Lynching Committee at this point. He polled the various members of the committee, asking them how Peabody's money should be spent, and then reported their responses to the board. The Anti-Lynching Committee decided, in the end, that Peabody's money should be used primarily to accomplish three goals: to gather and compile facts about lynchings (which the NAACP was already doing, as indicated by the tabulation of 1915 lynchings that appeared in the February 1916 issue of *The Crisis*); to pay for the investigation of individual cases; and to organize southern business and political leaders to speak out against lynching.[132]

Roy Nash also prepared a thorough and comprehensive report to be submitted to Peabody. It reviews the entire history of lynching in America and concludes that "the tortures are becoming more frightful year by year," and "the death penalty [lynching] is being inflicted each year for more and more trivial offenses." Among the offenses for which black people had been lynched, Nash lists "gambling, quarreling . . . throwing stones, unpopularity, making threats . . . bad reputation . . . enticing servant away, writing letter to a white woman . . . slapping a child . . . and disobeying ferry regulations."[133] Nash's report concludes that, with Peabody's $10,000, the NAACP should present the facts of lynching "clearly and exhaustively"; widely disseminate a "literature" based on these facts; enlist the interest of "influential folk in every State"; present a model antilynching law to Congress and state legislatures; establish permanent local committees to prosecute offenders; and raise more money to pursue these same activities.[134]

Perhaps the NAACP did its job too well. Nash's study was so thorough and so comprehensive that it seems to have convinced Peabody that $10,000 was *not* enough money to accomplish the desired goals. In truth, Peabody had seemed very reluctant to actually hand over the money without impossible guarantees from the beginning. Instead, he offered a substitute proposal: He promised to give the NAACP $1,000 if the group could raise an additional $9,000 for the Anti-Lynching Campaign by August 15. Moorfield Storey tried to revive the flagging spirits of those who had worked so hard on the proposal by offering to contribute $1,000 to the fund himself, so that the group would have only to come up with $8,000 from other sources.[135]

Even though the $10,000 from Peabody did not materialize, the exercise had not been useless. The Peabody offer inspired the NAACP's leading members to focus on the lynching problem even more intensely than before and to develop a precise and concrete program to deal with it. When the next terrible lynching occurred, that of Jesse Washington in Waco, the NAACP was prepared. But before it could unleash its most aggressive effort yet to expose lynching in all its hideousness, the right investigator had to be found to go to Waco and gather the facts.

In the years leading up to the Waco Horror, a young American woman was unwittingly preparing herself for the task. After what she had already braved as a "militant" in Emmeline Pankhurst's campaign for women's suffrage in Britain, she was not likely to be intimidated by the postlynching climate in Waco, Texas.

CHAPTER 3

"YOURS IN A GLORIOUS CAUSE"

The Investigator

Bruised, battered, but not broken in spirit, after hours of this ghastly
turmoil, 119 women were arrested, and those who were not went
home to patch themselves up . . . Yours in a glorious cause.

—Elisabeth Freeman, "Letter from an American"

O N September 15, 1911, Elisabeth Freeman, a twenty-six-year-old American woman from New York, returned to New York City on the
steamship *Baltic* after six years in England.[1] In a speech she gave at
Convention Hall in Buffalo two weeks later, Freeman explained to her audience how a "few months vacation abroad" had lengthened into six years overseas because of her passionate involvement in the British women's suffrage
movement as one of Emmeline Pankhurst's "militant" suffragettes.[2] The *Buffalo Courier* reporter who covered Freeman's September 29, 1911, speech, obviously quite taken with the fiery young speaker, describes her as "a slip of a
blonde young woman — sweet faced, eyes alight with the fires of resolution
and consecration to a cause." The journalist representing the *Buffalo Express*
at the same event comments that young Miss Freeman took the stage at Convention Hall following a fashion show. Many of the women in attendance had
come only to see the fashions, but they were tempted to stay on after the mod-
erator announced "a speaker who suffered the tortures of an English jail."

When the slight young woman came out on the stage, the whisper ran around the hall, "My she does not look a bit militant!"[3]

Elisabeth Freeman was indeed "sweet-faced," petite and dainty, only weighing about 110 pounds.[4] Photographs of her confirm the fact that she was a young woman with refined, delicate features and carefully groomed hair and clothing. But, despite her dissimilarity to the popular image at the time of the outspoken suffragist as a hatchet-faced, Carrie Nation–style shrew, Freeman was also a seasoned and unrelenting militant in the battle for women's suffrage. She may have gone to Europe as a young American woman of leisure on vacation, but she returned as a kind of suffragist soldier of fortune — restless, devoted to her cause beyond any other attachment, and ready to go anywhere to rouse women to action and help them win the vote.

Elisabeth Freeman. Inscriptions on the back of three identical copies of this photo read, "Eliza-beth [sic] Freeman of New York. Working with the Garment workers in New York. Went through the Ohio campaign with Rosalie Jones." *Courtesy* National Woman's Party Records, Group I, Box 161, Manuscript Division, Library of Congress.

Freeman's history in the movement, according to her own testimony, stretches back to 1905, but there is no way of knowing what speech she might have heard, which woman she might have met, or what street demonstration she might have seen in England that originally inspired her to take up the cause. By the time she appears in the pages of the *Woman's Journal*, the organ of the National American Woman Suffrage Association (NAWSA), in August 1910 — one year before her return to America — she had already given so much time to the suffragist cause in England that she had been chosen to lead the American delegation in an enormous parade of women through the streets of London on July 23, 1910.[5]

On this particular summer day in London, the crowds who watched the massive women's parade were friendly and supportive. Even the police, said one observer, were "the best-natured, most kindly officers I have ever seen."[6] According to official estimates, as many as a million people crowded into Hyde Park at the end of the march to hear the suffragist speakers. The park was packed with people — an ocean of upturned faces in every direction as far as the speakers could see.

But on the very day of the triumphal women's march to Hyde Park, Prime Minister Herbert Henry Asquith, an implacable enemy of women's suffrage, announced that the Conciliation Bill, the bill for women's suffrage, would *not* be given a third reading in Parliament. The failure to schedule a third reading meant the bill would not be passed, despite the support of a large majority of members of Parliament.[7]

The increasingly violent clashes between Asquith's Liberal Party government and the "suffragettes" of Emmeline Pankhurst's Women's Social and Political Union (WSPU) had a lengthy history, with both sides convinced that they were entirely in the right. And the tactics of the "militants" under Emmeline Pankhurst had a powerful influence on a number of young American women, who would carry the uncompromising attitude and wily ingenuity of the British suffragist back to America. New Jersey–born Alice Paul, for one, who was to form the National Woman's Party and lead the last push of the militants for women's suffrage in the United States, learned tactics, strategy, and relentless devotion to the cause in England.

The aggressive tactics of Pankhurst's group were born of intense frustration. British women had been agitating for the vote since the mid-nineteenth century. John Stuart Mill had introduced a bill for women's suffrage in Parliament as far back as 1866; in 1869, 255 petitions on women's suffrage were presented to Parliament.[8]

Some more conservative women's groups in England, linked under the umbrella of the National Union of Women's Suffrage Societies, continued to use traditional methods of "peaceful propaganda and persuasion" throughout the struggle for the vote for women.[9] But after years of stagnation in the movement, Emmeline Pankhurst was determined to draw public attention to the issue by engineering public actions that were much more dramatic than the traditional pamphleteering and polite lobbying of politicians.

Pankhurst was said to have been motivated in her impassioned quest for the vote by the suffering of the poor, which she observed firsthand as Labour Party representative to the Chorlton Board of Guardians in 1894. Much as Margaret Sanger became convinced of the need for birth control when, in the tenements of New York City, she saw the sufferings of women exhausted by repeated childbirth, Pankhurst, having seen the misery of women in the poorhouse, decided that conditions for poor women would never improve until women could vote.[10]

WSPU members under Pankhurst's leadership regularly heckled anti-suffragist government ministers, attempted to make suffragist speeches in the lobby of the House of Commons, marched in ever larger numbers through the streets of London, sent deputation after deputation to Parliament, and willingly submitted to arrest. Over time, WSPU tactics that at first aroused amusement, or even begrudging admiration, began to inspire violent attacks by the police and sometimes by angry male bystanders. On June 29, 1909, WSPU members ratcheted up the intensity of their protests by throwing bricks and breaking the windows of several government offices.[11]

On July 2, 1909, WSPU member Marion Wallace-Dunlop added another element to the WSPU arsenal. She inscribed a passage from the 1689 Bill of Rights on the wall of St. Stephen's Hall: "It is the right of the subject to petition the King and all commitments and prosecutions for such petitions are illegal." She was arrested for defacing the wall. When she was jailed and was refused the special rights of political (versus criminal) prisoners, such as the right to wear her own clothes, Wallace-Dunlop became the first suffragette to go on a hunger strike in prison.[12]

In October 1909, for the first time, Britain's home secretary ordered that suffragette prisoners engaged in hunger strikes be forcibly fed — which meant that jailers held the women down, pushed tubes through their noses and down their throats, and pumped mashed food through the tubes — an atrociously cruel treatment that has been described as being "akin to rape."[13]

There is no precise record as to whether the "slip of a blonde young woman," Elisabeth Freeman, went on a hunger strike or was force-fed in the precincts of London's Holloway Gaol, but Freeman later said that she had been arrested seven times during her service with the WSPU, and on one of these occasions was jailed for a month.[14] Her name is listed on the official Roll of Honour of WSPU women who went to jail in the battle for suffrage.[15]

The Conciliation Bill presented to Parliament in 1910 represented a paltry beginning for women's suffrage in England. Had it passed, the bill would have extended the vote only to a relatively small group of unmarried and well-to-do married British women.[16] But British suffrage leaders all agreed that the Conciliation Bill was a wedge that would establish the principle of the right of women to vote; suffrage could be expanded to more women later. While the bill was under consideration, suffrage groups promised to refrain from "violence and threats of violence" in order to give it every chance to pass.

Prime Minister Asquith, however, betrayed the women of England in July 1910 and again in November. When Parliament reconvened in November

1910, he announced on November 18 that it would adjourn in ten days and did not mention the Conciliation Bill in his list of legislation to be considered. It was clear that, once more, a third reading would not be permitted and the bill was dead.

This, then, was the background leading up to the day the suffragettes of the WSPU were to call "Black Friday," November 18, 1910. Black Friday was a turning point in the commitment of activists to more and more aggressive actions in the name of the right of women to vote. While Asquith was speaking on November 18, the WSPU was meeting in Caxton Hall. As soon as the women heard about his speech, they decided to send a deputation of three hundred women to the House of Commons to protest.

Although many of the women who went to the House of Commons to peacefully protest Asquith's decision were wives of distinguished men or had won high posts in their own right, they were viciously beaten, shoved and sexually mishandled for six hours by the police. Policemen threw women to the ground, tripped them, pushed them in front of cars, choked them, twisted their fingers and arms, and grabbed their breasts. In the end, to add insult to injury, the authorities arrested 115 women and four suffragist men.[17]

Freeman reported on the events of Black Friday in a letter to the *Woman's Journal* in the United States. She begins by saying that she had been afraid initially to go with the deputation to the House of Commons on November 18. Violence against suffragist demonstrators had been increasing and Freeman suspected what was coming. But then she felt herself to be such a "blank coward" that, "sacrificing . . . my business and my mother's displeasure," she had joined the group. When she was first attacked, she says, a policeman grabbed her by the throat, "pushing my head back till I thought my back was broken." During another suffragist demonstration a few days later, Freeman says, "I was footballed from one policeman to another," and another policeman "turned his undivided attention to making a corkscrew of my arm, until he had me on my knees, and then he kicked me and then took me into custody."

Freeman concludes her letter with an expression of bitterness: "It takes all my spare time not to be anti-man; this movement in England has shown the men up in a hateful light; women are for their pleasure and nothing else. God help them and their so-called Pride of Empire, for built upon such a rotten foundation it is sure to fall! One is thankful for those brave men who have come forward and are helping us in our fight. They have been the saving grace to us, and have kept our hearts sweet. Yours in a glorious cause, Elizabeth [*sic*] Freeman."[18]

Far from being intimidated by the violence of London constables, Elisabeth Freeman, along with many other suffragettes, continued her activities for the cause. In the spring of 1911, she was still giving speeches in Hyde Park on behalf of women's suffrage. On April 25, 1911, after delivering one of her Hyde Park harangues, Freeman encountered two American girls, Florence Luscomb and Margaret Foley, who were on their way through England to attend the International Woman Suffrage Congress in Stockholm. Luscomb was keeping a diary of their trip; excerpts reporting on their meetings with Freeman appeared in the *Woman's Journal.*

In her initial conversation with the two American girls, Freeman revealed one of the secrets of her success among the English — her shrewd adaptability, which was later used to good advantage in Waco. Freeman had observed in England that, when she was perceived to be an American, she had less effect on her audience, so she trained herself, as she put it, to "speak and dress English, which is very different from American." During her time abroad, she had also been to Germany and France, had learned to speak both German and French, and had visited prisons and given speeches on prison conditions in Germany and England.[19]

Every description of Elisabeth Freeman by Luscomb and Foley mentions her irrepressible vivacity, immense energy and generosity, and unquenchable enthusiasm for the cause. "Miss Freeman seems to be our good angel," Luscomb confided to her diary in the *Woman's Journal.*[20]

Elisabeth Freeman left England to return to the United States in September 1911, but the activities of Freeman and other suffrage activists in America came to be viewed partly through the prism of the increasingly fierce tactics of the militants in England. Infuriated by cruel treatment and the unresponsiveness of the government, some of Pankhurst's followers progressed from throwing stones to setting fires. Between April 23 and November 15, 1913, for example, there were forty-two major cases of arson, fires most likely set by suffragettes.[21] In the months leading up to Britain's entrance into World War I, suffragettes slashed several important paintings, placed bombs in Westminster Abbey and other churches, and, in the course of one night, burned down a library in Birmingham and three Scottish castles. One British suffragette, Emily Wilding Davison, in a desperate bid to gain public support for the suffragist cause, even committed suicide by throwing herself in front of the king's horse on Derby Day, June 8, 1913.[22] She broke through the barriers that separated the crowds from the racecourse and grabbed the bridle of the king's horse, which was in the lead. The horse fell, throwing the jockey and crushing Davison.

Davison died four days later without recovering consciousness. Her funeral was attended by thousands of grieving suffragettes dressed in white. She had told her friends that "the conscience of the people would awaken only to the sacrifice of a human life."[23] Despite the WSPU's relentless efforts, British women failed to attain full voting rights until 1928.

Having more than earned her stripes in the movement, however, Freeman decided to leave England in 1911, at long last, because she had been offered a paid position in the United States as a suffrage organizer for Carrie Chapman Catt, leader of the National American Woman Suffrage Association.[24] Freeman would find the battle for the vote to be almost as prolonged and wearisome in the United States.

By the winter of 1912, Elisabeth Freeman was the toast of the women's suffrage community in New York City. She was featured in a front-page article in the *New York Times;* the reporter, perhaps confused by Freeman's continued use of an English accent, identifies her as an Englishwoman and comments that she "does not weigh more than 100 pounds." He goes on to declare that she "created the most enthusiasm" of any speaker at a packed suffrage event in the Metropolitan Temple at 14th Street and Seventh Avenue. Freeman's topic was whether militancy hurt the cause of suffrage. "I don't think it does," [said firebrand Freeman]. "You have only to read the history of the United States to get the answer to this question . . . In Boston they destroyed the tea. In London we broke the windows. In both cases it was the merchant who suffered, and the suffering was for a great cause."[25]

By winter 1913, Freeman was well entrenched as a front-line fighter in the American women's suffrage movement. On February 12, 1913, she embarked on what was perhaps her most spectacular adventure in the suffragist cause in the United States: She joined a group of fourteen women calling themselves the "Army of the Hudson," under the leadership of "General" Rosalie Jones, who planned to walk the 225 miles from New York City to Washington, D.C.[26]

The long walk was to culminate with the hikers joining in the great women's suffrage parade to be held on March 3 in Washington, the day before Woodrow Wilson's first inauguration as president. All along the way, the marchers were to be fed, housed, and entertained by members of local suffrage societies — some of whom would join the march for a few miles.

Elisabeth Freeman was invited to go along with Rosalie Jones's "Army," not to hike, but to speak for women's suffrage whenever the suffragist "soldiers" or "pilgrims" stopped in a town or city along the way. Freeman's vehicle was a

Elisabeth Freeman with her "gypsy wagon" during the march of the "Army of the Hudson" from New York City to Washington, D.C., February 17, 1913. *Courtesy* George Grantham Bain Collection, LOT 11052-2, Prints and Photographs Division, Library of Congress [LC-USZ62-53218].

newsworthy feature of the march. Dressed in vaguely "gypsy" style herself, Freeman rode in a yellow "gypsy wagon" decorated with Votes for Women symbols and filled with suffrage literature. The marching women called the gypsy cart their "ammunition wagon." When the women came to a town, the wagon doubled as a speaker's platform.

The march to Washington by the Army of the Hudson turned out to be an enormously successful publicity gambit. According to the *Woman Voter*, organ of the New York State Woman Suffrage Association, "No propaganda work undertaken by the State Association and the Party has ever achieved such publicity."[27] All the New York papers and the national news syndicates covered the march. Day after day, from New York to Washington, the marchers were surrounded by reporters, special correspondents, and news photographers.

A *New York Times* reporter accompanied the march during the entire journey and filed copy that was by turns sympathetic and mildly derisive. The reporter notes the courage of the marchers as they faced bleeding, blistered, and swollen feet; freezing temperatures; and roads covered with snow and ice alternating with mud and slush — as well as the cheering and support given them by many townspeople. But he (she?) also slyly records petty disagreements among the members of the army, obstinate cows that planted themselves in the path of the marchers, and an inconvenient tendency of the marchers to frighten horses as they passed by with banners waving. The comments of less-than-enamored bystanders are also duly documented, such as those of the eighty-year-old woman in New Brunswick who admonished one of the marchers by declaring, "We are all home women here . . . and you ought to be home mending your husband's clothes."[28]

With a tendency to draw black Americans in caricature that was all too typical of the period, the *New York Times* journalist reports the comment of a black woman who was hanging clothes on the line in front of a small house outside of Princeton, New Jersey, as the suffragists went by. One of the suffragists asked the woman if she was with them. "I got enough to do looking after Rastus," she reportedly said. "I don't want no vote."[29]

Other black women, however, very much wanted to vote. Twice during the march, groups of black women joined the suffragists for short periods. The *Times* articles give the impression each time that Jones's pilgrims did not exactly tell the black women to go away, but did not receive them with any friendliness either.[30]

When Rosalie Jones's army reached Wilmington, Delaware, a delegation of southern men came to call on "the General," demanding to know "how the army stood upon the question of suffrage for negro women." The southern men announced that they favored votes for white women but, if the Army of the Hudson wanted votes for black women as well, "your way to Washington lies through the enemy's country." Jones sidestepped the controversy by saying this issue was up to the men and women of individual states to decide.[31]

A telling event took place in Baltimore on February 25 — revealing the daring character for the time of the woman who had devoted so much of her young life to single-minded pursuit of "Votes for Women" (the incessantly repeated suffragist slogan). In Baltimore the hikers were hosted at a luncheon at the Emerson Hotel by a group of young men who called themselves the "Sons of Jove." Mrs. Donald Hooker, president of the Just Government League of Baltimore, also attended. (It is tempting, though perhaps unjust, to picture Mrs. Hooker as a clone of the imperious and clueless Margaret Dumont of the Marx Brothers' movies.)

After the meal, when cigarettes and cigars were passed around, one of the mischievous Sons of Jove suggested to Elisabeth Freeman that she "ought to enjoy all the rights accorded to men" and offered her a cigarette, which she — never one to refuse a challenge — promptly accepted.[32] "Miss Freeman," comments the *Times* reporter, "is a militant suffragist. She broke windows in

London and served two terms in the Holloway Jail." Elisabeth Freeman puffed away for a moment or two. Mrs. Hooker spotted her and, rather startled, declared with an air of finality, "We don't do that in Baltimore."[33] Freeman ignored Mrs. Hooker, but soon after, one of the Sons of Jove, seeing that conversation had come to a halt as everyone stared and waited to see, perhaps, if Freeman would be struck by lightning, quietly took the cigarette out of Freeman's hand and put it out.

The women experienced their worst treatment near the end of the march, as they entered Bladensburg, Maryland, seeking shelter from a driving rain. They were jeered at, harassed, and jostled by two hundred rowdy boys from the Maryland Agricultural College at College Park. The boys knocked down one woman, tore banners off the accompanying automobiles, and tried to steal the women's baggage.[34]

The hooligan pranks of the Maryland college boys were just a prelude to what would happen when more than five thousand — perhaps as many as ten thousand — women marched through the streets of Washington, D.C., on March 3, led by the beautiful, charismatic Inez Milholland Boissevain wearing a white cape and riding a white horse. The march had been carefully planned to be a magnificent spectacle with nine bands, twenty floats, and women grouped and garbed according to their profession or place of origin.

The crowds of mostly male spectators, "a mob of the worst element," according to the Woman's Journal, surged into the street and blocked the way of the marchers while the D.C. police looked on, laughed, and made no attempt to help the women.[35] "Women were spit upon, slapped in the face, tripped up, pelted with burning cigar stubs, and insulted by jeers and obscene language too vile to print or repeat," wrote an angry suffragist reporter.[36]

Some of the suffragists who had cars drove them along the edge of the crowd to force the men back and allow the marchers to pass. One hundred of the women were injured seriously enough to be taken to the hospital. Secretary of War Henry Stimson finally called in a troop of cavalry from nearby Fort Myer to control the crowd.[37] The Woman's Journal notes that there were no similar problems during Wilson's inaugural procession the following day.

The Washington police, however, were mistaken when they thought they could enjoy the spectacle of over five thousand women being mistreated by a bunch of street toughs with impunity. Many of the women had connections at the highest levels. Congress held an inquiry into the misbehavior of the crowd and the failure of the police to intervene to protect the marchers. In the end, the superintendent of police of the District of Columbia lost his job. The suffragists also reaped a huge windfall of public sympathy and positive publicity—although that did not translate into instantaneous passage of suffrage legislation.

During the summer of 1913, Elisabeth Freeman was still slogging away in the suffragist trenches, raising money for the cause by selling copies of the *Woman's Journal* in New York City and environs, and organizing groups of girls and young women to do the same. For this tedious work Freeman was paid $125 a month. In her passion to serve the cause, she even agreed to cover her own expenses for the first month of her employment.[38]

In one of a series of letters to Agnes Ryan, business manager of the *Woman's Journal* in Boston, Freeman apologizes for not being able to do more: "I only wish I was a rich woman . . . But alas I am only poor and can do so very little."[39] This complaint seems to be real enough; at least one of Freeman's many letters to Ryan refers to "the beastly landlord" who "wants his rent."[40]

Freeman's reward for her hard work during this period seems chiefly to have consisted of praise from Ryan plus the satisfaction of advancing the cause of "Votes for Women." "There is no other person who can do the organizing job as you can,"[41] wrote Ryan, and, a few days later, "You are a wonder."[42]

The business of hawking suffrage newspapers on the streets of New York for five cents a copy—and trying desperately to inspire groups of other young women to perform the same task—was exhausting, discouraging work. "New York City is so hot," Freeman says in one midsummer letter to Ryan, "life hardly seems worth living."[43] Yet, soon after, on a better day, she declares, with only a touch of self-irony, "My soul shouts with joy!" just because an unexpectedly high number of *Woman's Journals* had been sold that day.[44]

Even on those blistering hot days when the papers did not sell and men on the street teased her and suggested that she stay home and "try nice quiet means to get your vote," Freeman stood up to them, telling them that "nice quiet means" hadn't worked for sixty years—and drew satisfaction from the fact that she had gotten "many good thrusts home."[45]

"Your spirit is the kind I love and you are making me love you," replied Agnes Ryan to one of Freeman's letters. "I wish that every woman who cares for suffrage in this country might have a little English training. It seems to me that it engenders the right spirit. Then too those who have served in England seem to have learned how to do things."[46]

By this time, "Votes for Women" had obviously become more than a matter of politics to Elisabeth Freeman. It was a religion to which she devoted herself, heart, mind, and soul. Even though she complained of heat and fatigue—and, at the end of a long day selling newspapers on the sun-baked streets, her handwriting widened across the page to a barely legible scrawl — even though she said later she was so ill at the end of the march from New York to Washington that she was hardly aware of what happened when they reached Washington — Freeman's enthusiasm never flagged.[47] She was engaged in what was for her the adventure of a lifetime.

Occasionally, Freeman took time out from her work in the suffrage trenches to attend other kinds of events, such as an "Author's Night for Woman Suffrage's Sake" that took place at Cooper Union on January 12, 1914. It was common for the reform movements of the day to cross-pollinate each other, so there was nothing remarkable about the fact that one of the attendees at this event was none other than W. E. B. Du Bois, then director of research and publications for the NAACP.

Du Bois had consistently expressed a strong belief in women's suffrage and had reacted in outrage in *The Crisis* to the mistreatment of the women during the Washington suffrage parade of March 1913.[48] Perhaps Du Bois and Freeman engaged in some conversation on the evening of January 12, 1914; perhaps Freeman expressed some sympathy for the plight of blacks in America, and Du Bois conveyed his understanding of women's desire for the right to vote.

Also present at the Author's Night were the famous muckraker Lincoln Steffens; poet and playwright Percy MacKaye; Frederick Howe, sociologist and author of *The City, Hope of Democracy*; and Edwin Markham, the poet best known for his sympathetic portrayal of the beaten-down farmer in *The Man with the Hoe* (1899). In the midst of these literary luminaries, in a photograph taken for the *New York Evening Post*, stood Elisabeth Freeman, whose only "literary" products were her letters and speeches.[49]

In the photo, Freeman, now approaching thirty, appears for the first time to be a bit worn and drawn, the planes of her face more angular than before, as if being on the road day and night for suffrage was beginning to take its toll. But the corners of her mouth are still slightly turned up in a faint suggestion of mischief, as if to say, especially to men, "I am not the demure creature you expect me to be. I am someone quite different altogether." This event may or may not have been the initial meeting between a representative of the NAACP and Elisabeth Freeman, but the photograph documents the fact that a contact had been made that would not be forgotten.

In July 1915, Freeman wrote a letter to Caroline Lexow Babcock from Women's Political Union headquarters in Syracuse. Babcock was right-hand woman to Harriot Stanton Blatch, who headed the Women's Political Union, the primary suffrage organization in the state of New York. All the WPU women

"A Literary Gathering in Support of Women's Suffrage" at Cooper Union, January 12, 1914. Seated *(left to right)*, Will Irwin, Edwin Markham, Lincoln Steffens, Arturo Giovannitti, Percy MacKaye, W. E. B. Du Bois; standing *(left to right)*, Mrs. Flora Gaitlin, Ellis O. Jones, Elisabeth Freeman, William Hard, Mrs. Paula Jakobi, Frederick Howe, and Mrs. Frederick Howe. *Courtesy* NAACP Archives, Library of Congress, Prints and Photographs Division [LC-USZ62-108198].

were feverishly working to achieve victory in the statewide referendum on votes for women, scheduled for November 2, 1915. Freeman reports in her letter to Babcock that she is about to set off for Ilion, Herkimer, and Little Falls on her way to Schenectady, planning "mainly to do factories and street meetings." She also says that she is going to speak at a prizefight in Syracuse that very night. "I think this is the first time this has been done," she proclaims proudly, exhibiting her usual willingness to plunge in where angels feared to tread.[50]

New York women lost the 1915 New York referendum on votes for women by less than 200,000 votes. It was probably a coincidence that one of the few places outside of New York City where the referendum succeeded was Schenectady, one of the cities where Freeman had made speeches. Other activists were disheartened by the loss; Harriot Stanton Blatch reacted with enormous bitterness following this defeat and vowed she would never make another suffrage speech on a street corner.[51]

Elisabeth Freeman probably had a few choice words to say to her friends, too, about the male voters of New York State, but she picked herself up quickly. Sometime during late 1915 or early 1916, the restless warrior removed to faraway Texas. Freeman and another peripatetic activist for women's suffrage, Lavinia Engle of Washington, D.C., busied themselves organizing the entire state. Because of their efforts, according to a prominent Houston suffragist leader, the number of suffrage clubs in Texas during 1915–16 increased to eighty (from only twenty-one as of April 1914).[52] The *Dallas Morning News* supported this claim, reporting that between 1915 and 1916, suffrage enrollment in Texas grew from two thousand to eight thousand, with each of the eighty suffrage clubs in the state averaging about one hundred members.[53]

Freeman's suffrage-related travels through Texas took her to Waco. On April 2, 1916, about six weeks before the Waco Horror, society editor Kate Friend of the *Waco Morning News* informed her readers that Elisabeth Freeman had been in Texas since midwinter as "state organizer for women's suffrage clubs." She continued: "Almost daily, she has reported another equal suffrage club organized." The women of the various suffrage clubs in Texas had been hard at work, doubtless under Freeman's experienced tutelage, preparing a "mammoth petition" asking the Texas Legislature to permit a referendum on women's suffrage in Texas. "Thousands upon thousands of names are on that petition," wrote Kate Friend.[54]

From May 10 to 12, 1916, the annual convention of the Woman's Suffrage Association of Texas, under the leadership of the wily Minnie Fisher Cunningham of Galveston, was held at the Adolphus Hotel in Dallas. Elisabeth Freeman attended. Although she is mentioned only once briefly by name in the lavish *Dallas Morning News* coverage of the convention,[55] the paper comments that "several well-known advocates of votes for women from the North and East" were to be featured speakers and names Freeman's carpetbagger partner from the East, Lavinia Engle.[56]

A massive follow-up story about the suffrage convention in the newspaper includes pictures of many of the local heads of suffrage organizations; one of those pictured is the fetching Mrs. W. E. Spell of Waco.[57] Mrs. Spell, the *News* reports, made a "rousing" speech at the convention, declaring that suffragists should work vigorously to defeat every legislative candidate who was opposed to women's suffrage.[58]

When Minnie Fisher Cunningham gaveled the suffrage convention to a close on May 12, it must have seemed to Elisabeth Freeman that she knew exactly what she would be doing for the next few months — traveling from one steamy town to the next, stirring up the women of Texas to seek the vote. But she was about to take a prolonged and unforeseen detour from the political demands of women into a darker place.

The good citizens of Waco probably thought in early May 1916 that the fine reputation of their city would continue to grow and spread to the four corners of the earth, and prosperity would increase and beckon like a straight road, newly paved and sprinkled. But the new road was about to double back into an ugly time the city had never really left.

William Walling, Moorfield Storey, Joel Spingarn, Oswald Villard, Mary Ovington, and, above all, W. E. B. Du Bois were in the best position to anticipate what was coming because they had seen it all before. Even they would be shocked, however, by the daytime nightmare they were about to confront.

Elisabeth Freeman was right on the spot, just one hundred miles from Waco, when the news came three days after the suffrage convention ended that Jesse Washington had been burned to death in Waco's town square.

All three primary aspects of the Waco Horror story were about to come together: a violence-prone city steeped in virulent racism that all the self-improvement clubs, prosperity banquets, and civic pride had neither moderated nor disguised; a brash new national protest organization led by an idealistic group of white reformers and one black man with a stunningly eloquent and powerful literary voice; and a clever young devotee of women's suffrage who had been proselytizing and outwitting hostile strangers on the streets of unfamiliar towns for many years. When these phenomena met, something new would happen, something that would begin to change the way people in America thought and felt and talked about the worst form of abuse of black Americans, the pestilence of lynching.

CHAPTER 4

PRELUDE TO A LYNCHING

"Slogan Is Harmony and Efficiency"

Officials take over city reins: New administration is
begun when John Dollins is inaugurated Mayor—
slogan is harmony and efficiency.

—*Waco Morning News*

ON April 12, 1916, John Dollins, former police and fire commissioner of
Waco, a tall, rotund man "with a big smile and a heart of equal proportions," was inaugurated as mayor. He was the only man in the history of Waco—at least until his death in 1930—to be elected mayor without
opposition.[1] Over a mass of "freshly inspiring flowers" on the round desk in the
city commission chamber, Dollins addressed the crowd assembled to welcome him, expressing his fond hope that, with his arrival, "all factionalism and
strife" in city government would come to an end.[2]

Dollins took office at a time that was more unsettled than usual. For one
thing, a small article in the *Waco Times Herald* two days after his induction announced that the boll weevil was destined to infest all cotton acreage in the
South and nothing was going to stop it.[3] A *Waco Semi-Weekly Tribune* story in
June continued the theme, warning that the loss to Texas farmers could be as
high as thirty million dollars for the year—a sinister prognosis for a community where cotton was the mainstay of the economy.[4]

78

Waco Mayor John Dollins. *Courtesy* Archives Division of The Texas Collection, Baylor University, Waco, Texas.

Popular amusements of the day, however, helped distract Wacoans from worrying too much about whether available remedies like calcium arsenate dust would control the plundering of Texas cotton by the boll weevil.[5] One of the record-smashing entertainments of the months just prior to the Waco Horror was the first local screening of D. W. Griffith's *The Birth of a Nation*, the epic racist paean to the glories of antebellum society and the rise of the Ku Klux Klan after the Civil War.[6] White Wacoans in general were delighted with Griffith's portrayal of slavery as a misunderstood and happy way of life and the depredations of Reconstruction as akin to the torturing of early Christians in the Roman Coliseum.

Local reviews of *The Birth of a Nation* in November 1915 plainly express the intense racism the film encouraged and justified. The following is a excerpt from a typical review in the *Waco Times Herald*: "The production of D. W. Griffith, masterful in its delineation will linger long in the memory of all who witness it, presenting as it does the birth of the woes and miseries of a subjected people, who, when denied the right of freemen [*sic*], produced an army of men, whose work was swift, sure and silent: who visited stern justice on the despoilers of their homes, and who fought only that the superiority of the white race might prevail."[7]

The climax of the film focuses on the cautionary tale of a freed slave, Gus, intoxicated by his newfound equality, who attempts to "marry" Flora, the lovely, blonde youngest daughter of an old southern family, the Camerons. He pursues her until she throws herself off a cliff in order to save her "purity." Flora's brother Ben thereupon leads the Klan to seize the villainous Gus and lynch him on the spot. *The Birth of a Nation* was telling southern audiences exactly what they wanted to hear: that their way of life was right and correct and necessary to keep the persecutions of Reconstruction from ever recurring.

A few southerners, however, were making sincere, if rather feeble, efforts to end the lynching mania. Only a few days before the much-lauded premiere of *The Birth of a Nation* in Waco, a group of presidents of Texas church-sponsored colleges, including the president of Baylor University, met in Georgetown, Texas, and produced "An Address to the People of Texas." It was printed in full in the *Waco Morning News*. The surprisingly frank "Address" laments the nearly four thousand "mob murders" committed in the United States during the previous thirty years and condemns the "thousands" who participated in the murders, the "many other thousands" who looked on approvingly "with a sense of the satisfaction of the spirit of vengeance and race hatred," and the rest who regarded the incidents as something they could not control and therefore "dismissed them from [their] minds as [they] laid aside the newspaper which contained their gruesome story." The "Address" postulates "a complete revolution of sentiment among all classes of our people" as the only cure for "this deep-seated moral disease" and eloquently calls on "the press, the pulpit and the school" to remedy the situation by teaching better values. It also demands more courage and better behavior from officers of the law, whose job it is to protect life and maintain order.[8]

Laudable as such attempts to end lynching were, and admirable as the men were who pursued them, often courageously opposing public opinion, their efforts all seemed to take the same form. Good men — righteous, religious men — would plead with the mass of southerners to mend their ways and stop the moral deterioration of society and the besmirchment of the South's reputation throughout world. But their well-meant pleas did nothing to move the populace to whom they were addressed because there was no clear penalty — legal or social — attached to this moral deterioration. A white man could hang or burn a black man with enthusiasm on Thursday and still be welcomed at the general store the same afternoon, at the bank where he deposited the proceeds from the sale of his cotton on Friday morning, and in his pew at church on Sunday.

Other concerns pressed more closely on the people of Waco in May of 1916 than the fear of "moral disease." On March 9, 1916, about a month before Dollins's inauguration, Pancho Villa and over five hundred of his followers attacked the tiny American border town of Columbus, New Mexico, and killed eighteen Americans. On orders from Pres. Woodrow Wilson, Gen. "Black Jack" Pershing formed what became known as the Punitive Expedition, crossed into Mexico with ten thousand troops, and set out to find Villa and bring him to justice.

None of this touched Waco directly at first. On May 7, the day before the murder that set the events of the Waco Horror in motion, the *Waco Times Herald* announced that Villa would soon be apprehended — a declaration that appeared over and over again in the Waco papers over the next several weeks.[9] But on May 8, the *Waco Morning News* told anxious Wacoans that there had been another border attack by Mexican bandits at Glen Springs, Boquillas, and Deemers in the Big Bend area. This time three American soldiers and a ten-year-old boy had been killed and two other Americans — a shopkeeper and his clerk — had been kidnapped.[10] As usual, it was rumored that the fearsome Villa was leading the raiders himself, but no one knew for sure. The day after the raid in the Big Bend, the militias of Texas, Arizona, and New Mexico were ordered by President Wilson to report to Gen. Frederick Funston for duty on the border.[11]

Companies K and G of Waco were called up immediately, about three hundred local men.[12] "Boys Ready to Go" brags a subhead to a story in the *Waco Times Herald*, which is followed by more chest-thumping copy: "No city in the state will be better represented, population considered, than Waco. Members of the local militia have been holding themselves in readiness, for just such a call as was sent out today from Washington. They have realized the gravity of the situation on the border for the past few weeks, and they have been kept on a state of preparedness for instant response by Captains Weatherred and Torrence."[13] This overblown pride in the readiness of young Wacoans to go to war was punctured by subsequent events, as will be seen.

As if the calling up of local companies of the National Guard was not enough to make a mother's heart beat a little faster, another danger lurked at the edge of consciousness — further removed from Waco than the muddy river that meanders between Texas and Mexico, but, in the end, a much greater potential threat. "Germans Make More Gains in Offensive at Verdun," whispers a smaller headline on the front page of the *Waco Morning News* on May 8, tucked below the story about the marauding bandits.[14] The Great War in Europe was continuing into a third year with no sign of resolution. In the meantime, Wilson was threatening to break off diplomatic relations with Germany if German submarines continued to menace American ships, and there was the chance that Texas boys might eventually have to go overseas to fight the Hun.[15]

It is a safe bet, however, that in May 1916, the sheriff of McLennan County, one Samuel Simpson Fleming, was not lying awake nights worrying about the boll weevil, Pancho Villa, or German progress through the thick forests and trenches of France. Fleming was facing a bitter battle for reelection against his arch political rival, Special Officer Bob Buchanan. The Democratic primary, the only election that counted at that time in Texas, loomed before Fleming like a ghost in the night. It was set for July 22, a little over two months away, and Sam Fleming knew it would be a squeaker.

Fleming was not a native Wacoan, hailing originally from St. James, Missouri.[16] Before he ran for sheriff of McLennan County, he had worked for eight years at the McLendon Hardware Company in Waco, selling buggies and cultivators.[17] From his very first campaign in 1912, Fleming's paid political ads in the Waco newspapers were unusually long-winded, florid, and obsequious. He spoke to the voters at great length with something of the attitude of a stray puppy — tongue out, panting, eager for approval, longing to be petted and perhaps thrown a vote or two in lieu of bones. Because he could not claim any law enforcement experience when he first ran for sheriff, Fleming expatiated instead on the fact that he was a "southern man" and that his father was a "southern soldier." "I have lived in the south all my life," he declared, "coming to Texas in my earliest manhood days." In other words, having suffered the misfortune of being born elsewhere, Fleming had hurried to Texas as soon as he could.

Fleming deeply regretted, he said, that he had not actually been able to meet each voter personally, although he had tried manfully to do so. He continued: "Elect me your sheriff and every duty shall be performed; the high, the low, the rich and the poor shall be upheld with the strong hands of justice . . . Your wives, daughters, mothers and sisters, the noblest and sweetest creation of all this world, shall receive every care and protection that blood can give. I will appreciate your support and make you a worthy servant" (emphasis on the word *servant*).[18] By contrast, the ads for Fleming's opponent, Bob Buchanan, were blunt, unapologetic, straightforward: "Why not vote for Bob Buchanan for Sheriff? . . . He is brave. He is honest. He is fearless. He is clean. He is active. Bob hates crime."[19]

Fleming's obituary, many years later, includes the assertion that "old-timers speak of Fleming as one of the best vote-getters the county ever saw."[20] This was back in the days when all politics was retail. Bob Poage, congressman from Waco from 1936 to 1978, liked to describe the fine art of campaigning for public office in Waco back in 1924, when he first ran for the Texas Legislature while he was still a law school student at Baylor. Any political campaign in McLennan County in those days, recalled Poage, began with the hopeful candidate stationing himself at the rotunda of the McLennan County Courthouse and distributing his card to everyone who passed by. "There were a great many people," said Poage, "who would not vote for any candidate who had not given them a card. That was a customary thing for a man to say . . . If he doesn't think enough of me to ask for my vote, I'm not going to give it to him . . . [You would say to the potential voter:] I'm running for the legislature, and I hope you can support me. You didn't give him any reason why he should support you . . . for the local officials, it was almost entirely a personality contest."[21]

A heavyset man in the days when girth suggested a man of substance, Fleming was a born salesman and probably knew just about everyone in Waco who had ever thought about buying a buggy or a cultivator. Apparently, he was very effective at selling himself as a candidate for sheriff, even though in 1912, he was running against the incumbent sheriff, G. W. Tilley, in addition to Bob Buchanan, another experienced peace officer.

In his passion to get himself elected, however, Fleming made a mistake that would come back to haunt him in 1916. He promised in his campaign ads that he would serve as sheriff for only two terms. "I do not believe," he told voters, "that it is to the interest of good government that a man should be sheriff more than two terms, and I promise you now that if I am elected, I will prepare myself to serve you in a greater capacity and not run for the sheriff's office the third term."[22]

Despite his charm, however, Fleming barely got himself elected in 1912. He won the primary that summer by the paper-thin margin of 21 votes over G. W. Tilley, out of 8,110 votes cast; he ran only 101 votes ahead of Bob Buchanan. Each of the three major candidates in the race, Fleming, Buchanan, and Tilley, received around 2,300 votes. The contest turned out to be such a cliff-hanger that the results were not announced until four days after the election.[23] There must have been a faction in town that was impressed by Fleming's friendly, hearty manner, while those who preferred a professional lawman in the office were almost equally split between the two more qualified candidates, Tilley and Buchanan.

Fleming was probably reelected in 1914 without opposition. Tilley did not run again, and Bob Buchanan indicated in campaign ads in later years that he had not challenged Fleming in 1914, deciding to let the man have his "two terms."[24] But there is no doubt that in 1916, Bob Buchanan was running again and running hard. Knowing he had beaten Buchanan by only a handful of votes in 1912, Fleming could feel his rival nipping at his heels.

By contrast to Fleming, Bob Buchanan was lean and sported a big, black handlebar moustache and an equally intimidating black ten-gallon hat. In his campaign photos, he looks precisely the part of the lone marshal in an old-time western. By 1916, Buchanan had already served fifteen years as a Waco policeman, part of that time as assistant chief. Some of his political ads make a big point of the fact that, unlike Fleming, Buchanan was a native of Waco whose father, Jack Buchanan, had helped rid the county of "the most depraved band of marauding cut-throats and horse thieves that ever cursed any country with their presence." Buchanan, by implication, was not only a local, but, unlike Fleming, had inherited a talent for law enforcement.[25]

One of Bob Buchanan's additional claims to fame (not mentioned in his campaign ads, as Elisabeth Freeman was to report to the NAACP later) was that he already had "three dead 'niggers' to his 'credit.'"[26] One of the three killings had occurred as recently as November 1915. A black man named Will Bradley, whose age was reported as fifty-four, allegedly tried to break into Buchanan's house on the night of November 8. Buchanan's wife called her husband and handed him a revolver. When Buchanan appeared, according to the newspaper account, Bradley turned and tried to run. Buchanan shot Bradley the first time as he was trying to escape. Bradley then turned back toward Buchanan and threw an axe at the officer, whereupon Buchanan shot Bradley a second time and killed him. In the spirit of a paid political ad, the newspaper story remarks, "[Officer Buchanan] is regarded as efficient, cool under dangerous sit-

Waco lawmen: *(seated on left)* John Dollins; *(standing on left)* Bob Buchanan. *Courtesy* Archives Division of The Texas Collection, Baylor University, Waco, Texas.

uations and slow to use a gun in handling difficult cases."[27] Apparently, no one seriously questioned Buchanan's version of how he had come to kill one more black man.

Under the circumstances, Sam Fleming may have determined that he could not afford to let Bob Buchanan appear to be more effective in handling crimes committed by blacks than the duly elected sheriff. Everything Fleming did from May 8 through May 16 demonstrated that he was well aware that the case of Jesse Washington would end his career as sheriff if he did not handle it with due deference to the sentiments of the majority in the community.

And so May 8, 1916, arrived, a warm day with temperatures already spiking into the upper eighties and the local populace perhaps a little more on edge than usual as they worried about Pancho Villa, the kaiser and, more trivially (except to those directly involved), the upcoming Democratic primary. Nevertheless, the *Waco Times Herald* made a point, as was customary, of celebrating the fact that two organizations, the Texas Christians and the Southwestern Water Works, were holding conventions in Waco. The *Waco Morning News* good-naturedly enjoined out-of-town visitors to "enjoy your presence."[28]

Wacoans were about to learn, however, that there was no need to travel to Boquillas or Verdun in order to meet a violent death. Death — a brutal and shameful death — could overtake one without warning right at home in McLennan County in the middle of a sunny spring afternoon.

CHAPTER 5

AN "EXCITING OCCURRENCE"

The Lynching

> Yesterday's exciting occurrence is a closed incident.
>
> —*Waco Times Herald*

THE story of the Waco Horror begins with the discovery of a body. Just about sundown on the evening of Monday, May 8, 1916, near the town of Robinson,[1] eight miles south of Waco, twenty-one-year-old Ruby Fryer and her brother, fourteen-year-old George Fryer Jr., returned home from chopping cotton on the family's two hundred–acre farm.[2] In the heavy heat and quiet of the late afternoon, they noticed that their mother, Lucy Fryer, was not in the house as usual. Just as George was going out to look for her, Ruby peered through the window and saw Lucy lying in a pool of blood in the doorway of the seed house, about thirty steps away.[3]

A neighbor, Cris Simon, had been away from home all day and had just come back through the big gate at the main road when he heard Ruby and George screaming and crying over their mother's body. It was probably Simon who ran for George Fryer Sr., who had been working in a different part of the field from the children, about a mile from the house. The *Waco Times Herald* reported that when George Fryer Sr. learned that his wife was dead, he "was overcome."[4]

The young George and Lucy Fryer. By permission of Lucy Wollitz Kirkland.

According to Lucy Fryer's granddaughter, Lucy Wollitz Kirkland, who still lives in Robinson, there was a quiet romance connected to the history of George and Lucy Fryer — a story of suffering, separation, and exile for the sake of true love, which may have made George Fryer's grief at the loss of his wife all the more terrible. George and Lucy Fryer grew up in central England. George was said to have been a stable boy on a large estate while Lucy was the daughter of the upper-class family who employed him. Lucy's parents did not want the young couple to marry, so George crossed the ocean, entering the United States at Galveston in 1882. He settled in Cottonwood, Texas, and worked for four years to earn enough money to send for Lucy.[5]

There is some evidence that this often-told tale of two lovers divided by class may not be strictly accurate. According to United Kingdom birth records, a Lucy Davis was born on July 1, 1862, the same birth date recorded for Lucy Davis Fryer in Fryer family records and on her death certificate. This Lucy Davis was born in Callaughton Wenlock, County of Salop (now part of Shropshire), the daughter of Henry Davis and Elizabeth Pope Davis. But Henry Davis, Lucy's father, is identified in the official birth record, not as a lord, merchant, or landowner, but as an "agricultural labourer."

Whatever the true story of their births and original circumstances, George Fryer and Lucy Davis did immigrate to the United States from England and were married in McLennan County on April 30, 1890.[6] At the time of their marriage, Lucy was twenty-seven and George was within a couple of weeks of his thirtieth birthday.

The couple settled in the Lorena area in the southern part of McLennan County. Their first child, Ruby, was born in 1894. In 1898, they had another little girl named Beatrice Pearl, who died in 1907 at the age of nine and was buried in the Lorena cemetery.[7] George Jr. was born in 1901.

At the time of Lucy's murder, the Fryers had been living in Robinson for six to eight years and were "among the most highly esteemed and respected residents of the Robinson community," according to the newspapers.[8] The couple had just celebrated their twenty-sixth wedding anniversary. Lucy was fifty-three. But all that was past now.

Lucy Fryer lay in the doorway of the seed house "almost brained and criminally assaulted."[9] Her skull had been bashed in at several points and her clothing was disheveled. Dr. J. H. Maynard examined her and reported at the trial

The mature Lucy Fryer. By permission of Lucy Wollitz Kirkland.

that "a quantity of brain had escaped from the cranial vault" and at least two of the six wounds on her head, made with a heavy, blunt instrument, could have killed her.[10]

Deputy Sheriffs Lee Jenkins and Barney Goldberg arrived on the scene first and were followed soon after by Sheriff Samuel S. Fleming, Constable Leslie Stegall, and Deputy Phil Hobbs. Both Stegall and Jenkins were highly regarded peace officers. Jenkins began his career in law enforcement as a Texas Ranger in 1880 at the age of eighteen and was elected constable in 1883. Later he served as deputy sheriff, detective, and chief of police. When he died in 1929, he was described as "the best criminal detective the Lone Star state has known."[11]

About fourteen years younger than Jenkins, Stegall also began his career as a peace officer as a very young man when he became a deputy sheriff in 1897. He served Waco as constable from 1912 to 1922, and then was elected McLennan County sheriff for the next ten years. Stegall, like Jenkins, was described by admirers as "a detective type officer [who] used modern methods of detection in the days when strong arm methods were prevalent."[12] Stegall and Jenkins have important roles to play in this story. Together they helped to turn the tide of Waco's ugly history.

At this point in their illustrious careers, however, both men were subordinate to friendly, accommodating Sheriff Fleming. Although Fleming got most of the credit for solving the murder of Lucy Fryer, it was Lee Jenkins, according to at least one newspaper report, who immediately found evidence that pointed to a suspect. The "evidence" may simply have been the fact that Cris Simon had that morning seen a black farm laborer, seventeen-year-old Jesse Washington, planting cotton about 250 yards from the Fryer house — closer to the house than either Mr. Fryer or the children and close enough to know that after the noon meal no one else was around.[13] As Simon arrived home that evening, he saw Jesse Washington coming in from the field and going to the mule lot near the seed house just a few minutes before the children cried out.

Jesse Washington, with his mother and father, Henry and Martha, and at least one brother, William, possibly about sixteen, had been living and working on the Fryer farm for only five months or so, since the beginning of the year.[14] According to Elisabeth Freeman's account of the lynching, there were also some younger children in the family.[15] Jesse Washington was a large, strong young man, but was illiterate and possibly retarded. When Freeman went to Waco to investigate the lynching for the NAACP, one of Washington's teachers told her that no one had ever been able to teach Jesse to read or write.[16]

One lifelong resident of Robinson, Thomas Hague, claimed in an interview that he was told by his father, Hugh Hague, who was a close friend of George Fryer Sr., that Jesse Washington was not retarded, but "a little bit thick-headed" and "just plain ol' lazy." The elder Hague tried to get Jesse Washington to help him with some carpentry work, but the task seemed to require more effort than Washington wanted to put out.[17] (Or perhaps carpentry was simply beyond Jesse's abilities.)

During this period, there were other black men who allegedly committed crimes and were lynched who fit the same pattern as Jesse Washington: "illiterate and feeble-minded," as lynching victims were often characterized in the literature of the Association of Southern Women for the Prevention of Lynching.[18] Henry Smith, the victim of vicious, prolonged public torture and burning in 1893 in Paris, Texas, was "out of his head for weeks" at a time, suffered from attacks of delirium tremens, and should have been in an asylum, according to a local black minister.[19] George Hughes, the victim of the burning of the courthouse in Sherman, Texas, in 1930, was also said to have been illiterate and feeble-minded.[20] Lynch mobs, which were coagulations of cowards and bullies, naturally tended to focus on the most defenseless and friendless black men they could find.

One of the best indications that Jesse Washington was "absolutely deficient," as Elisabeth Freeman puts it in her report, is not, according to her reasoning, the fact that "he attacked an old woman of 53 when this young girl [Ruby] was in the family."[21] Enough is known about rape now to know that the impulse is not activated by the victim's sexual appeal. The more revealing detail is, rather, the fact that, after Jesse Washington supposedly raped and killed Lucy Fryer, he went placidly back to planting cotton as if nothing had happened and made no effort to escape or to cover up his crime other than hiding the hammer that was later said to have been used in the attack. Freeman reports that when Jesse Washington was arrested, he was frightened at first, but then "curled up in the automobile and went fast to sleep."[22]

Freeman also reports a rumor she was unable to verify, which, if true, would indicate that, in the context of the times, Jesse Washington was a hothead with very poor judgment. Freeman was told by one of Waco's leading black men that the Saturday night before the murder, Washington went to Rosenthal, another small town south of Robinson, and, while there, accidentally stepped on the toes of a white man. "The white man smashed him," writes Freeman in her report to the NAACP. Washington fought back until finally the white man said, "If you get in my way again, I will blow your damned head off." On his way home, Washington supposedly drove into the man's yard and said, "Now blow my head off."[23]

Whatever the intelligence or temperament of the alleged assailant, as soon as word of the murder of Lucy Fryer got out, a general hue and cry arose in the Robinson neighborhood. The male residents, "thoroughly aroused and greatly incensed over the terrible crime," reports the *Times Herald*, organized to try to help the officers find the culprit.[24]

From the first, the *Herald* seasoned news stories about the murder with incendiary language designed to make the tale more dramatic. Helpful asides include the following: "That Mrs. Fryar [sic] had made desperate resistance against the brute who assaulted her and then completed his fiendish crime by killing her, was unmistakable"; and, "That she was given no chance for her life is apparent, and the lustful brute waited until he was absolutely sure no help was in sight before he attacked his helpless victim."[25]

Fortunately for Jesse Washington, the officers found him before the men of Robinson did. He was sitting in his yard, unconcernedly whittling a piece of wood.[26] Lee Jenkins later testified that he found blood on Jesse Washington's clothes, undershirt, and pants.[27] Washington claimed the blood had come from a nosebleed, but Jenkins arrested him on the spot. By then it was about nine o'clock in the evening, only three hours after the body was found.[28]

Jesse's brother William, and later his parents and a woman named "Moore" who lived with them, were all arrested along with Jesse. Officers stated that they had arrested family members not because anyone other than Jesse had participated in the crime, but so that "no avenue of obtaining information may be lost by the officers."[29] The real reason was probably to apply more pressure on Jesse to confess.

Jesse was taken to Waco, where he was questioned by both Lee Jenkins and County Attorney John B. McNamara. At first, he "denied, stoutly" that he had had anything to do with the rape and murder of Lucy Fryer.[30] Later he told McNamara that he had indeed beaten Lucy Fryer with a "piece of iron"; finally, he admitted that he had killed her with a blacksmith's hammer.

The most incriminating element in Washington's confession, according to newspaper reports, was that he told his questioners exactly where he had hidden the hammer. While Washington was being interrogated, a group of officers was turning the Fryer farm upside down trying to locate the murder weapon — they even replowed ground in the area where Washington had been working — but they failed to find what they sought.[31]

The hammer was finally discovered right where Washington said it would be, at the end of the rows where he had been plowing, in some high brush and weeds near a hackberry tree along the main Robinsonville road. According to testimony at Washington's trial, it was covered with blood and bits of cotton-seed lint.[32]

Sheriff Fleming knew, of course, that the citizens of Robinson and the vicinity were on the prowl and would soon hear that Jesse Washington had been arrested. Fleming made arrangements to transfer him, the very night he was arrested, to the jail in Hillsboro, some thirty-five miles north of Waco. Sometime on Tuesday, the Waco newspapers were informed that Jesse Washington had confessed to the crime to Sheriff Fleming on Tuesday morning in the Hillsboro jail.

Fleming could see that Hillsboro was not far enough away, so he had Jesse moved again, this time to the Dallas County jail, a further sixty-five miles from Waco. In Dallas, Washington repeated his confession before witnesses. The confession was officially recorded and read back to him. Washington signed with an X.[33]

In the meantime, there were ominous developments in McLennan County. On his way out of town to serve some papers Tuesday night, Sheriff Fleming encountered "a determined body of citizens from Robinson, Rosenthal and other towns in the southern part of the county" on their way into Waco to get Jesse Washington.[34] Another lawman might have taken a different approach to this challenge to his authority, but Fleming's method of dealing with the crisis was to get out of his car, gather the men around him, and talk to them earnestly in the middle of the road. He pleaded his case to about five hundred angry citizens, reminding them that he had solved the crime, arrested the culprit, and obtained a confession in less than twenty-four hours and was now obligated by his oath of office to protect the man in his custody. He told the men that Jesse Washington was out of their reach in Dallas, but encouraged them to come into Waco and search the jail if they did not believe him. A long line of "grim-visaged farmers" took Fleming up on his offer, caravaning into town in a line of "buggies, autos and men on horseback," after the leader of the group declared, as reported in the *Times Herald*, "When we left home tonight our wives, daughters and sisters kissed us good bye and told us to do our duty, and we're trying to do it as citizens."[35]

The newspaper coverage, however, leaves no doubt of the general climate of sympathy for the would-be lynchers. "It was admitted by the officers last night," reports the *Morning News*, "that if there ever was a justification for the formation of a mob, the Robinson crime was one of them." The *News* even compares the mob to their glorious forebears who had fought the Redcoats for freedom from Great Britain: "Resembling the forefathers who dared anything for their country's sake, the determined band of farmers and neighbors last night declared to the sheriff that they didn't want trouble, but that their blood would not stand for a fiendish brute to trample the chastity and sacredness of life and their women folk."[36]

What ensued, however, was hardly the "shot heard 'round the world"; it more closely resembled a farcical episode from one of the popular traveling vaudeville shows that occasionally passed through Waco. Sheriff Fleming led the delegation of farmers into town and encouraged the entire group to search the jail — which they proceeded to do most thoroughly, climbing on the steam radiators to be sure no one was hiding on top of the cells, exploring the section where demented prisoners were kept, and even clambering up into the belfry.

When they were done, Fleming helpfully suggested that they might want to search the Hillsboro jail and even offered to "pay their way" to Hillsboro. But by now, it was very late, and the men, exhausted from their exertions in the name of good citizenship, decided they had had enough excitement for one night. The five hundred outraged citizens went home.[37]

In the midst of all this commotion, Lucy Fryer's burial went almost unnoticed — a couple of paragraphs at the end of stories that feature lengthy descriptions of Washington's confession, the Robinson mob, the confrontation between Fleming and the mob on a rural highway, and the search of the jail. There was a simple ceremony at the Fryers' home, and Lucy was buried in the Lorena cemetery near the daughter who had died in childhood.[38] One of the men who officiated at Lucy's funeral had earlier said that there was "no better woman living" than Lucy Fryer, but Lucy's tale was not told in the Waco papers.[39] One of the sad consequences of the chaos and turbulence that surrounded the Waco Horror was that the story of Lucy Fryer's life was lost. She was remembered only as the inert, "almost brained" victim of a "negro brute."

Waco's newspapers then proceeded — all three of them — to publish Jesse Washington's confession in full. Even bowdlerized of the worst of the original language, the confession is disturbing and a fine exemplar of what Jacquelyn Dowd Hall calls the "acceptable folk pornography" of newspaper descriptions of the alleged crimes of "black fiends" during this period.[40] The modern reader may find the confession disturbing in other ways, as well. Portions in brackets show the words in the original confession that were changed or eliminated in the newspapers to make the piece fit for public consumption. The italicized words are the substitutions for the original language:

On yesterday May 8th, 1916, I was planting cotton for Mr. Fryar near Robinsonville close to Waco, Texas, and about 3:30 o'clock P.M.[41] I went up to

Mr. Fryar's barn to get some more cotton seed. I called Mrs. Fryar from the house to get some cotton seed, and she came to the barn and unfastened the door and scooped up the cotton seed. I was holding the sack while she was putting the seed in the sack, and after she had finished, she was fussing with me about whipping the mules, and while she was standing inside of the door of the barn, and still talking to me, I hit her on the side of the head with a hammer that I had in my hand. I had taken this hammer from Mr. Fryar's home to the field that morning, and brought it back and put it in the barn at dinner. I had picked up this hammer and had it in my hand when I called Mrs. Fryar from the house, and had the hammer in my right hand all the time I was holding the sack.

When I hit Mrs. Fryar on the side of the head with the hammer she fell over, and then I *assaulted her* [pulled up her clothes and crawled on her and screwed her. By screwing her I mean that I stuck my male organ into her female organ, and while I was going (doing?) this she was trying to push me off. When I got through screwing her I got off of her and] I then[42] picked up the hammer from where I had laid it down, and hit her twice[43] more with the hammer on top of her head. I saw the blood coming through her bonnet.

I then picked up the sack of cotton seed and carried it and the hammer to the field, where I had left the team. I left the sack of cotton seed near the planter and went about forty steps south of the planter and the mules, and put the hammer that I killed Mrs. Fryar with in some woods under some hackberry brush.

I knew when I went to the barn for the cotton seed that there wasn't anybody at the house except Mrs. Fryar, and when I called her from the house to the barn, I had already made up my mind to knock her in the head with the hammer and then *assault* [screw] her.

I had been working for Mr. Fryar about five months, and first made up my mind to *assault* [screw] Mrs. Fryar yesterday morning and took the hammer from the buggy shed to the field with me, and brought it back and put it in the barn at dinner time, so that I could use it to knock Mrs. Fryar in the head when I came back for seed during the afternoon.

I planted cotton the rest of the afternoon, then put up the team and went home *to* [at] my daddy's house where I was arrested.

There wasn't anybody else who had anything to do with the killing or *assaulting* [raping] of Mrs. Fryar except myself.

Signed Jess Washington X, his mark [Signed by arrested party][44]

The first thing one notices about this ugly tale of premeditated violence blended with common daily routine — besides its being published in full in three newspapers where it would certainly be read by every literate potential juror in McLennan County — is the strange combination of the grossest vernacular with rather stilted speech that probably does not represent the way Jesse Washington really talked. But Jesse Washington could not read the confession he was told to sign.

Oddly, while the whole city of Waco had read Jesse's confession and knew that he was supposed to have "criminally assaulted" Lucy Fryer, there was no testimony about the rape at the trial. Even Dr. Maynard, who testified about the wounds to Lucy's skull, was not asked about the rape, which makes one wonder if there was any solid evidence, other than Washington's confession (which was probably coerced), that Lucy was raped at all. But, in the context of the times, it was the rape story more than the murder that inflamed the populace and served as a pretext for the lynching. Elisabeth Freeman initially accepted the story of the rape,[45] but, after investigating the Washington lynching exhaustively, came to believe that Lucy Fryer had not been raped.[46]

Why did Jesse Washington suddenly attack Lucy Fryer on May 8, 1916? Apparently, until that day Washington had never given any member of the Fryer family any reason to distrust him. Lucy did not seem to fear Jesse's temper. She did not hesitate to berate him for whipping the mules; she did not anticipate that he might react violently. Maybe Jesse killed Lucy simply on an impulse because he was angry that she had scolded him. Maybe no rape was ever involved.

There is also, of course, the possibility that the attack appeared to be unanticipated and inexplicable, and that Jesse Washington plowed all afternoon after Lucy Fryer's murder because he was, in fact, innocent and knew nothing of what had happened. What if the blood on his clothes really did come from a nosebleed, as he claimed? What if Fleming's men found the hammer or placed it in the brush and *then* forced Jesse to "tell" where he had put it? What if Jesse only "confessed" because, as he said when asked by his defense attorneys if he was concerned about the possibility of a mob coming after him, "They promised they would not if I would tell them about it."[47] In other words, Washington claimed that the officers of the law who questioned him promised that if he "confessed," they would protect him from being lynched.

Nona Baker, Sank Majors's great-niece, has suggested that Jesse Washington might have been brutally interrogated and beaten in three different jails —

in Waco, where he was initially taken along with his whole family; in Hillsboro, where he confessed; and in Dallas, where he "signed" a confession he couldn't read.[48] Defense attorney Joe Taylor Jr. later told Elisabeth Freeman that "the boy had not had the third degree."[49] But there may have been no need to beat Jesse Washington into confessing; he was no match for his interrogators.

There is also an odd story that has lingered for more than eighty years in the little town of Robinson. According to this tale, George Fryer killed his wife or hired Jesse Washington to do it.[50] The origin of this rumor was most likely an article that appeared in the *Chicago Defender* on June 10, 1916, declaring that "the truth has come to light that this woman's husband is the murderer," but that "not one word has been sent to the daily papers; not one word has gone out to the Associated Press." The article does not detail how the truth supposedly "came to light" or what this new "truth" is exactly, but the author cries out against Waco for lynching an innocent and demands to know if the true perpetrator of the murder will now be tried and hanged.[51]

The *Chicago Defender* story drifted south to Waco and was reprinted locally on June 17, 1916, by twenty-seven-year-old A. T. Smith, managing editor of the *Paul Quinn Weekly*, the newspaper of Paul Quinn College, one of Waco's two colleges for black students.[52] After the story was published in the *Paul Quinn Weekly*, Smith was indicted for criminal libel. Although the NAACP was notified about the Smith case, the organization, which picked its causes with care from among the great swamp of injustices committed against blacks across the South, did not involve itself in Smith's problems, because, as NAACP secretary Royal Freeman Nash, put it, "he [Smith] must have known it was untrue, at least the charge that Mr. Fryar had been arrested."[53]

Elisabeth Freeman, while in Waco, heard a rumor that George Fryer had confessed to the crime, had gone insane, and had been confined in a local hospital. She visited the hospitals and did not find Fryer, but later did meet and speak with him: "He was very quiet and reserved," she reports, "and said little or nothing. He did not talk about his troubles — and a man who does not talk about his troubles is not likely to talk about his crimes."[54] Freeman eventually concluded that Jesse Washington was probably guilty of murdering Lucy Fryer. She was convinced primarily by the discovery of the hammer precisely where he had allegedly left it and the absence of hard evidence pointing to anyone else.[55]

Even those who repeat the tale that George Fryer might have murdered his wife have no knowledge of any friction between husband and wife or of any other motive for murder. Martha Kettler, a lifelong resident of Robinson who was six when Lucy Fryer was killed, characterized Lucy Fryer as "just a normal nice little lady." Kettler described George Fryer, who never married again and lived in Robinson until his death in 1938, as "average, friendly, neighborly."[56]

The violent death of Lucy Fryer and the maelstrom of violence that destroyed Jesse Washington provided rich soil for the sprouting of rumors and suppositions. The darkest crimes never seem to be forgotten. They blight the locale where they occur. Buildings may be torn down and replaced, fields replanted, thousands of sweet, ordinary days may pass after the one day of monumental evil, but the shadow, however faded, lingers.

The methods used by the justice system of the time also encourage endless speculation about Washington's guilt or innocence. In that poisoned climate, it would have been up to Jesse Washington to prove he was innocent, and Jesse had only the dimmest understanding of what was going on. For the purposes of this story, however, it makes little difference in the end whether Jesse Washington was innocent or guilty. Nothing he could have done would have justified what happened to him.

On Thursday morning, May 11, the grand jury convened in special session and within thirty minutes indicted Jesse Washington for the murder of Lucy Fryer. A special venire of fifty men was summoned for possible service as jurors in Jesse's trial. "It is not expected," remarked the *Times Herald*, "that the trial of the negro, who is charged with the heinous crime, will occupy much time."[57]

The whole idea was to rush through the trial and the execution as speedily as the arrest and confession, in order to convince the public that the evildoer would be punished almost as fast by legal means as by lynching — and, therefore, there was no need for the upheaval and disorder of a lynching. Jesse Washington was to be put on trial for his life on Monday morning, May 15, 1916, one week to the day after the murder of Lucy Fryer. He would be tried in the 54th District Court, presided over by fifty-eight-year-old District Judge Richard Irby Munroe.

A wiry little man, Munroe was a unique character well known in Waco for his dry, salty wit. He grew up in Florida, one of a family of twenty-one brothers and sisters. The Florida Munroes must have been famous hell-raisers. Munroe was fond of telling a story that when he first arrived at Emory College in Atlanta, one of his professors peered at him over the top of his glasses and asked him, "Are you one of the Florida Munroes?" Munroe admitted that he was, and the professor replied, "Then God help your soul."

Munroe came to live in Waco in 1881, served as city attorney, wrote an early Waco city charter, and, while in private practice, appeared before the U.S. Supreme Court in a complex probate case. By 1916, he had already served on

Judge Richard Irby Munroe, in front of his home on Ethel Avenue. *Courtesy* Archives Division of The Texas Collection, Baylor University, Waco, Texas.

the bench of the 54th District Court for eight years. He would serve in the same court for fifteen more years, until his retirement in 1931.

Munroe spoke his mind in and out of court and was fond of leavening his remarks with folksy maxims that must have seemed endearing when he was eulogized as an exemplar of days-of-yore local color in his 1942 obituary. He had a habit of referring to friends and foes alike, in fun, as "horse thieves" and once described an acquaintance as "a cross between a dried apple and a cracklin'."[58] On one occasion, a lawyer practicing in Munroe's court was disgusted with the bail set for his client and remarked sarcastically, "Why don't you set it at a million dollars?" Munroe did. On another occasion Munroe set bail for a poor black defendant at one penny.[59]

When Elisabeth Freeman inquired about Judge Munroe in Waco in 1916, she heard less appealing descriptions. "The judge is a rotter . . . a reprobate . . . His moral character is unspeakable," she reports. "He has been a gambler and drunkard and of low repute — but a splendid criminal lawyer, though representing only the liquor interests and their victims — respectable people would not have him as their lawyer."[60]

Was Munroe an amusing but honest judge, or the disreputable creature of those who had put him in office? He speaks for himself later in this story and may be judged on that basis.

Six very young and inexperienced lawyers were appointed to represent Washington: Joe Taylor Jr., known to all as "Little Joe" because of his small size, was the leader of the group. Taylor was twenty-seven and had been practicing law for about six years. He was the son of one of Waco's most prominent attorneys, Joe Taylor Sr. His mother, Sally Sears Taylor, was the daughter of early Waco pioneers and for many years one of Waco's most-admired social luminaries. In 1873, when Sally Sears was a dazzling eighteen-year-old beauty, she had hosted the inaugural ball on the arm of the newly installed governor, Richard Coke.[61]

The other young attorneys appointed as defense counsel were Frank Fitzpatrick, C. H. Machen, Kyle Vick, Percy Wilie, and Westwood Bowden Hays Jr. Fitzpatrick was twenty-five and had been practicing law for all of two years. He had just recently been appointed secretary of the county Democratic Executive Committee,[62] and was described as "one of the very prominent among the younger members of the bar here" in Waco newspaper articles that appeared in June 1916,[63] when he announced that he was running for "flotorial" representative to the Texas Legislature representing McLennan, Falls, and Limestone counties.

Chester Machen was about thirty at the time of the Washington trial.[64] Kyle Vick was twenty-four, had barely received his law license, and did not even open an office in Waco until the following year.[65] Hays was only about twenty-three — another socially prominent young attorney, son of the founder of an important fire insurance business in Waco and grandson of a pioneer settler of Waco.[66] Only five years later, Hays was implicated in one of the first violent acts by the Ku Klux Klan in Waco, the abduction and tarring and feathering of a local man, allegedly for selling dope to Baylor University students.[67] Many of Waco's most prominent citizens, including Kyle Vick, offered to provide bail for Hays and the other culprits.[68]

The youthful defense attorneys were allowed a grand total of two days to prepare for a capital murder trial.[69] Jesse Washington was not to be returned to Waco until Sunday night; there is no record that any of the defense attorneys went to Dallas to talk with him before the trial.

The young attorneys were probably appointed to the case because they were viewed as manageable fellows who would take their elders' advice and not make too much of a fuss about defending Jesse Washington. Some of

Waco's leaders apparently had not forgotten that the Sank Majors lynching, eleven years earlier, had been triggered because defense attorney George Barcus convinced the judge that the jury had not been charged properly, thus forcing the judge to grant Majors a new trial.

Times had changed, according to one newspaper report. Defense attorneys had learned to be less finicky about constitutional rights and suchlike: "There has been a complete change in the manner of handling cases of this kind, by common consent in Texas, and after parties charged with criminal assault get a fair hearing in the trial court and are found guilty, there being no reasonable doubt of guilt, then attorneys withhold further effort, no technical points are raised or delays occasioned and executions take place quickly. This has had the effect of stopping many of the lawless demonstrations which formerly characterized the commission of the diabolical crime of which Washington stands accused and to which he has confessed."[70]

One bystander commented before the trial, "I hope he [Washington] waives his thirty days [before hanging] and allows the officers to hang him at once; otherwise I fear trouble."[71] In other words, Jesse Washington himself was to prevent his own prospective lynching by voluntarily giving up whatever bit of life was left to him. The practice of lynching was to be ended by hustling defendants through fast-paced trials and straight on to eternity in record time — in effect, converting illegal lynchings into legal ones.

Sheriff Fleming did take one more precaution — or seize one more opportunity to be seen doing his duty. On Saturday morning, May 13, he went to Robinson to address farmers from the area again, this time at Joe Swayne's store. Fleming and other local leaders pointed out to the assembled crowd, one more time, that the criminal had been identified, apprehended, and charged as quickly as was humanly possible, and that the trial would take place immediately. They asked their audience to let the law take its course.

Fleming was received respectfully. Members of the Robinson community urged "calmness and forbearance" on their fellow citizens. At that point the situation appeared to be under control.[72]

But a vapor of unrest and anxiety continued to hang in the air. Some citizens felt that Jesse should have been granted a change of venue to avoid trouble. Despite all the assurances of the men of Robinson, "the feeling of uneasiness was found pretty general," says the *Waco Morning News*.[73]

In a brief paragraph buried in the lower left-hand corner of the editorial page on Friday, May 12, the *Waco Times Herald* makes its own plea to the citizens of McLennan County — which suggests that the newspaper's editors were not convinced, despite Fleming's efforts, that all was well and that the danger of mob action had been averted: "The *Times Herald* begs the citizenship of McLennan County to at this time put their confidence in the judicial tribunals of their own creation. Judge Lynch has no proper place in a community where courts are properly organized and conducted. Let the law be supreme. Let the law take its course."[74]

On Saturday, May 13, it seemed that McLennan County just might squeak by without another "lawless demonstration." But events on Sunday, May 14, should have set off warning bells for those who hoped to maintain order.

All day Sunday and into early Monday morning, people poured into Waco from the outlying areas. "The railroad trains," says the *Waco Morning News*, "brought in a good many people from practically every town within twenty-five miles of Waco."[75] At that point Fleming should have seen that, with so many curiosity seekers thronging the city and anticipating excitement, the situation was likely to get out of hand. On Sunday, Fleming or Mayor Dollins or Chief of Police Guy McNamara, brother of County Attorney John McNamara, should have considered bringing in reinforcements to help local officers or asking Judge Munroe to postpone the trial and possibly to consider a change of venue.

But Fleming did nothing and, apparently, no other city leader suggested that he should. Instead, late Sunday night Jesse Washington was brought back to Waco from Dallas and secreted in Judge Munroe's little office behind the courtroom. "Attorneys for the defense," says the *Waco Morning News*, "remained with Washington until nearly midnight Sunday, hearing his gruesome tale, looking for some mitigating circumstances. They declared they found none. One declared that he told the negro that there was no possibility of his life being saved, and it was suggested that he had better spend the night in prayer. The negro seemed unmoved, they declared."[76]

Such was Jesse Washington's defense — a suggestion that he should pray. This late-night interview appears to have been the first time that any of the six rookie lawyers saw or spoke with their client.

The crowd that surrounded the county jail the next morning hoping to get a glimpse of Washington "was the largest ever seen," says the *News*.[77] The *Waco Times Herald* estimated that as many as twenty-five hundred people crowded into Judge Munroe's courtroom,[78] "churning around the chamber for an hour, flooding the balconies and standing two persons high wherever a railing or a bench permitted."[79]

There were hundreds more milling around inside and outside of the

Waco courtroom, 1919. *Courtesy* Archives Division of The Texas Collection, Baylor University, Waco, Texas.

courthouse, including a number of black people who, reported the *Morning News*, were "quiet and seemingly not much excited."[80] It seems more likely that they were terrified and trying to attract as little attention as possible. Sure enough, in Gildersleeve's best-known photograph of the lynching, there are a few black faces on the fringes of the crowd. Their expressions are unreadable.

The reporters did not interview any of the black spectators, so it is impossible to know if members of the Washington family were among them. Freeman comments in her report that "the family has been arrested and taken away from Robinson."[81] This is the last mention found in the record of Washington's relatives.

The courthouse was so packed with people that a farmer named Brown fainted in the crush in the corridor on the first floor and had to be taken outside. The solemnity of the crowd might be gauged by the remark of a young white girl, about eighteen, who had managed to force her way up to the third floor but could not get inside the courtroom: "I would just give anything to see that negro," she declared.[82]

A path had to be cleared for the judge to get into his own courtroom. The court reporter, Warren Hunt, barely found a place to sit, and the defense counsel and the county attorney, John McNamara, who was prosecuting the case, abandoned all thought of getting chairs. Spectators occupying the chairs in the jury box had to be cleared out so the jury could be seated.[83] Some witnesses and some of those called for jury duty had to be lifted over desks and people to the front of the courtroom.[84]

As proceedings were about to begin, Sheriff Fleming begged the crowds to stand back if they possibly could: "It's not *if* you possibly can," said Judge Munroe, less deferentially, "but you must, else there won't be any court today."

"We don't need no court," someone yelled, but no one paid any attention to him.[85]

Munroe made no effort to clear the courtroom but did repeatedly demand that the boys in the balcony quiet down and all "gentlemen" present remove their hats.[86] He did not ask anyone to remove their guns, however. When Jesse Washington, wearing overalls and a calico shirt and looking no older than the seventeen years he claimed, was brought into court, a young man in the crowd reached for his revolver, muttering, "Might as well get him now."

"Let them have their trial," admonished an older man sitting near him. "We'll get him before sundown and you might hurt an innocent man."[87]

By some accounts, Washington seemed unmoved by the spectacle he saw — the mass of white humanity glaring at him, all those eyes fixed on him with barely controlled rage. But one reporter noted that "the negro's heavy lips were trembling and he seemed to be muttering to himself."[88]

The trial began about 10:00 A.M. A jury was seated quickly; the six young defense attorneys did not challenge a single juror. The foreman was W. B. Brazelton, a leading citizen. Brazelton was a longtime, prominent Waco lumberman and a member of the school board.[89] After the jury was impaneled, Judge Munroe read the charge and asked Jesse Washington if he wanted to plead guilty or not guilty. Jesse, who must have been entirely lost, did not answer at first and plainly did not understand the question. The judge explained the charges and the consequences of pleading guilty. "Washington's plea of guilty," said the *Morning News*, "was a muttered 'Yeah.'"[90]

Prosecutor McNamara then called Dr. J. H. Maynard to the stand. Dr. Maynard described the battered condition of Lucy Fryer's body, but did not testify that she had been raped. A succession of officials then testified either to having heard Jesse Washington making his confession in Hillsboro or to having witnessed him signing the confession with his X in Dallas. Cris Simon told how he had arrived home, glimpsed Jesse Washington walking into the mule lot, and heard the Fryer children crying over their mother's body. Fleming, Jenkins, and Stegall all testified as to how they had identified Washington as a suspect, how they had arrested and interrogated him, and how the murder weapon had finally been found after he had told them where it was.

The only question asked by defense counsel was put to Sheriff Fleming by Joe Taylor: "Who were present when the hammer was found?" Fleming replied that John McNamara and deputy sheriffs Lee Jenkins and Joe Roberts were present, along with Fleming himself. Jenkins added in his testimony that, before the hammer was picked up, the group had stopped a passing car and the driver, Mr. Reeder, plus another man who lived nearby, a Mr. McCullough, were asked to come and see where the hammer had been found.[91]

Washington's confession was formally introduced into evidence; then, finally, he was allowed to speak on his own behalf. According to the court record, he said only, "I ain't going to tell them nothing more than what I said . . . that's what I done." Then he mumbled something that could not be heard by the court reporter. Joe Taylor interpreted the mumble for the court as, "He says he is sorry he did it." Taylor then asked Washington if there was anything else he wanted to say. There was no answer. Taylor said, "That is all."[92]

John McNamara made use of his summation to pat everyone on the back and made a special point of congratulating the defense attorneys for doing their duty. Then, declaring that "the prisoner has been given a fair trial as fair as any ever given in this court room," he demanded that Jesse Washington be assessed the death penalty.[93] The crowd broke into loud applause and yells. The defense contributed no final argument.

Outside, as soon as the cheer was heard in the courtroom, voices cried, "Let's go in and get him"; "Throw him out of the window"; "They're goin' to take him out the other way—we'll have to watch all sides for him"; and "Oh, we'll get him; they can't keep him from us." One reporter describes the increasing tension in the scene outside, with men and boys "running here and there with straining eyes and faces growing more excited each minute. Boys not more than fifteen years of age were running wildly around and around the building, either to get a view through curiosity or else to have some part in the gruesome work ahead . . . [they] were running with the speed of wolves or hounds it seemed, almost, and were frantic lest the officers should manage to spirit the negro away."[94] There were also girls and women on the courthouse lawn. They seemed more nervous and more serious than the men, but, says the same reporter, as they got used to the situation and relaxed, they began laughing and chatting, though their faces were still pale.

The jury retired for a total of four minutes and then returned to the court-room. Foreman W. B. Brazelton read the verdict: "We the jury find the de-fendant guilty of murder as charged in the indictment and assess his penalty at death." By then the time was 11:22 A.M.[95] Jesse's entire trial had taken a little over an hour. "Is that your verdict, gentlemen?" asked Judge Munroe. The members of the jury answered that it was. Munroe began writing in his docket, "Plea of guilty and verdict of guilty, and pun . . ."[96] The actual docu-ment remains in the old courthouse files: it is obvious that the judge broke off at "pun . . ." and added the remaining ". . . ishment assessed at death" in haste afterward. "As he wrote there was a hush over the entire court room. It was a mo-ment of hesitation, but just a moment," writes the reporter for the *Waco Semi-Weekly Tribune*.[97] The officers were preparing to take Jesse Washington away.

Suddenly, all hell broke loose. A tall young farmer at the back of the room put his hands on the heads and shoulders of the people in front of him and lifted himself over them, leaping on a table as someone cried, "Get the nig-ger!" A man standing by the judge looked up and said, "They are coming after him," and "the wave of people surged forward."[98]

According to Elisabeth Freeman's report, by then Sheriff Fleming and the court stenographer, Warren Hunt, who both knew what was coming, had slipped out of the courtroom. One deputy, Barney Goldberg, pulled his re-volver. He had not heard that Fleming had given orders to his men to let the crowd get Washington. A rumor later made the rounds in Waco that Goldberg had struck two men in the mob with his gun, injuring one of them severely. Members of the mob threatened revenge.

Goldberg was apparently so afraid of the public's reaction if it became gen-erally known that he had made even a feeble attempt to stop the lynching that he convinced several friends to swear out affidavits and publish them in the newspapers claiming that he had never left his grocery store all day and was not even present at the trial.[99] It seems unlikely that Goldberg did anything more than draw his gun and stand there for a moment until he realized that he was all alone.

The unidentified "tall man" grabbed the collar of the terrified Jesse Wash-ington, and the mob carried him down the back stairs behind the courtroom and out into the alley, tearing off his clothes as they went. The lynchers paused for a moment on the east side of the courthouse, long enough to put a chain around Jesse's neck, and proceeded to drag him down Washington Street.[100] "Then," wrote one reporter, "he became the plaything of the mob."[101]

Door through which Jesse Washington was dragged out of the courthouse and into the alley between the courthouse and the jail on May 15, 1916. Photo by the author.

At first, Washington fought them, "squealing like a crazed animal," according to one newspaper account. He managed to bite one man's finger "almost to the bone," but released him when another man "stamped him in the face."[102] Freeman reports she was told that Jesse cried out, "Haven't I one friend in this crowd?"[103] By this time, men in the crowd had begun slashing at Jesse with their knives so that "he was covered in blood long before the square was reached."[104]

Now that they had their chance, it seemed that nearly every man in Waco wanted to take his turn at Jesse Washington. Along the way, people in the crowd beat him with shovels, bricks, clubs, and anything else that came to hand.[105] One paper reports that "a yellow negro boy who was raised here in Waco" hit Jesse on the head and cried, "You're getting just what's coming to you, you d——— rascal."[106] Despite their delicacy in not printing words like *damned* in full, the Waco newspapers spared their readers none of the details of the lynching. Such details became as much a part of the "folk pornography" of the time as details of rapes.[107]

Part of the crowd surged toward the bridge, thinking Jesse would be hanged where Sank Majors had been hanged eleven years earlier, but the ringleaders already had another plan in mind. Hanging would be too easy a death. They turned on Second Street, to take Jesse to the town square by City Hall and burn him alive. Piles of kindling and wood had been left along the way; dry goods boxes and inflammable material like excelsior seemed to appear out of nowhere.

"The shouts attracted attention," reports the *Tribune*. "They were shouts like those a crowd will give when leading a triumphal procession from a ball game that has been a big victory."[108] The *Times Herald* takes refuge in a kind of imperial passive voice, as if the lynching had been ordained by some abstract overlord or diety: "Others from Waco followed the crowd to the place where *it had been decreed* that Jess Washington should pay with his life the penalty for the terrible crime of which he admitted he was guilty."[109] But it was individual men who killed Washington. They can be seen doing their work in Gildersleeve's picture.

Jesse was pulled over the fence around City Hall and the chain attached to his neck was flung across the limb of a tree in the rear of the building. "They drew the chain over the tree and the boy grabbed it. They then cut off his fingers so that he could not hold the chain," reports Elisabeth Freeman.[110] "Fingers, ears, pieces of clothing, toes and other parts of the negro's body were cut off by members of the mob that had crowded to the scene as if by magic when the word that the negro had been taken in charge by the mob was heralded over the city," says the Times Herald.[111]

Leona Lester, a young manicurist at the Goldstein Migel Department Store — "a child," Freeman calls her — told Freeman during a manicure that she had seen someone in the mob "unsex" Jesse Washington. "Men state that they did not do anything of the kind and would swear to it," says Freeman in her report, "but others say they did and that they were carrying the proof around in a handkerchief showing it as a souvenir."[112]

Thomas Hague, third-generation resident of Robinson, claimed to have seen years ago a by-then thoroughly moth-eaten shirt full of blood that was supposed to have been taken from Jesse Washington. A friend's father had purchased it.[113] Nona Baker remembered that a friend, now deceased, had picked cotton on a white man's farm when he was a boy. One day the boy's employer showed him a finger in formaldehyde in a jar and told him it was Jesse Washington's finger.[114] According to one report, children were occasionally even given these relics to play with and show their friends.[115]

Thousands of people came rushing to the town square to see the sight. "Not all approved, but they looked on because they had never seen anything of the kind," reports the Tribune.[116] Before the fire was lit under the tree on the town square, Jesse Washington, "half alive and half dead," was propped briefly against the tree and then suddenly yanked up by the chain around his neck and dangled in the air, his tongue protruding from his mouth and his face smeared with blood. He was cut in so many places, "his body was a solid color of red, the blood of the many wounds inflicted covered him from head to foot."[117] Freeman comments that just as the chain was jerking Washington into the air, "the big man" smashed him on the back of the neck with a knife; this violent blow may have been "practically the death blow."[118]

By now all the kindling material that had been gathered was piled into a huge dry goods box placed at the base of the tree. Washington's body swayed in the air and then was gradually lowered into the box. Coal oil was poured over him. "No sooner had his body touched the box than people pressed forward, each eager to be the first to light the fire, matches were touched to the inflammable material and as smoke rapidly rose in the air, such a demonstration of people gone mad was never heard before . . . shouts of delight went up from the thousands of throats."[119]

After that, Washington's body was lowered into the fire several times and then raised again. Unfortunately for him, he was a strong young boy — "from the pictures, a wonderfully built boy," says Freeman.[120] Death had not yet

The crowd around the courthouse on the day of the Jesse Washington lynching. *Courtesy Archives Division of The Texas Collection, Baylor University, Waco, Texas.*

come to him. He even managed at one point during the burning to kick himself free of his funeral pyre, but his executioners quickly grabbed the chain and pulled him back into the fire.[121]

Estimates of the number of spectators range between ten thousand and fifteen thousand, "crowding the city hall lawn and overflowing the square, hanging from the windows of buildings, viewing the scene from the tops of buildings and trees . . . Onlookers were hanging from the windows of the city hall and every other building that commanded a sight of the burning."[122] A number of small boys had climbed into the top of the tree from which Jesse was hanged and into other trees nearby.[123] At least one little boy had to be removed from the tree from which Washington was hanging when it got too hot for him to stay there.[124]

Mayor John Dollins and Chief of Police Guy McNamara observed the proceedings in comfort from the mayor's office on the second floor of City Hall. Local photographer Fred Gildersleeve was advised ahead of time where the lynching would take place and had his photographic equipment set up and ready to go in the mayor's office. He took photographs of the waiting crowd during the trial and photographed Washington's body up close at various points during the burning, just as he would have shot the high school football team before the big game, just as he had shot the pictures of Waco's Prosperity Banquet in 1911. To Gildersleeve, it was one more slice of life in Waco. Freeman declares in her account that the picture taking was a "cooked business" between the mayor and Gildersleeve and implies that the mayor was getting some kind of "rake-off" from the sales of the photos afterward.[125]

"Many turned away [from the scene of Jesse's torture]," reports the *Tribune*, "but many lingered to talk about it and to watch it. Some stayed in the outskirts of the crowd not caring to rest their eyes upon the actual scene."[126] Some watched with more enthusiasm than others: "Two tall farmers held on their shoulders a man said to have been George Fryer so that he could see the assaulter and murderer of his wife burn. There were probably fifteen thousand people in the crowd, many of them women, and one well dressed woman clapped her hands when a way was cleared so that she could see the writhing, naked form of the fast dying black." There were also boys and girls about, who had left school to go home for lunch. Some of these children actually saw the burning.[127]

Jesse Washington's body burned and smoldered for about two hours until there was nothing left but a skull, a torso, and the stumps of limbs. Even then the crowd was not satisfied. Spectators searched the area for bits of charred bone, links of the chain, and pieces of the tree that could be kept or sold as souvenirs. Links of the chain sold for twenty-five cents.[128]

"And then the worst happened," says the *Waco Semi-Weekly Tribune* with unintended irony, although by now Jesse Washington was dead.[129] About midafternoon, a horseman came along, lassoed what was left of Washington's body and began to drag it around the square and then through the streets of town while waving his hat in the air. Somewhere along the way the skull bounced loose from the rest of the body and was placed on the doorstep of a prostitute on "Two Street," where it was picked up by a group of small boys who extracted the teeth and sold them for five dollars each.[130] The rest of the body, now tied behind a car, was dragged all the way to Robinson, put in a sack, and hung from a telephone pole in front of a blacksmith's shop for everyone to see. Toward the end of the day, Constable Les Stegall went out and picked up the sack and brought it back to town, where the little that was left of Jesse Washington was buried in the local potter's field. The Washington family was either gone or so terrorized that even after Jesse was dead, they were afraid to claim his remains.[131]

Some of the good citizens of Robinson were actually embarrassed by this last excess. One Robinson man called the *Morning News* and a group of men visited the offices of the *Times Herald*, in each case to say that the people of

The infamous Gildersleeve photographs of the Jesse Washington lynching. These were published in the July special supplement to *The Crisis*. *Courtesy* Archives Division of The Texas Collection, Baylor University, Waco, Texas.

Robinson condemned — not the lynching — but the dragging of the body through the streets.

And thus ended the Waco Horror.

There are suggestions at the very end of the long article about the lynching in the *Waco Morning News* that not every resident of Waco approved of what was done that day. Under the paragraph header, "Some Grave Faces in the Frantic Crowd," the reporter notes: "Here and there — but rarely — some man walked with sober stride, downcast head and grave expression, talking in a subdued voice of his regret over what was taking place, declaring that if it had been at all possible every step should have been taken to spare the community the cataclysm of human passion which was turned loose within a few minutes' time."[132] But the same reporter immediately follows that comment by noting that the vast majority of spectators seemed "satisfied" with what was going on or at least passive about it. Note, also, that these "grave" men spoke of "sparing the community," not of sparing the victim the ordeal that was visited upon him.

An "old Confederate veteran" was said to have commented before the uproar began that any spark would set off the crowd. "It would be wrong, of course," he said, "but that is what would happen if a movement should start."[133] Another observer described by the reporter only as "a man connected with the courts," speaking before the lynching, blamed the sheriff for having "conferred too much with the citizens of Robinson, though it was well meant." This observer thought the people of Robinson should just have been told firmly that "the negro" would be legally tried and legally executed.

There is a little picture offered here by this same "man of the courts," who seems to have a very good opinion of his own insights. He notes that wherever a group of eight men gathered in the days before the lynching, one or two expressed a hope that the incident would end legally and in good order, but the others said nothing. This sketch suggests in a thumbnail the comparative ratio of those who wanted Jesse Washington to be legally convicted and legally hanged to those who either wanted him lynched or did not care.

One poignant note in the *Morning News* story implies in a more oblique way that some folks were horrified by what had been done: the reporter repeats a conversation between two men which he overheard after the lynching. One man said "he would not have had his son, fourteen years old, witness the incident for all the money in Waco." The other answered that he would have been glad to have his son "witness the tragedy" — as a salutary moral lesson perhaps? "Each was sincere," adds the reporter, "just a different viewpoint."[134]

So much for the more thoughtful crowd in Waco. No doubt, some citizens were deeply troubled by the lynching of Jesse Washington, but no one took any action to stop it.

The *Waco Morning News* responded to the lynching by running a poem on the editorial page composed by editor E. G. Senter. Salient passages of "Vengeance Is Mine, Saith the Lord" (apparently originally written in 1905 in response to a different lynching) include the following:[135]

> *The maddened crowd its fury feeds with flame,*
> *Nor recks of God, nor feels the sinful shame.*
> *Thou fool — the serpents which thy passions breed*
> *In whirling fury on thyself shall feed . . .*
> *Who is the doubter of God's justice? Tell*
> *Him of the dark abyss that curtains Hell.*
> *Man's fitful wrath adds nothing to the woe*
> *Of guilty wretch about to leap below.*
> *'Round the avenger shadows grimly draw,*
> *Father, forgive him — he forgot thy law.*

Senter was new to the position of editor at the *News* and probably new to Waco, as well. He had been introduced to the business community at a Young Men's Business League event in early April, at which time he had forecast "a splendid future for this city" and also a splendid future for the *Waco Morning News*, which he intended to make a "great statewide" newspaper.[136] But Senter apparently did not stay in Waco long enough to appear in even one edition of the *Waco City Directory*. In 1917, Charles Marsh and E. S. Fentress, who had come to Waco from Des Moines, took over both the *Waco Morning News* and the *Waco Semi-Weekly Tribune* and created the *News-Tribune*, which competed for ten more years with the *Times Herald* until Fentress's company acquired that paper, as well.[137]

At the time of the Waco Horror, however, before the Fentress/Marsh takeover, the *Times Herald* was a much stronger paper than the *Morning News*. According to E. S. Fentress's son Harlon Fentress, "The morning paper had been kicked around a good bit, various ownerships, none of which had made any particular success." The owner of the *News* in May 1916 was Artemas R. Roberts who, at his death in 1933, was remembered principally as the man who had erected the Amicable skyscraper. His ownership of the Waco newspaper seems to have lasted only about two months, after which he sold his stock back to the previous owners.[138]

It was natural, then, that the weaker daily, the *Morning News*, should take refuge in the oblique, symbolic language of a poem as a way of making a faint effort at a critical commentary on the lynching. Elisabeth Freeman met a director of the *Morning News* who "deplored the whole thing,"[139] but she reports that the Waco newspaper owners she interviewed were, for the most part, afraid that a strong criticism of the lynching would "injure their circulation."[140]

The *Waco Semi-Weekly Tribune* was something of an exception. It was owned by old-time journalist A. R. McCollum, who had founded his first newspaper in Waco in 1878 and had been running some sort of paper in the city ever since.[141] The *Tribune*, published only twice a week, was also probably the weakest of Waco's three newspapers. McCollum was sixty-seven and in poor health at the time of the Waco Horror and would expire in 1918, only a year after selling his last newspaper venture to Fentress and Marsh. Elisabeth Freeman reports that, in May 1916, A. R. McCollum was almost blind and said "anything he please[d]."[142] He was also, however, a state senator running for reelection.[143]

McCollum's *Tribune*, like the *Waco Morning News*, published a poem on the editorial page — an anonymous poem contributed by an unknown citizen of Waco. The poem, entitled "The Mob," ends dramatically:[144]

> Then burn your laws, your bill of rights,
> Your constitution and your code,
> Proud guaranties that were your lights
> Whose searching rays swept clear the road.
> You do not need their guidance now,
> A tyrant's hand is on the reign,
> And subjects, self-enslaved must bow
> And follow blindly in his train.
> Disdainful of your valiant past,
> Without a sigh or muffled sob,
> Plunge on — while on your skies is cast
> The grinning shadow of the Mob.

But McCollum dared to print an editorial as well, the only newspaperman in Waco who did so immediately after the lynching. "The Work of the Mob" is a fascinating artifact of its time because it so plainly illustrates the mental contortions of a man who thought he was a good person, a serious person, a man who loved his community. Clearly, McCollum (assuming he wrote the piece himself) was steeped in the near-universal racism of his time, but he was still uncomfortable about what had happened. He was attempting somehow to simultaneously excuse what the mob had done and express his discomfort.

McCollum begins, as many similar editorial writers of the period did, with a half-jocular personification of the lynching that seems highly offensive to the modern reader: "Judge Lynch held assizes in Waco last Monday, displacing the tribunal that the people of the state had established for the orderly and sure processes of justice." He goes on to say that everyone was expecting the lynching, it would have been next to impossible to avert it, and Sheriff Fleming and his deputies should not be blamed — but, rather, should be given credit for preventing the lynching for as long as they did. As was customary in these pieces, McCollum expends a lot of energy reviling the murderer and the horrors of his crimes and makes the usual nod to "the sacredness of our womanhood," a "consideration that overshadows all others." He never describes or decries the vicious sadism of the lynchers. "We cannot repress regret, though," he adds, "that the men who took execution of the law into their hands had not forborne and allowed the law to take its course." He goes on to warn that "the influences of mob action must ever hold menace and danger to morals and civilization." McCollum acknowledges that some argue that lynching is a deterrent to crime, but he comments, after listening to this argument "in a respectful spirit," that the so-called deterrent effect of lynching has not been proved and can probably never be proved.

In closing, McCollum congratulates the city by insisting on the silver lining, also mentioned repeatedly in the *Tribune*'s coverage of the event. The saving grace for Waco, as McCollum sees it, is the fact that no black people other than Jesse Washington were injured or threatened in any way — unlike in such places as "Springfield, Illinois," and "Canton, Ohio" (it is no accident that he mentions "northern" cities) where, after initial violence directed at one or two men, many blacks were attacked or driven out of town. In Waco, says McCollum, "there is no evidence of hostility to the negro simply because of his race, and we should feel regret if it were otherwise."[145]

The editorial is a self-serving piece, designed primarily to uphold the good name of the community, and McCollum's criticism of the mob action is muted to the point of ineffectuality, but at least it is there. At least, he made some effort to face the facts and take a look at them.

And what of the paper that Harlon Fentress called the strongest in Waco at the time, the *Times Herald*, run by George and Fred Robinson? Much-admired veteran newspaperman E. M. Ainsworth was probably working for the *Times*

Herald at this time.[146] Elisabeth Freeman comments in her report to the NAACP that "Mr. Ainsworth of one of the newspapers seemed the only man who wanted to start a protest."[147] But Ainsworth's admirable impulses must have been overruled by higher-ups.

The day after the lynching, the *Waco Times Herald* published a very short wrap-up story covering the judge's failure to complete his entry on the docket because he was interrupted by the mob action, the burial of the pitiful remains of Jesse Washington, and a defense of the young attorneys assigned to represent Washington for doing their duty. After that, the *Times Herald* never published another word about the Waco Horror. The three-paragraph story, buried on page five, ends with the hopeful conclusion, "Yesterday's exciting occurrence is a closed incident."[148] The author of those words could not possibly have known how mistaken he was.

CHAPTER 6

"ENOUGH TO MAKE THE DEVIL GASP"

How Could This Happen?

It is enough to make the devil gasp in astonishment, seeing that
we have in our own country such communities as Waco, Texas.

—James W. Johnson, "Chance for Humanity"

IF you had been picked up from wherever you were and dropped into
Waco, Texas, on the morning of May 15, 1916, and if you, devoid of all context, had watched the Waco Horror unfold, you would surely have thought
you were no longer on earth but had fallen into the bottom pit of Hell. How
could such a thing take place? Waco was not an isolated South Seas island
where primitive tribes sacrificed outsiders to their gods. It was not medieval
London where spectators picked each other's pockets while some unfortunate
notable was disemboweled, quartered, and decapitated or some adherent to
an out-of-favor religion was burned at the stake. Waco was not even a back-
woods outpost, peopled with inbred crackers driven mad by moonshine and
pellagra. The people of Waco considered themselves to be thoroughly civilized and modern. They were not our ancient ancestors; they were our grandparents and great-grandparents. They had electricity, automobiles, running
water, and flush toilets, by golly.

My father was raised in a small town in Central Texas in the 1920s. All of his life he talked about the freedom and joy of his upbringing, running wild with boys his age, learning to swim by being thrown into the old swimming hole, riding home from school on a neighbor boy's donkey cart. A bucolic existence it was, to hear him tell it, with no fear of robbers or child snatchers, or things that go bump in the night. Life for boys growing up in Waco in the early part of the last century was probably much the same. But that was for white boys.

For black boys growing up anywhere in the South in the early part of the twentieth century, things were quite different. Set foot outside the "colored" part of town and there were dangers everywhere. Some could be anticipated and possibly avoided; others might strike without warning from an unexpected quarter. Quiet living, education, hard work, sometimes even the patronage and protection of powerful white people were not enough to ward off victimization or bring redress for wrongs.[1] As John Dollard, author of the classic *Caste and Class in a Southern Town*, sums up the constant fear, "Every Negro in the South knows that he is under a kind of sentence of death; he does not know when his turn will come, it may never come, but it may also be at any time."[2]

Unlike my father's little town of three thousand souls, Waco had supposedly benefited from the presence of several institutions of higher education, including the august Baylor University and two black colleges. To imagine the townsfolk of "refined" Waco unleashing the Waco Horror is to step inside a grotesque fantasy in which the townspeople are, by random turns, both human and demonic. Rational bystanders who witnessed the Waco Horror must have wondered if they were hallucinating the whole episode.

It is beyond the scope of this book to examine in detail the causes of so complex a phenomenon as lynching. There are many theories; the issue has been addressed by some of the most brilliant and thoughtful American sociologists and historians of the past one hundred years (some of the important sources on the subject and on the whole problem of violence in American history are included in the bibliography). But after all the books have been read and all the theories of lynching carefully considered, separately and in combination, there remains an essential darkness at the heart of the lynching epidemic that none of the analyses adequately illuminates: How could otherwise absolutely conventional twentieth-century people living in a prosperous, industrialized society suddenly metamorphose into a wild mob howling for blood and then, within two or three hours — their blood lust sated — revert to being inoffensive, everyday folk again?

Voices from Waco — of elderly people still living and of others who are now dead but whose words are preserved in taped and transcribed memoirs — do open a small window on this particular time and place, this particular lynching town. These voices offer vivid glimpses into how contemporary minds framed and viewed the Waco Horror, how they felt about it, how they excused or rationalized or "regretted" the episode and others like it, how they absorbed it and still managed to continue to live in Waco.

George Moses Fadal, longtime resident of Waco whose parents came to the city from Lebanon, recalled a lynching in Waco that took place five years after the Jesse Washington lynching. Fadal would have been about fifteen years old at the time of the lynching of a crippled white man named Curley Hackney in 1921. Although Fadal was fuzzy about the details of the crime Hackney allegedly committed, he captured the atmosphere of the crowd that came to "enjoy" the event: "I did witness a mob hanging. This old boy raped a little old girl down at a circus — not a circus but a carnival. And they went up in this little hotel where this fellow was staying and they got ahold of him and drove him out in the country and we just followed like a bunch of boys would. We's all hanging around the drugstore there . . . And drove way out here on Third Street somewhere and put him up on top of a gate and put the rope around his neck and he told them he said, 'Now listen, boys, you may hang me but I don't want you all to shoot me.' Well, anyway, they shot him full of holes and then took the gate out from under him."[3]

This eyewitness account contradicts the newspaper report of the event, which claims that the victim was hanged and then shot once (or shot once and then hanged).[4] More striking is Fadal's casual attitude about the entire event, which is typical of that of many of the men who lived through that period. Fadal is even described by the transcriber of the interview as "chuckling" when he recalled how the lynching victim tried to dicker with the mob and asked them not to shoot him to bits; but the mob riddled his body with bullets anyway.

When asked what his feelings were at the time, Fadal responded, "I just don't recall anything right now — what the feelings were — well, like it was the wrong approach all right. But nothing you can do about it. When you have mob rule there's not much you can do."[5] This easy generality was brought forth by a man who was a voluntary spectator at the lynching, even though he may not have personally taken part. Residents of lynching towns tended to refer to the "mob" as if it were an abstract entity or natural force. But the mob was made up of individuals like George Fadal.

Newspaper printer and union activist Francis L. Pittillo was about eighteen and already at work helping his father print the *Waco Semi-Weekly Tribune* at the time of the Jesse Washington lynching. Pittillo, a little cannier than

Fadal, did not confide to the interviewer exactly what *he himself* was doing on the day of the Washington lynching, but did comment, "Well, naturally there was a spirit of hysteria there . . . But it would die down in a short time and go right on just business as usual . . . that was an emotional incident that happened right at that particular time. And it's all over with and that was the end of it." After adding that he didn't believe in taking the law into your own hands, Pittillo repeated several times that, once it was over, it was over. As for the respectable portion of the community, said Pittillo, "They just kept quiet. They said nothing because as soon as it's over with — there's nothing they could do anyhow. But that's — that's just the old saying about the law west of the Pecos."[6] When asked if the lynchers were ashamed of themselves afterward, Pittillo replied indirectly that they did not come from the "top society" in the community. He explained their actions by taking refuge in a platitude that, under the circumstances, is a grotesque understatement: "They let their emotions run away with their better judgment."[7]

The conspiracy of silence seemed to envelop everyone after these "lawless demonstrations." The Rev. Joseph M. Dawson, pastor of the First Baptist Church of Waco for many years, said in a 1971 interview, when he was ninety-two, that mob violence in Waco was usually caused by "the poorest classes" and that the rest of the populace remained silent or indifferent "when this element became aroused to a violent point." Most Wacoans, he said, agreed that, afterward, the best thing to do was "let the issue drop."[8]

James R. Jenkins, who was an attorney in Waco in 1916 and a retired judge at the time he was interviewed in 1971, explained that "mob violence . . . was simply an impulse with no thought behind it." This is a comfortable assumption that we know to be untrue in the case of Jesse Washington. His lynching was thoroughly premeditated. Jenkins said that attorneys at the time told themselves that lynchers could not be prosecuted because the whole mob had been gripped by "temporary insanity."[9]

Wilford W. Naman, another Waco attorney, was far more dramatic in his assessment of the Washington lynching. He called it a "blood sacrifice" which enabled the people to "return to their senses" after it was over. "Respectable citizens," Naman said (admitting that not every participant in the lynch mob was a lowlife barely clinging to the bottom rung of society) "caught in the mob psychology turned like mad dogs on Jesse Washington and were returned to their senses by his blackened and dismembered body."[10] But certainly the man who lassoed Jesse Washington's remains and dragged them through town and the men who dragged what was left of him to Robinson to hang in a sack in front of the blacksmith's shop were not suffering from postlynching remorse.

The imperative for women of the better classes seems to have been to ignore the entire sordid episode. Mildred Richter, the daughter of a man who owned farms, ranches, and a chain of food stores, was raised in Waco. Her memory of an event associated with a lynching was still sharp and clear more than eighty years after the fact (when she was ninety-two). She recalled that she was a young teenager at the time, shopping with her mother at Goldstein Migel for clothes to wear to a camp for girls in North Carolina. "We were on the third floor of the store where ready-to-wear was," said Richter, "and we heard quite a commotion out the windows down on the street. Well, everybody in the area rushed to the windows to look out and see what was going on. They were dragging the body of a black man up the street fastened to the back of a car or truck."

The incident Mildred Richter remembered was probably not the lynching of Jesse Washington; she was born in 1908 and would have been only eight at the time of the Washington lynching. She was probably remembering a lynching that took place in Waco in 1922, when she would have been about fourteen.[11] The reaction of Richter's mother to the hideous sight in the street outside the department store was probably typical of what was expected of well-bred young women and matrons. She jerked Mildred back into the store, declaring, "We'll not see this!" Nothing more was said about the incident. Mildred Richter asked no questions (she was focused, she said, on her upcoming trip), and her mother volunteered no answers. Yet Richter could still remember vividly, in the year 2000, the gruesome spectacle she had glimpsed in 1922, though her mother had probably hoped that what was "not seen" and not discussed would soon be forgotten.[12]

Mrs. Ike Ashburn, in a 1971 interview, was more forthcoming about the climate of fear and polarization in Waco following the Washington lynching. Women were more closely guarded, she said, and the activities of daughters were more carefully supervised after the Washington lynching until the fears of rape gradually subsided. Tension remained while, outwardly, the town seemed to settle back into normal pursuits. Racial prejudice increased and white fear of the black race worsened as the lynching polarized the races even more than before.[13]

Amidst the general acceptance of mob murder and the near-universal effort to hush up and cover up afterward, the recollections of Harold Lester Goodman, who was eighteen in 1916 and who grew up to become the founder and first president of the American Income Life Insurance Company, seem to offer a little more hope for Waco. Goodman saw the lynching of Jesse Washington and had the grace to be highly disturbed by what he saw. He attended the trial and reported, "There was a lot of screaming and hollering and screams of 'Get him, get him.' And then there were screams of 'We've got him, we've got him.' It's — I've had some nightmares about it in my lifetime . . . I was on the perimeter of the mob; and as they moved on away from this area down to the city square I followed. I was with two or three other boys around my age . . . my feeling was one of great fright. I stayed well away. Even at the square I was a block away when all of this happened. And I could only see glimpses of things, and I was very frightened when they seized this man. I was not far away there, and the mob surged down the street with him."[14]

When his interviewer asked if the whole thing took a matter of minutes, Goodman refused to minimize the time it took to kill Jesse Washington: "Oh, the thing went on for an hour or so," he said.[15] Although Goodman, like others, was quick to identify the leaders of the mob as "the riffraff of the town," he did not take refuge in the prevailing fatalism when it came to the question of whether the lynching could have been prevented: "If there'd been a determined effort made to keep control of this man and keep him out of the hands of the mob it could have been done. He [Fleming?] could have had thirty or forty deputies and made an announcement that they were not going to take him . . . it could have been avoided."[16]

The aftermath, Goodman said, was very subdued. "There [were] many regrets about the whole incident."[17] He added that a "Negro man" who worked for his father told him later that a new black teacher had just come to Paul Quinn College from Ohio or Illinois. The day after the lynching of Jesse Washington, the young teacher resigned his job at Paul Quinn and moved his family away from Waco.

Perhaps Goodman was more thoughtful about the lynching than other Waco males who were his contemporaries partly because he was Jewish and had been teased quite a bit as a young boy growing up in the tiny town of Lott, about twenty-seven miles south of Waco: "All the tricks and jokes and — were first tried out on me," Goodman explained. One of his childhood friends once told Goodman he didn't know whom to "hate" most, Gerald Strange [a newcomer to Lott] because he was a Yankee or Harold Goodman, because he was a Jew.[18] The sense that he was different from the other children, though he was generally accepted, might have made Goodman more sensitive to the mistreatment of others.

Perhaps Goodman was also aware, at age eighteen, that Leo Frank, a Jew, had been lynched in Marietta, Georgia, the year before the Waco Horror.[19] He might have experienced an unspoken sense of increased vulnerability. He might not have been quite as certain as others that his white skin would protect him from ever becoming "the plaything of the mob." He insisted, however, that "Waco has been as free as any community I ever knew of in the United States from any [religious conflicts] . . . People have always been polite and easy about the situation."[20]

Black Wacoans had their own comments to make about the lynchings of Washington and others. In contrast to the fuzzy recollections of many whites, Nanette Booker Hutchison, in particular, remembered these events with clarity. Hutchison, daughter of Ellis Booker, the longtime foreman of the Dr Pepper Bottling Company, was a schoolteacher for forty years. When I interviewed her in 2000, she was still intensely proud, bitter, and outspoken about Waco's treatment of blacks, though advanced age had left her nearly deaf. She had an intense memory of the aftermath of a Waco lynching, which might have been the lynching of Jesse Washington in 1916, but was more likely the lynching of Jesse Thomas in 1922, when Hutchison was twelve. This is probably the same lynching that Mildred Richter remembered.

"I remember tenseness that day," Hutchison began. "Mother kept us in the house right around her. We didn't have telephones. As different ones came from town [out to North Sixth Street, where the Booker family lived], they told us they were building a platform and laying logs and things for the fire . . . We were afraid to go outside. The white people were all mad and in an uproar . . . 'They burning him, they got him tied onto the back of a truck, they going up North Sixth Street,' passersby telling us."

Hutchison's younger brother and sister had taken a bucket and gone down the street to buy some barbecue from a neighbor for dinner. Nannette was frightened by all the commotion downtown and was standing on the porch watching nervously for her brother and sister to return. Just as she saw them heading back toward the house, she also spotted a truck coming up the street. The truck, packed with people of all ages, was dragging a body that was "charred like an old charred bird," said Nannette, "like you burn a chicken or something." When she called out to her little sister and brother, "Did you get the barbecue?" a man riding in the truck hollered back at her, "Here's your barbecue!" For a long time after that, Hutchison said, she was afraid to walk into the street in front of her house barefoot, for fear she might walk on the remnants of the burned man's flesh.

Hutchison had other ugly memories of white men in Waco from that era. When she was ten or twelve, she often carried her father's dinner up to the Dr Pepper plant. White men she passed, young and old, would pinch her anywhere they could and say, "Two bits," or "Four bits," as if they were dickering with a prostitute over price; then they would laugh themselves silly.

She recalled a memory from a later time when she was better able to take care of herself. She climbed on the streetcar one day on her way to work and a white man grabbed her behind and said, "Two bits." Hutchison turned around and knocked him down. The streetcar conductor yelled, "Stop that!" at her. She held her ground, declaring angrily, "Tell him to grab some of these white behinds!"

"I used to hate white men," said Hutchison, "but I'm getting too old and too close to the Lord." But even as she said this, her eyes flashed and her lips pursed, and it was clear that she had forgotten none of the indignities heaped on her by the white men of Waco in the bad old days.[21]

These are the voices and the memories of the people of Waco. These are the lies they told themselves, the excuses they used to blanket over what had happened, and the occasional flashes of clear sight that penetrated the haze. For many of Waco's whites, the elaborately interwoven and often wholly illogical lies about black men and the danger they posed to white women formed a thick veil that distorted the spectacle of a retarded seventeen-year-old boy chained to a tree, bleeding from dozens of wounds, without fingers, ears, toes, or genitals, writhing in a fire.

Harold Goodman, however, spoke of his nightmares. Perhaps, no matter what they told themselves at the time, the sight of this burning boy was scorched onto the retinas and branded into the brains of that crowd of men wearing their summer straw hats. Perhaps, at least for some, the unwanted image returned, over and over, to haunt sleepless nights and lonely hours, and the lynching of Jesse Washington was never a closed incident.

CHAPTER 7

"THE NEWS WILL GO FAR"

The Immediate Aftermath

For wherever the news of it goes—and the news will go far—it will be asserted that
in no other land even pretending to be civilized could a man be burned to death in
the streets of a considerable city amid the savage exultation of its inhabitants.

—*New York Times*

THE reaction to the Waco Horror across the state of Texas, across the
country, even outside the country, was overwhelming. It was as if the
Associated Press accounts of the lynching carried with them a sizzling
current of revulsion and disgust. Newspaper readers were becoming accustomed to reading about southern lynchings, but this one, most people acknowledged, was something special.

The *Dallas Morning News* covered the incident as a news story, but did not
publish an editorial, perhaps because an elderly black man had been thrown
out of a second-story window of the Dallas courthouse, dragged along the city
streets, and hanged from a telephone pole only six years earlier.[1] But both of
Houston's major dailies excoriated Waco without any reservations. The *Houston Post* called what had happened a "shocking exhibition of mob rage." The
editorial begins: "There has not occurred in Texas within the *Post's* knowledge
such a savage outlet of unrestrained mob passion as that which attended the
burning at the stake Monday of the negro boy, Jesse Washington, on the public

square in Waco in the presence, it is said, of 15,000 persons. From no angle viewed, can there be the least excuse, much less justification, offered for it."[2] The *Post* goes on to express particular anger over "the shame and humiliation that has been brought upon the State" and comments that the inhabitants of Waco enacted "the role of veritable demons in tormenting to death the condemned prisoner."[3]

The *Houston Chronicle* was even harsher and also anticipated the world's condemnation of the state because of what the people of Waco had done: "It is with gloomy forebodings that we await the stinging lash of criticism and reproach — criticism thrice hard to bear because it is merited, reproach thrice difficult to endure because it is justified. Not a word of defense is there to offer; not an extenuating circumstance to plead."[4] The *Chronicle* notes that the criminal had already been condemned to die with remarkable swiftness: "What could the mob hope to do that the state had not already done except to satiate that blood lust and morbid antipathy which have no place in civilized communities?" The *Chronicle* editorial writer also expresses the fear that other communities will use the Waco lynching as justification for more of the same: "'They did such a thing in the cultured, reputable City of Waco,' men will say. 'Why should not we do likewise?'"[5]

The *Chronicle* editorial writer foresaw that regional pride, so important to southerners at the time, would come under intense attack: "Georgia, that we scolded so excitedly because of the Frank affair, what will Georgia have to say? New York, that we ridiculed because of the Thaw case,[6] what will New York have to say?" The only response Texans could make to any criticism, says the *Chronicle*, would be "to bow our heads in shame." How, the writer continues, could the United States hold its head up among the nations of the world when such an enormity had been committed on American soil? "We have denounced the Germans for certain alleged atrocities in Belgium; we have called upon the world to ostracize Turkey for her treatment of the Armenians; we have worked ourselves into horrified repugnance at the French revolution for more than a century; we have pretended to be humane, Christian and tolerant and have called upon others to emulate us . . . Now we stand before the world, confessedly involved in one of the most revolting tragedies of modern times; a tragedy which for sheer barbarism has seldom been paralleled in American history."[7] The editorial writer was particularly struck by the fact that the deed was not done in the dead of night, but in broad daylight, before an audience of "40,000" people, in plain and open defiance of the law, and that no one made any attempt to stop it.

The *Austin American* expressed disgust and horror on a par with that of the Houston newspapers. The Austin paper's editor comments on recent lynchings in Oklahoma and Florida, but finds the Waco lynching more terrible than any of these: "The press of Texas had condemned these open violations of the law and it is now called upon to record an even greater outrage, more humiliating to the good people of the state because it occurred in one of its great centers of learning, of boasted civilization — Waco, a city that has produced more 'reformers' than any other city in the state. A city of good people, of fine homes, of refinement, admittedly so, but in their own contentions, far surpassing the other cities of the state."[8] The *Austin American* editorial writer seems to be particularly outraged, not by the burning, which he considers bad enough, but by accounts of the dragging of the body through the streets of town by a 250-pound man riding a big white horse. The writer even dares to propose that *this* miscreant at least should be identified and punished: "Who was the 250-pound man? Whose was the big white horse? The people of Waco know. Will they tell and aid in wiping this stain from the honor of Texas? Will they show to the world that the state of Texas does not condone acts like this?"[9]

It was the *Houston Chronicle* editorial writer's headline, "The Horror at Waco," and the *New York Times*'s headline, "Punished a Horror Horribly" that first used the word *horror* in connection with the lynching of Jesse Washington.[10] It was W. E. B. Du Bois, as will be shown later, who made it stick, though. The *New York Times* editorial, acid and brief, also emphasizes the fact that what the people of Waco did brought "disgrace and humiliation on their country as well as on themselves," because nothing like this could happen in any other so-called civilized country. And "it is not reported," says the *Times*, "that anybody protested or objected."[11]

The *San Francisco Bulletin* published two successive editorials on the Jesse Washington lynching. The first one begins, "A description of life in the United States which omitted lynching would be incomplete. Lynching is an American institution," and it goes on to state emphatically, "Waco did more than burn a negro; she burned her own courage, decency and character, outraged the imaginations of her young people and smeared a foul disgrace across her civic life." Other newspapers mention German and Turkish atrocities in connection with the lynching of Jesse Washington, but many, like the *Bulletin*, compare the lynching to barbarisms committed by Mexicans during the six years of the Mexican Revolution: "When such things can happen in an American community we have no call to civilize Mexico. Civilization is at least as safe in Mexico as it is in Waco, Texas."[12]

The *Philadelphia Press* reports that "in the whole revolting history of mob violence in America, no episode is recorded that for ferocious lawlessness matches the deed of the Waco, Tex., mob that burned a negro boy to death in a public square while 15,000 men, women and children looked on . . . Primitive red Indians could not have done worse." The Waco episode is called "a blistering disgrace to the entire nation."[13]

The *Chicago Evening Post* was sarcastic: "'Over 15,000 men, women and children see negro boy lynched in Texas.' This, if we remember rightly, is the noble State that is always hollering to be allowed to 'clean up barbarous Mexico.'"[14] In the same vein, the *St. Louis Globe-Democrat* comments that "Texans never get so occupied with Mexican troubles that they have not the time to burn a negro."[15]

Only two days after the lynching, the story of Jesse Washington appeared in the *Times of London* — a one-line item in a column of briefs under the heading "Imperial and Foreign News Items": "A negro who had been convicted of the murder of an elderly white woman was dragged from the Court at Waco, Texas, by a mob and burnt at a stake before 5,000 people."[16] Although the story was accorded minimal space, it is remarkable that the tale of Washington's death made its way to London so quickly and was included at all in a newspaper that was packed from start to finish with news of the Great War in France, lists of British dead and wounded, and lists of soldiers who had received honors or promotions.

But the most unrelenting coverage of the Waco Horror in the early days appeared in the nation's black newspapers and in the liberal journals. Editorial writers at America's black newspapers were, as one might imagine, beside themselves with rage, even though they reported tales of lynchings on a near-weekly basis. The *Dallas Express*'s reaction was the mildest of the batch — perhaps because it was so close to the scene, and the editor thought he had better be cautious. The editorial writer expresses himself in an earnest but rather mild vein: "This is not a time for the 15,000 white people who are said to have participated in the awful holocaust (nor as for that matter, any other number of white people), to damn and berate the Negro race; nor is it a time for colored people to condemn all the white people, but it is a time for the men and women, who love humanity and who uphold public order, to soberly consider the prevention of crime, the absence of which will dissolve the mob forever."[17] The *Express*'s proposed solution to mob violence is to abolish "the idler in our midst . . . with the going of these will go the mob." Only at the very end of the editorial does the writer permit himself a stronger statement to the ef-

fect that American statesmen who are so worried about fighting a foreign enemy should give more consideration to episodes like the Waco lynching,
which, "if not checked, will in due time overthrow the republic and destroy its
institutions."[18]

Other black publications were less restrained. The *Washington Bee* published a long letter purporting to be from a former resident of Waco, one
"I. Gustavus R. Ford," who describes the scene of the Waco Horror as "fifteen
thousand merciless maniacs swoop[ing] down upon one defenceless creature
just because they have the power."[19] Ford notes, as did others, the discrepancy
between American ideals and the actual treatment of black Americans. At the
end of his letter Ford suggests that blacks have been quiescent for too long: "If
rebellion against such actions is the only means of cure, then I say to the Negro race at large, rebel."[20]

James Weldon Johnson, the widely respected black writer, educator, and
diplomat who would soon be directly involved with the NAACP, wrote an editorial on the subject of the Waco Horror for the black newspaper called the
New York Age: The National Negro Weekly. Johnson's prose is controlled but
dense with fury: "The people who composed the mob that perpetrated this act
of savagery and the mob that witnessed it feel themselves superior to the Mexicans across the border, but they are not only lower in the human scale than
Mexicans, but lower than any other people who at present inhabit the earth;
for not in Europe, nor Asia, nor Africa, nor South America, nor the islands of
the sea could be found a people so close to the brute but they would have done
such a deed. In comparison with them, a crowd of Mexican bandits is a company of high-souled, chivalrous gentlemen . . . It is enough to make the devil
gasp in astonishment, seeing that we have in our own country such communities as Waco, Texas."[21]

Johnson followed up about a week later with another piece that oozed
even more sarcasm. His comments were based on reports that 116 members of
the Texas militia called up by President Wilson to protect the border were either refusing to report for duty or refusing to enter the service once they arrived
at the mustering point.[22] The reasons for their refusal to serve were unclear.
Perhaps they were alarmed by the fact that guard service now actually required
something more than parading and wearing a dashing uniform. The prospect
of fighting and possibly dying in the deserts of northern Mexico was unsettling.

Even sympathetic stories about "our boys" in the Waco papers at the time
dismantled the popular image of Texans as tough guys and fearsome fighters.
Quite a number of the Texans who were called to active duty fainted while

waiting in line to be inoculated with antityphoid vaccine.[23] Some of the men also complained bitterly about being made to dig trenches in the hot sun, "it [being] extremely hazardous for those who were totally unaccustomed to that kind of work."[24] But, after they were threatened with a court martial, most agreed to do their duty.[25]

"During the past three years," recalls Johnson in the *New York Age*, "in which we have been harrased [*sic*] by Mexico, in which Americans have been murdered and despoiled, both on this and on the other side of the Rio Grande, the nation has been made to look upon the fierce and fearless denizens of Texas as hounds straining at the leash."[26] Now, Johnson informs his readers, 116 members of the Texas militia are about to be court-martialed for refusing to serve in Mexico. In the meantime, Johnson notes, thousands of black soldiers have been out in the Mexican desert fighting and dying to protect those self-same Texans. (Not long afterward, even the Waco newspapers were celebrating the courage of the black buffalo soldiers of the Tenth Cavalry, who were battling supporters of Venustiano Carranza against impossible odds at Carrizal in northern Chihuahua.)[27]

And how are Texans responding to the courage of black soldiers defending their land? asks Johnson: "They are burning black men at the stake. When it comes to tramping across the hot sands of Mexico and being shot at by bandits, the valor of the precious Texan does not appear to rise to the boiling point; but when it comes to a mob of several thousand seizing a Negro boy, dragging him through the street, chaining him to a stake and burning him alive in the public square of one of their cities, the gallant Texan is Johnny-on-the-spot."[28]

The *Chicago Defender*, the most successful black newspaper of the time, covered the Waco Horror in its own idiosyncratic way, with plenty of emotion, but little attention to accuracy.[29] The *Defender* story on the Jesse Washington lynching, which ran under the banner front-page headline "Southern White Gentlemen Burn Race Boy at Stake," carries the byline of one "Henry Walker," who declares himself to be a white man hailing originally from the state of Massachusetts and an eyewitness to the lynching. It is not clear whether this mysterious Henry Walker is supposed to be a visitor to Waco who just happened to be in town when the lynching occurred, or a full-time resident. There is no Henry Walker listed in the 1916 *Waco City Directory*.

The *Defender* article begins dramatically enough: "I am a white man, but today is one day that I am certainly sorry that I am one. Fifteen to twenty thousand men and women intermingled with children and babes in their arms witnessed one of the most outrageous crimes that has ever been committed in the history of the American republic."[30] The report then declares, erroneously, that Jesse Washington made dying statements "praying and crying to 'God Almighty' to have mercy on his soul that he was innocent."[31] Apart from the fact that no one else reported such a speech, it seems unlikely, from what we do know of Washington and the way he expressed himself (or failed to express himself) in the courtroom, that he was capable of this kind of impassioned eloquence. In any case, by the time he had been chained to the tree on the public square, when he could have made a public statement, he had already been beaten and stabbed half to death and was probably only partially conscious. Henry Walker also reports that there were two trials, and "the judge on hearing the evidence said that there was some doubt as to the youth's guilt." Of course, there was only one trial, and Judge Richard Munroe never expressed any uncertainty as to Washington's guilt.

"Henry Walker" could have been a pseudonym used by some Wacoan, black or white, who did not dare publish a story in the *Chicago Defender* under his real name. But the confusion about the facts of the case suggests another explanation. In the process of researching his biography of Robert S. Abbott, founder and owner of the *Chicago Defender*, Roi Ottley interviewed Henry D. Middleton, a post office employee who had known Robert Abbott for years and often helped him produce his newspaper. Middleton reported that J. Hockley Smiley, who performed the functions of managing editor for the *Defender* from 1910 to 1915, established a tradition of publishing exciting fabrications: "'From his vivid imagination,' said Middleton, 'came lynchings, rapes, assaults, mayhems and sundry *crimes* against innocent Negroes in the hinterlands of the South, often in towns not to be found on any map extant. If there was a dull week in the quality and quantity of news, he would fortify himself with jiggers of gin and simply manufacture stories' — so inflammatory in fact that galley proofs often came back from the printer with the notation, 'Our women proof readers refuse to handle this copy!'"[32]

By May 1916, the dapper Smiley, with the chronic cough that was not improved by his drinking habits, was dead of pneumonia. It is likely, however, that his custom of sensationalizing stories by adding flourishes beyond the simple facts continued after his death. The *Defender*'s staff might have taken the Associated Press wire copy about the lynching of Jesse Washington and decided to make the story more interesting to black readers by creating a fictional on-site observer who was supposed to be both white and a Yankee and could therefore revile whites with greater dramatic effect than could an impersonal wire service account or a black reporter.

On June 3, another story was published in the *Defender* reporting the burial of the "seared and scarred torso" of Jesse Washington in an unmarked grave in a potter's field and condemning the local black men for their lack of resistance. The writer comments that local black women wanted to raise the money to give what was left of Jesse a decent burial, but were unable to do so before the burial took place. By this time, the writer had obviously read newspaper accounts from Waco and was able to add a few accurate details about the unfinished entry in the court docket and the fact that Jesse was hidden in the judge's office behind the courtroom before the trial.[33]

But on June 10, the *Defender* suffered another serious outbreak of fiction with the report that George Fryer had been arrested and jailed for the murder of his wife. The *Defender* headline demands to know if Fryer will now be convicted and hanged for committing the crime for which an "innocent boy" was murdered. "The *Chicago Defender* was the only paper that stated the boy was innocent," comments the writer in self-congratulatory mode. It was this inflammatory and patently untrue *Defender* story, reprinted by assistant editor A. T. Smith in Waco's own *Paul Quinn Weekly*, that got Smith into trouble and initiated the rumor that lingers today in the environs of Robinson that it was George Fryer who murdered his own wife.[34]

Reprinting an article from the *Chicago Tribune*, the *Defender* also covered with undisguised delight the same story that had so disgusted James Weldon Johnson—the tale of the Texas troopers called up for National Guard duty who refused to serve. The paragraph introducing the *Tribune* story, however, is pure *Defender*, referring to the recalcitrant troopers as "southern skunks" and expressing the hope that the cowards will face death by firing squad.[35]

The most sustained coverage and discussion of the Waco Horror, however, took place in several of the noted liberal journals of the day. Hamilton Holt's *Independent* magazine reported the event in the May 29 issue under the headline, "A Terrible Crime in Texas." "In the town of Waco, Texas, last week a crowd of 15,000 persons watched a human being burned to death," says *The Independent*. The three-paragraph item describes Washington's crime and the lynching and concludes, "His lynching was simply an orgy of mob brutality and savage lust. The young negro's crime was a horrible one. The crime of the people of Waco was more horrible and a deeper stain upon the fair name of Texas."[36]

The *New Republic*, where Walter Lippmann, who was later to become America's best-known intellectual and social commentator, was associate editor from 1914 to 1917, aggressively attacked the kind of sectional pride that would lead southerners to defend a "filthy crime" like the lynching of Jesse Washington. "To minimize the horrors of lynching and to exaggerate the horrors of criticism is infantile," says the *New Republic* editorial writer.[37]

Some of the reports on the lynching in the days and weeks immediately succeeding the event were comparatively brief and tempered in tone. But as time passed and the debate became more heated, longer, more impassioned stories followed. This was not a matter of natural happenstance — as will be shown in subsequent chapters.

It is no surprise that some of the most intense early writing about the Waco Horror appeared in Oswald Garrison Villard's *The Nation:* "Thus Texas for the moment outdoes Georgia in infamy,"[38] says a *Nation* writer, "and the good people in both States doubtless thank the Almighty daily that we are not as the Mexicans with their Pancho Villa! How long is the South, how much longer is the whole country, to permit such revolting criminality?"[39]

The Nation item set off a wave of letters to the editor that continued for months after the appearance of the original story. In the June 22 issue, one J. T. Winston of Bryan, Texas, defends lynching in the usual way, by insisting that it is the only way to protect southern white women from hideous rape and murder. (No one ever addresses the fact that, despite thousands of lynchings, these dreadful crimes against women apparently continued. Lynching would seem to have been a poor deterrent.)

Winston begins his diatribe by declaring that he was born a northerner, never went south until he was twenty-eight, and would have said, before he came to live in the South, that lynchers "were barbarians and deserved the same torture they dealt to the negroes." But he had now resided in the South for fifteen years and was "a convert." Blacks of "the better class," says Winston, went north, where they were few in number. In many parts of the South, "negroes greatly outnumber the whites" and "are inclined to be troublesome and insolent to the whites."

After describing an intolerable incident of disrespect in which a Negro "jostled me from the walk," Winston launches into an extended, melodramatic account of the gruesome rape and murder of an eleven-year-old girl by "a dehumanized fiend, swelling with bestial lust" who had been "a trusted farm hand." "Devise plans to prevent the negro from causing the South to wreak vengeance on him," says Winston, "and then black bodies hanging from telephone poles will be as rare as dead pirates hanging from the yard-arms of present-day ships. Lynching is a horrible disease. Remove the cause, and the disease disappears."[40]

A July 13 letter from L. P. Chamberlayne of Columbia, South Carolina, "a Southerner born and bred . . . and the son of a Confederate soldier," neatly decimates Winston's arguments. Says Chamberlayne of Winston, "He has no case whatever." Whatever the provocation, Chamberlayne responds, "we Southerners are no more privileged than other people to maintain man-hunts and torturing orgies, and yet at the same time enjoy the repute of high civilization." Chamberlayne goes on to note that most lynched blacks are not even accused of rape: "A negro was murdered in this State," he says, "within the last three years for hiding under a house." He also points out that southern white men accused of the same crimes ("rape and criminal assault") were never lynched.[41]

Another letter in the same issue of *The Nation* blames sex crimes committed by blacks against white women on the "easy-going tolerance" of promiscuity within the black community, the promiscuity of white men with black women, and excessive tolerance of minor crimes by blacks, because "he is a negro and nothing is expected of a negro." The writer of this letter, "J. M. S." of Morrilton, Arkansas, adds, "It is but a step from being a bad negro to being a rape fiend."[42]

In the July 27 issue of *The Nation*, Oscar Woodward Zeigler of Baltimore warns that "the uncontrollable sex instinct of the negro is often, if not most often, a perversion of the very strength of the negro character, the veneration of the superman he builds for himself in the white race." With great earnestness, Zeigler declares that what is needed to prevent black sex crime is to remove from all public places "artistic" posters and calendars that depict white women in suggestive poses. These pictures, he suggests, are a greater temptation than most black men can withstand.[43]

On this foolish note, national discussion of the Waco Horror might have petered out, as had discussions of many other lynchings. But the leaders of the NAACP were determined that this time the nation's reaction to a lynching would not exhaust itself so quickly. They had a plan to set in motion that would prevent rapid extinction of the story.

CHAPTER 8

"WHO IS SHE; A DETECTIVE?"

The Investigation

Once I saw a bunch of men standing talking and could tell from
their movements that they were discussing the lynching. I sauntered by. They all
closed up and stood perfectly still, with absolutely no expression on their faces, until I
had gotten out of hearing. I heard them say—"Who is she; a detective?"

—Elisabeth Freeman, "The Waco Lynching"

WHILE the newspapers and the journals chewed over the grisly story of the Waco Horror, the NAACP took immediate action. On May 16, 1916, one day after the lynching of Jesse Washington, Royal Freeman Nash, the white social worker who was then secretary of the NAACP, wired Elisabeth Freeman in Fort Worth, where she remained following the statewide suffrage convention in Dallas.[1] "Desire confidential report on recent Texas tendencies along lines of my Georgia investigation," said Nash with tantalizing vagueness. "Fifty a week and expenses. Will forward check and instructions by mail tonight if you can give us any time. A week should be enough. Wire address."[2]

Freeman wired back that she was mystified as to the "nature of business" Nash wanted done—at least until she received Nash's follow-up letter, also written on May 16. In the letter Nash tells Freeman that the evening papers had all carried a brief AP story on the Waco lynching: "Such a spectacle in the public square of a town of over 25,000 inhabitants, a young boy condemned to

137

death and then taken from the court-room, affords one of the most spectacular grounds of attack on the whole institution of lynching ever presented."
Nash's next remark makes it clear that the NAACP had been lying in wait for
a lynch mob to strike again: "Mr. Villard of the *Evening Post*, our treasurer,
asked me when I came back from Georgia to get the inside story of the next
horrible lynching so that he can write it up and spread it broadcast through the
Southern press over his own name."[3]

Nash advised Freeman that her suffrage work throughout Texas would
give her a cover to investigate the lynching and an excuse for being in Waco.
He suggested that she "locate liberals or Northerners" and contact the state
secretary of the Socialist Party to put her in touch with "trusty radicals." Local
priests or ministers, he thought, might also help her get at the truth. "We want
all of them," Nash said, "the crime in detail, who the boy was and who his victim, the Judge and jury that tried the case, the court record, and the ghastly
story of the burning." He also wanted anything that could be used as "legal evidence" against the mob, since the intent was to try to bring charges against the
lynchers. "Photos of the places mentioned," said Nash, "the town, the courthouse, the square, the suspension bridge, the scene of the murder, and any of
the actors will make the thing vivid for news purposes." A cashier's check for
$100 was enclosed with his letter, against which Freeman was to render an
account of her time and expenses.

Nash also sent Freeman a copy of his "findings in Georgia" to use as a
model for her investigation. The "findings" Nash refers to in his wire were
summarized in a lengthy story published in the March 1916 issue of *The Crisis*, which describes in detail how poor whites had driven every single black
person out of Forsyth and Dawson counties in northern Georgia following the
rape and beating of a white girl by three black men.[4]

Even after she received Nash's sample of comprehensive investigative
journalism to guide her, Freeman was still puzzled about what, exactly, she
was supposed to do in Waco. The first few letters she sent to Nash from Waco's
elegant ten-story Raleigh Hotel are full of confused and self-deprecatory remarks: "I am terribly 'green' at this work & scarcely know what you want to
know . . . Of course, I am working in the dark—not quite knowing what you
want me to get. Mayhaps I am not getting what you want."[5] Her uncertainties,
however, did not slow her down. By the end of her second day in Waco, following a "Texas storm" on the first day during which she made phone calls and
set up appointments, Freeman had already seen the newspaper editors, the
"leading colored men," the black ministers, the head of one of the black col-

leges, and "a few of the 'bad' negros" — which group she later defines as "the lower element of colored folk."[6] She had also acquired newspaper clippings and photographs of the lynching, despite the fact that the photographer had been forced to "make a sworn affidavit not to sell — give — or show them to anyone."[7] Freeman thanked Nash for giving her the opportunity to do the work, declaring that the project was "terrifically interesting." Because she had visited Waco before in her suffrage work, she said, she already had entrée to people whom she otherwise never would have been able to see.

In the process of acquiring the photos, Freeman reports in her full account of the investigation, she "made about five visits to the mayor." She sweet-talked John Dollins with a line she would use successfully throughout her investigation: "I told them that I had been in Waco before and had been treated very nicely, that I had been in Texas four months and would like to go back North and see if I could not show the people that Waco was not as bad as they would expect."[8]

Freeman soon learned that she had to call on all of her considerable skills to extract the information she wanted from the people of Waco. It seems that, at first, the investigation of the Jesse Washington lynching was almost a game to her. She saw it as a challenging assignment, a departure from her customary work of making speeches and inspiring women to join the suffragist cause — an exciting new project which she attacked with her usual energy and optimism. But before long, the tone of her letters to Nash changed. As she gathered one hideous detail after another — first, the details of Washington's crime, and then the details of the lynching — Freeman was clearly weighed down by what she had learned.

She also began to sense that what she was doing was dangerous. "Am being closely watched," she scribbled upside down at the beginning of a long letter describing her activities in Waco. Elsewhere in the same letter she writes, "The net is tightening. Every one is closing up as tight as a clam."[9] Later she reported that she had almost been arrested twice for being out alone at night and that her hotel room had been searched at least twice.[10] She decided that it was too dangerous to mail much of the material she had gathered and that some of it was not fit to be mailed; she promised to deliver everything she had to Nash in person.[11]

In point of fact, what Elisabeth Freeman was doing — investigating a lynching in Waco only a few days after the event on behalf of the NAACP — was perilous in the extreme, as later events would prove. NAACP representatives who tried to investigate racial incidents in the South in similar circumstances were threatened with bodily harm or actually attacked. John Shillady, a white social worker (like Roy Nash) who became secretary of the NAACP in 1918, traveled from New York to Austin, Texas, in August 1919 to try to work out a local dispute between the state and the NAACP. There were rumors in Austin that local blacks were arming themselves following a race riot in Longview, Texas, a month earlier, and the NAACP was blamed for stirring up unrest. While Shillady was in Austin, he was violently beaten on a public street by Constable Charles Hamby, County Judge Dave J. Pickle,[12] and Ben Pierce — all of whom are identified by name in the newspaper — "until he was bleeding from the face and howled for mercy." After the beating, Shillady was forced to get on a train to St. Louis and was ordered not to get off the train as long as he was still within the borders of the state of Texas.[13]

Shillady never recovered from the terrible beating, either physically or mentally. Walter White reports that Shillady's "great gaiety and warm smile disappeared" and his former efficiency was replaced by a near paralytic indecisiveness. As the months passed, Shillady seemed to grow, not better, but worse, until he ultimately resigned his position, entered a hospital, and died not long afterward.[14]

In the same year, Walter White, then assistant executive secretary of the NAACP, was almost lynched while investigating an outbreak of racial violence in Phillips County, Arkansas. White was warned by a local black man that the white folks in Helena, Arkansas, were planning to "get" him. As soon as he heard the news, White headed for the train station and caught the first train out, climbing on from the side opposite the platform and buying his ticket from the conductor on the train. As White paid his fare, the conductor admonished him that he was leaving "just when the fun is going to start . . . There's a damned yellow nigger down here passing for white and the boys are going to get him . . . When they get through with him, he won't pass for white no more!"[15] White, who identified with his black heritage although he was blond with blue eyes, realized that he was the "yellow nigger" the conductor was describing. He had escaped from Helena just in time.

Elisabeth Freeman, nosing around Waco in May 1916 for bits of information about the Jesse Washington lynching, was intuitive and sensible enough to be aware that her inquiries into the lynching were not welcome and that she was under suspicion and possibly in some danger, but she seems to have been stimulated, rather than discouraged, by the difficulty of her task. If the direct approach failed, Freeman went at her target — a witness or an actor in the drama — from a more oblique angle.

The first time Freeman tried to get a statement from Judge Richard Munroe, she simply approached him on the street and announced without preamble, "I want to talk with you about something very important . . . I want to get your opinion of that affair." Munroe refused and then demanded to know why she wanted the information. "If you refuse to talk with me, there is no use of telling you what I want it for," she replied saucily.[16] Afterward, Freeman apparently recollected that her purpose, in this case, was not to maintain her dignity, stand up to recalcitrant, antisuffrage men, and score "many good thrusts home," but to get the information the NAACP needed, no matter how she did it. Here her experience in England, where she had changed her dress and her accent to fit in with the English, stood her in good stead.

She went back to see Munroe, wearing a different dress and affecting "a strong English accent" and found that he did not recognize her: "[I] said I was interested in clippings from New York papers which showed that Waco had made for itself an awful name, and I wanted to go back and make the Northerners feel that Waco was not so bad as the papers had represented." Of course, nothing could have been farther from the truth, but, as happened with Mayor Dollins, Freeman's appeal to the judge's local pride worked. Munroe gave her the court records and may even have introduced her to court stenographer Warren Hunt. Freeman proceeded to win over Hunt by engaging in "a plain, common, every day flirtation which I had to carry on to get what I wanted."[17]

Again she succeeded. Documents in the NAACP archives concerning the Jesse Washington lynching include a complete transcript of the testimony given at trial, along with a copy of Washington's original confession, which was entered as evidence during the trial. These documents are *not* found in the court records at the McLennan County Courthouse, although other documents relating to the case, such as lists of witnesses to be subpoenaed, do remain. Warren Hunt either removed the only record from the courthouse files and gave it to Elisabeth Freeman, or he took the trouble to make a special transcript just for her. At first, according to Freeman, Hunt said he would give her a copy of Washington's unexpurgated confession only if she paid him $50; in the end, utterly charmed by the visitor from New York, he said he would charge anyone else $50 for it, but he would give it to her for nothing.[18]

Savvy about the ways of the media, Freeman also managed to place a story in one of the Waco papers about her presence in town and her suffrage work, which she hoped might serve as cover.[19] But on May 24, the *Morning News* published a little item which seemed intended to warn Wacoans that strangers were snooping around. The article begins by describing the floods of letters into Waco, "some of them addressed to the district, others to the county, and some to the city authorities, regarding the occurrence here on May 15." It continues, "Most of the letters are couched in withering terms of criticism, and the terms employed in a part of them are of a character to show that this city has been placed in a most unenviable light before the world." The *News* expresses particular concern over the fact that the size of the crowd that witnessed "the incident" was "grossly misrepresented."

The final paragraph of the story seems to be an oblique reference to Freeman and her inquiries. It showed, says Freeman, that "they had become suspicious of me."[20] "One or two special writers for publication in the east [says the article] have appeared in Waco seeking information relative to the tragedy, and also seeking pictures which were made at the time; gruesome incidents connected with the affair are being sought out and the publicity of undesirable character appears to be just getting under good headway, insofar as some of the outside points are concerned."[21]

The *News* editors were clearly disturbed, not by the fact of what had happened in the Jesse Washington "occurrence," but by the injustice of outsiders who were condemning the city as a whole on the basis of a single event. After the May 24 story appeared in the *Morning News*, Freeman complained that the size of the crowd that witnessed the lynching, originally estimated by Waco's papers at fifteen thousand, was gradually being reduced in popular memory to only five hundred.

On the same day the story about mysterious "writers for publication in the east" appeared, the *Morning News* also printed an editorial, not so much about the lynching as about the response to the lynching. Stung by the scathing criticism, pouring in from all parts of the country, of a town that had up until then been widely admired, the *News* editorial writer took as his theme the convenient notion that all men are sinners and no one is qualified to "cast the first stone": "The News has not hesitated to voice the condemnation which every right-thinking person must feel with respect to the human holocaust which occurred on the streets of Waco. For that, it has no word of palliation or excuse," the editorial begins.[22] But the *News*, in point of fact, had *not* editorialized previously against the lynching but had only printed a poem written some years before.

Then came the excuses. The *News*, says the editorial writer, could accept fair criticism of "the deed," but not a denunciation of the South in general and Waco in particular. Waco was really a pretty good place, maintained the *News*, a place that was usually conducive to the development of good citizenship. But good citizenship is abandoned when (in the familiar and comforting metaphorical mode), "the torch has once been lit whose flames always obscure reason, paralyze law and transform men into savages." The editorial continues in the same grandiose exculpatory vein: "The outbreak of the spirit of revenge and passion which occurred here was simply an old, old story of human weakness which has blurred every page in history and thrown its shadows across the world since time began. No nation, no race, and no community has any just right to say to any other race or any other community: 'I am holier than thou.' All have sinned and sinned alike."[23]

In other words, the writer of the editorial refuses to recognize that the lynching of Jesse Washington was something above and beyond ordinary human sin, something quite extraordinary, an extravagant and prolonged display of public savagery celebrated by thousands of citizens. Instead, he reminds his readers of the Great War then destroying half the world and of the many crimes that "go unrebuked" and the "personal and social faults" of all of us. He concludes pompously, "Civilization is but skin deep, refinement a sham, education a disappointment, unless there is deeply lodged in the human heart an abiding reverence for God, veneration for His law, and that charity which believeth, endureth and hopeth, looking forward to an individual immortality, and to a personal citizenship in a Kingdom of Peace which shall never end." In short, you can't expect anything better of people until men become angels and all things are perfect. That vague philosophy offered precious little hope to black Americans any time soon.

The *Waco Semi-Weekly Tribune* reprinted the condemnatory editorial from the *Houston Post* in a reluctant bow to the tide of negative public opinion. In an introduction to the *Post* piece, the *Tribune* editorial writer refers to the "expressions on that matter ['the event of last Monday'] by several hundred Texas papers that have come to The *Tribune* office during the week." The *Houston Post* piece was being reprinted, says the editorial writer, "to show not only the fearfulness of the blow that was struck at Law, but the blow dealt at the good name of Waco and McLennan County."[24]

The *Tribune* writer continues the familiar attempt to blame "the riffraff" by expressing regret that "*irresponsible, non-representative men* can so work harm to a community," and then declares that the paper will now "dismiss the matter forever, for no good can come from further reference to it."[25] By May 20, Augustus McCollum, the probable writer of this editorial, had apparently come to see that his glib defense of the city in his May 17 editorial had not staved off the torrents of both regional and national disgust washing over his beloved Waco.

It must be said of both the *Waco Morning News* and the *Waco Semi-Weekly Tribune* that at least editorials were penned and published and the "incident" was acknowledged. The *Waco Times Herald* devoted its editorial pages to politics, local and national, and other safe subjects, and continued its imperturbable silence on the subject of the lynching of Jesse Washington.

By the weekend after the lynching, Elisabeth Freeman began to feel that her sources were drying up. "Suddenly everyone became silent," she reports to Nash. She decided to try another tack. She made an appointment to have her hair washed and her nails done at the Goldstein Migel Department Store and casually mentioned to the manicurist (whom she described as "a little girl"), "You had a terrible happening here the other day."[26] It was this girl, Leona Lester, who told Freeman that she had witnessed the castration of Jesse Washington from the windows of the department store and that her father, "Mr. W. Lester, 1605 Summer Street" (probably the man listed as Robert P. Lester, 2005 Summer, in the *Waco City Directory*) had also seen the mutilation take place. "Mr. Lester," writes Freeman, had been near City Hall and had climbed into a tree to get a view of the lynching. He had seen the mob cut off Washington's fingers and saw the blow to the back of his head by "the big man" that probably finished Jesse off.[27]

As she tried to absorb the disturbing facts she was uncovering, Elisabeth Freeman took comfort and solace from her visits with the black citizens of Waco. She had been advised to look up local "radicals" or Socialists, but, as she tells Nash wryly in one of her letters, "Radicals are rare in Waco."[28] Freeman went first to visit an unidentified "suffrage friend" in Waco. The friend's brother-in-law, a clerk in a lawyer's office, says Freeman, "has a very keen interest in colored people and is friendly with all the best class of colored people."[29] Thus Freeman was led to Waco's most prominent black citizens for information and help.

In her full report Freeman mentions particularly "'Dr.' Willis, a very fine colored man."[30] "Dr. Willis" would have been William S. Willis, president of Willis Realty & Construction, who also owned Lone Star Undertaking. Freeman also spent time with the Rev. John W. Strong, president of Central Texas College, and the Rev. J. Newton Jenkins, pastor of New Hope Baptist Church, Waco's most important black church, which had been founded by former slaves in 1866. Jenkins, a graduate of Fisk University, came to Waco from South Carolina and was pastor of New Hope Baptist Church from 1907 to 1950.[31]

A fourth contact was the New Hope Baptist Church choir director, Dr. George S. Conner.[32] Freeman identifies Conner as a dentist, but he was, in actuality, one of the first black physicians and surgeons in Waco.[33] In 1916, he was also superintendent of the Training School for Nurses at Central Texas College.[34]

"The feeling of the colored people," says Freeman, "was that while they had had one rotten member of their race the whites had 15,000."[35] Freeman recounts how the black residents of Waco waited patiently for the Sunday following the lynching to see if any of the white ministers of Waco would denounce the lynching. Among the white ministers, writes Freeman, "Dr. Colwell [Caldwell] was the only man who made any protest at all, and this was only after I had called him up about five times."[36]

Freeman's condemnation of Waco's ministers was not entirely fair. Dr. C. T. Caldwell, pastor of Waco's First Presbyterian Church, was the first, but not the only, white minister to speak out against the lynching. Soon after the lynching, most of Waco's prominent Baptist pastors left town to attend the Southern Baptist Convention in Asheville, North Carolina (where the entire group adopted a resolution denouncing mob violence, although principally with an eye toward protecting "persons lecturing on religious subjects").[37]

Caldwell's formal protest, endorsed by his congregation, stressed that the Presbyterian Church had "always dared to have a conscience ahead of the community" and had stood against all kinds of anarchy: "When the people or community overthrow His ordained method of administering justice, His wrath and curse have been invited, since nations, governments and communities have no future existence, but are punished here and now . . . I earnestly and solemnly protest against the fearful, lawless occurrence of last Monday . . . Let us fervently implore God to stay His vengeance and not deal with the whole community after *the sins of the few.*"[38] Caldwell goes on to express his confidence that the judicial and executive branches of government will "fix and execute such swift and dire penalties as unspeakable criminals deserve."[39] He was one of very few even to mention the possibility that the lynchers might be punished for their actions. Caldwell also vigorously urged other Waco pastors to take a public stand against the lynching. Dr. F. C. Culver of the Austin Avenue Methodist Church seems to have been the next to follow Caldwell's lead and preach a sermon against the mob. Two weeks after the lynching, nine Baptist pastors in Waco passed resolutions expressing the "intensest denunciation of this criminal violence on the part of persons composing *a mob manifestly made of the lowest order of society* collected from various communities, and drawn together by the prospect of an orgy of savage brutality, *possibly* emboldened by the encouragement of some who profess respectability."[40] Once again, community leaders were insisting it was the scum and the riffraff who had perpetrated the lynching, but the Baptist pastors did hint at the possibility that members of the more respectable classes might have been peripherally involved.

On May 27, the faculty at Baylor University, regretting that "the incident will evoke from the outside world reproaches unmerited by the majority of the people of our fair city and county," also formally denounced the actions of the lynch mob.[41] Faculty members declared that they abhorred and deplored the actions of the mob and disapproved of every form of mob violence. The law, they said, should be allowed to take its course.

In a paragraph on the editorial page, the *Semi-Weekly Tribune* referred to the article about the Baylor faculty resolutions and explained that, although the editors had already condemned the lynching and had not intended to print anything more about it, they were responding to the appeal of the Baylor faculty to print the resolutions and also admired the spirit of the Waco ministers in denouncing the mob action. "Here we leave it," the piece concludes, "a memory one does not desire to recall."[42]

As testimony to the power of selective memory, two of Waco's most revered long-time pastors, C. T. Caldwell and Joseph M. Dawson (of First Baptist), each insisted in later years that *he* had been the only local minister to speak out against the lynching of Jesse Washington. Caldwell recorded his thoughts in a memoir about the First Presbyterian Church: "When a negro was hung and burned by a mob, our church lifted up its voice in protest against such a procedure. The pastor was advised not to do so — that it would injure both himself and the church. But when the protest was presented to the congregation, the whole body rose to sanction the protest. This happened to be the only protest that was made in the city. It gave influence to our church."[43]

Joseph Dawson, in his autobiography, recalls his horror at the lynching of Jesse Washington but also his pride in the protest he made: "My resolutions adopted by the Waco Pastor's Association are still being quoted around the country." But, he continues, "One protesting man could do nothing against 5,000 senseless human beings turned into beasts. Nonetheless I swore then on the altar of God I would henceforth forever fight lynching, if every Baptist Church in the South kept silent."[44] Dawson then expresses relief that he was not dismissed from his position for his outspokenness.

Freeman records for posterity others who spoke out against the lynching:

"W. A." [W. B.] Brazelton, the lumberman who was foreman of the jury but thought he could not lead a protest because he had been directly involved in the trial; newsman Ed Ainsworth, who "seemed the only man who wanted to start a protest"; "Col. Hamilton," a northerner who feared he would be lynched himself if he spoke out but who "said he would never register in any hotel that he came from Waco"; former mayor "Allan Stanford" [Allen Sanford], who was assured by the sheriff and the judge that the lynching would not take place; Judge W. E. Spell, whose wife headed the local suffrage league and had made a fiery speech at the suffrage convention in Dallas — Spell thought it was all "deplorable but the best thing was to forget it"; and former mayor "Mackaye" [J. H. Mackey].[45]

When Freeman represented herself to former mayor Mackey as a newspaperwoman, he begged her to "fix it up as well as you can for Waco, and make them understand that the better thinking men and women of Waco were not in it."[46] Freeman sums up the feelings of the "best people" in the end as "shame for the whole happening. They realize it could have been stopped if they had had a leader — now they think they are right in trying to forget it and fancy the world will do so too."[47] Freeman was now determined that the Waco Horror would not be forgotten, despite the inevitable hurt feelings of the "best people," who had trusted her.

Freeman's feelings evolved during the several days she spent in Waco. Soon after she arrived, she began to hear the details of Jesse Washington's crime and was so disgusted that she first wrote Nash, "To put up a legal fight will be a bit unwise. The boy committed the foulest crime . . . frankly admitted his guilt, was coarse and beastal [sic] in the telling. Had there been any shadow of his guilt — I'd see a splendid opportunity to raise the legal side of the matter — but the crime was unspeakable."[48]

By the time she wrote her next letter, however, Freeman had heard more about the lynching and had changed her mind entirely. She now believed the legal angle should be pursued. "Have gathered some horrible details of the crime against the boy," she wrote.[49] By the time she left town, she was actively involved in the search for a lawyer to try to bring charges against leaders of the lynch mob. "Am working on the lawyer. That will be hard. No Waco man is to be trusted. Have written friends in Houston and Austin."[50]

One of Freeman's great successes as an investigator ("Who is she, a detective?" she heard a group of men asking each other as she passed) was that she succeeded in obtaining and recording the names of the reputed leaders of the lynch mob.[51] The five names were not published in Du Bois's account in

The Crisis, but they are included in Freeman's report. The following is the list she compiled — some of the names distorted by her chronic carelessness with spelling: "The man who led the mob is a driver for the Big Four Ice Company. Others who took part are Frazer, who works for Ludde, Jesse Mims, a brick-layer, Dillard, a saloon keeper, Hancock, the son of a saloon keeper, and Sparks, who also works for Ludde."[52] Initially, William Willis gave Freeman these five names; they were later confirmed by others.[53] Everyone in town knew who the chief lynchers were. Their actions had been observed by thousands; they had been photographed. The many clearly visible faces in Gilder-sleeve's photos who are now mysteries to us were well-known to residents of Waco at the time.

Did Elisabeth Freeman get it right? Did the men she named exist and were they credible suspects? Were they indeed the scum, the riffraff, the disreputable element in the community, as the embarrassed "better element" in lynching towns was always so quick to claim? The accuracy of her assertions can be tested by examining available records in Waco to see if the five men she mentions by name existed and if any information about them suggests that they could have been lynch mob leaders.

Misspellings notwithstanding, each man Freeman mentions can be identified as a real, documented Waco resident. It would also appear that the term "riffraff" might be an appropriate way to describe them. Freeman would probably not have cared to take tea with any of these characters at the Raleigh Hotel. There was, to begin with, a Jess T. Mimms, a bricklayer living in Waco, who was almost thirty-nine at the time of the Washington lynching. He died in Waco of apoplexy and bronchitis in 1927 at the age of fifty.

It is no accident that two of the reputed leaders of the lynch mob named by Freeman, Dillard and Hancock, were associated with the then thoroughly disreputable business of saloonkeeping. Saloons in 1916, unlike the speakeasies of a few years later, were places where respectable women did not go. They were dirty, rough, and sometimes dangerous. The drinking establishments around the town square in Waco at the time were probably among the worst in the city. Says Elisabeth Freeman about the condition of that part of town in 1916: "The City Hall is in the center of the worst part of the city. The people are all Mexicans, Negroes, and the lower class of people. It is, however, the beginning of the main street in town, and used to be a very nice section."[54]

"Hancock, the son of a saloon keeper," was probably James T. Hancock Jr., who was, in 1916, a bartender in the saloon of his father, James T. Hancock Sr., at 100 South 2nd Street. James T. Hancock Sr. ran several saloons in Waco at different times, which were all located in the immediate vicinity of the central town square. After the arrival of Prohibition, the elder Hancock was identified in Waco city directories at various times as the proprietor of a "billiard hall" or a "domino parlor."[55] In 1916, Hancock Sr., who fathered five sons in all, had two other sons living in Waco besides James T. Jr. Edgar Hancock was a printer for the *Waco Morning News*, and Leamon Hancock, who is listed as his father's partner in a saloon operation in the 1911–12 *Waco City Directory*, had become a salesman.

It was James T. Hancock Jr., however, who was most closely identified with his father's saloon in 1916; therefore, it seems likely that it was James, not Edgar or Leamon, who was the active participant in the lynching. Ironically, James T. Hancock Jr.'s last job in Waco, as listed in the 1917–18 *City Directory*, was driving a police patrol car. After that, he disappeared from the directory and seems to have left the area.

The other saloonkeeper identified by Freeman, Joseph W. Dillard, was a much more significant character in the history of Waco than either James Hancock. In 1916, Dillard, then in his mid-forties, was running a saloon at 110–112 South 6th Street. He and his brother Thompson, along with a younger brother named George, also owned and operated a famous chili parlor, which is celebrated in the Special Centennial Edition of the *Waco Tribune Herald* in 1949, in an article that begins: "[Joe Dillard] was a young night bar tender at Andy Anderson's bar on City Hall Square back in the 1880s. He used to step down the street a few doors and buy himself a bowl of chili at a little stand down there. He liked it so well he bought the stand for $150 and the recipe for $500 and he and Mrs. Dillard . . . started making and selling chili." After Dillard's chili parlor closed for good in 1917, he never sold the recipe for his chili, although, according to local legend, he was offered $10,000 for it by the "Gebhart [*sic*] chili people."[56]

A close reading of the folksy article about Dillard's chili, however, suggests that the person who was really responsible for its superlative quality was neither Joe Dillard nor his wife, Lucy — nor any of the other Dillard brothers — but "an old Negro named Ellis." It was Ellis, says the writer, who painstakingly prepared the red peppers that went into the chili every day by removing the seeds, simmering the pods, and then skinning them. Dillard's chili sold for a nickel a plate or fifteen cents a bowl, with or without beans, dry or "with grease," and with crackers. The crackers were kept in wooden boxes stacked above the cordwood behind the cook stove. The heat from the stove kept the crackers crisp. "The young fellows and their girls," rhapsodizes the Centennial

Edition article, "would go [to Dillard's] after dances to eat a bowl of chili; the gay young blades of the town practically lived there. They used to pawn their valuables with Joe Dillard when they needed money, and he always kept them safe and also kept their secrets."[57] There was a serving window between the chili parlor and Dillard's saloon next door, so a young man could get a mug of beer to drink with his chili without having to go outside onto the street and into the saloon.

Joe Dillard was apparently an immensely stubborn fellow, in addition to being closemouthed and trustworthy. The owners of the building where his saloon and chili parlor were located wanted to tear down the old building and build a new one, but they could not get Dillard to leave. The roof of the old building started to leak when it rained. The owners of the building refused to fix the leaks because they wanted Dillard out; Dillard wouldn't fix the leaks because he thought they were the landlord's responsibility. He took to giving umbrellas to his customers to hold over their heads whenever it rained. Finally, the building owners just went ahead and tore the building down. Dillard sold drinks up to the last minute as the wreckers worked around him.

After the demise of his saloon and chili parlor, Dillard, like James T. Hancock Jr., became a driver for the city police patrol in 1920 or 1921 and continued to work for the police department for twenty-five years. During the 1930s, when he must have been pushing sixty, he finally became a full-fledged policeman — in which capacity he was known as "Uncle Joe."[58] "Uncle Joe" Dillard was fondly remembered in Waco as a master chili chef, a trusted confidante to "gay young blades," and a friendly policeman who always wore a red flower in his lapel,[59] not as one of the leaders of a vicious lynch mob that stabbed, beat, mutilated, strangled, and burned a black teenager to death on May 15, 1916 — except in the pages of Elisabeth Freeman's report on the lynching.

The other two lynch mob leaders identified by Freeman, "Frazer" and "Sparks," were both said to work for "Ludde." "Ludde" was George H. Luedde, who was, in 1916, one of Waco's most prominent and prosperous citizens. Luedde managed both the Anheuser-Busch beer distributorship and the Geyser Ice Company, one of two companies in Waco that manufactured and delivered ice. In 1916, a Clarence C. Sparks was listed in the *Waco City Directory* as a "houseman" (possibly a bouncer or a general factotum) for Augustus A. Busch & Co. Clarence Sparks would have been about thirty-five in 1916.[60] He had lived in Waco since he was eleven.

Sparks's father was a cotton weigher. Clarence Sparks began his working life as a laboring man working for his father but, by 1906 or 1907, he was a "laborer" for the Busch company. He then became, in quick succession, a driver for Busch, a warehouseman, and an assistant shipping clerk and notary before becoming a houseman. By the time the 1917–18 edition of the *Waco City Directory* appeared, however, Sparks was no longer working for Busch. After that, he seems to have held a succession of low-level jobs, as a guard, a driver for Fields Beverage Company, a salesman, and a stockroom clerk at Hilltop Bakery, with periods of unemployment between jobs. In 1939, Sparks became an attendant at the Veterans Administration facility in Waco and remained in this position until about 1946. In 1954 he died at the age of seventy-three.

The likely lynch mob leader (as identified by Elisabeth Freeman) about whom we know the most — thanks to the kindness of his descendants — is William Henry Frazier, who was forty-two years old and a driver and stable boss for Augustus A. Busch & Company in May 1916. From what we know of Frazier, he was almost too bad to be true, a lynch mob leader right out of central casting.

Frazier's son Ammon was also working for "Ludde" at the time of the Waco Horror, as a clerk at the Geyser Ice Company. Ammon was twenty-one years old when the lynching took place. Traditionally, many of the most active participants in lynch mobs were young men in their teens or twenties, but Ammon Frazier was reputed to be an exceptionally gentle soul all of his life. During most of his adult life he worked faithfully as a salesman at the Harry Daum dry goods store in downtown Waco.

William Henry Frazier, Ammon's father, was an entirely different kind of character. No one would ever have called him gentle. Frazier was born in DeKalb County, Tennessee, in 1873 in an area known as Dry Creek. He married Zady (more commonly "Zadie") Vandergrift in DeKalb County on July 7, 1895.[61] William and Zadie had several children. It appears that the oldest of these, Ammon, was born about a year before the marriage, on July 22, 1894. Several years after the marriage, according to William Henry's grandson John Frazier, Zadie became seriously ill, and her half-sister Ada was sent for to help take care of her and her children.

John Frazier said that, while Ada was living with the family and trying to help out, William Henry and Ada "fell in love" and decided to run away together to Texas. Illiterate Zadie, left with no means of supporting her children, was so desperately poor that her church took up a collection to send her and her children to Waco after her husband.

Whatever the reasons for the move from Tennessee to Texas, the three Fraziers — William Henry, Zadie, and Ada — appear in Waco for the first time in the 1906–1907 *Waco City Directory*, all living together at 420 South 13th Street. Frazier is described in the directory as a dyer at the woolen mill; both of the women are listed as "Miss" (Miss Ada M. Frazier and Miss Zadie F. Frazier) and are identified as operators at the woolen mill. As the years passed, the Fraziers apparently settled on a story that Zadie was a widow living with her sister Ada and her brother-in-law William Henry. William Henry and Ada were presented to the world as a married couple.[62]

In the 1910 census records, Zadie is listed as "sister in law" and William Henry's children by Zadie — Ammon, Hassie, Johnnie, Hubbard, and Willie — are identified as his nieces and nephews. In the meantime, Ada had had children of her own: Rosie, born in 1906; Viola, born in 1908; and Leona, born in 1909. In 1910, Ada bore twins who died when they were two days old. Ada's youngest child, Lillian, was born around 1917.

It appears that, during the years that William Henry was living in Waco with both Zadie and Ada, he was having sexual relations with both of them. Zadie gave birth to two more children after she came to Waco, twins Evert and Evoline, born about 1912.[63]

William Henry Frazier was a very large man, weighing about three hundred pounds, according to John Frazier, with unusually long arms and a lot of excess girth around the middle. There is a stained, torn family picture of him in his prime that might have been taken at the Busch stables. He stands firmly planted in the foreground, holding the bridle of a sleek, dark horse. Behind him is a large, open brick building with tall, narrow windows that could be a stable or barn. Frazier is wearing suspenders, a collarless shirt, loose trousers, and a misshapen hat pushed back off his forehead. His eyes are pale. He looks solid and menacing.

Zadie and Ada, on the other hand, were both tiny women. Zadie was described by Kenneth Frazier, another grandson of William Henry, as "a very, very tiny little lady who dipped snuff and got cancer of the cheek." Toward the end of her life, Zadie wore a patch on the side of her face to cover the hole in her jaw caused by the cancer. Ada was also described in her old age as "a tiny little old lady, very slender."

One wonders if either woman felt she had much choice in her dealings with William Henry Frazier. "He was a forceful, me-oriented person," according to Kenneth Frazier. The two women believed they could not support themselves and their children without him; they may have felt they had to put up with anything he wanted and could not question or alter the strange, polygamous lifestyle he had chosen for them.

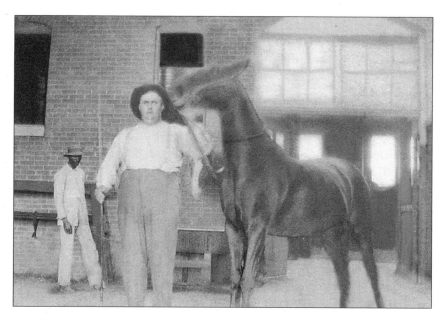

A middle-aged William Henry Frazier, possibly one of the lynch mob leaders. By permission of John Frazier.

By the time the 1907–1908 *Waco City Directory* was published, Frazier was already working for Anheuser-Busch as a driver. Subsequently, he was identified in various city directories as a barnman or a night clerk, as well as a driver. John Frazier still owns the account book William Henry kept as he made deliveries for Anheuser-Busch. The tiny red notebook contains notations like "1 barrell 1619 Wash. St. bar Monday nite" and "Guy Shelton get one keg Mondy."

During the years he worked for "Ludde," Frazier also farmed — or, at least, he owned a farm. His method of farming, according to Kenneth Frazier, was to "take the boys, he'd just get them up, feed them breakfast, throw them in the fields, he'd go drink all day, he'd come back and beat them up because they didn't do enough work." Frazier beat his sons with a buggy whip. "He would tell them that the rows weren't straight," said John Frazier. "He was a high-strung, hot-tempered man," said Kenneth Frazier, "with not a lot of remorse for what he did. Alcohol played a big part in what my grandfather did."

In addition, according to Kenneth Frazier, William Henry Frazier lied about the age of his oldest son, Ammon, to keep him out of school and at home working the fields. As a result, Ammon Frazier thought for most of his life that he was two years younger than he actually was; he believed that he had been born in 1896 instead of 1894. When Ammon applied for Social Security, he discovered his true age and the fact that he should have started receiving his Social Security checks two years earlier.

"All the love in the family," said Kenneth Frazier, "came from my grandmother [Zadie]. All the boys were crazy about her. She was always in the kitchen, and the big old boys would come in and swing her around." Kenneth remembered hearing talk from his father and aunts and uncles about Zadie's talent for canning fruits and vegetables and smoking meat. Zadie might have been unable to read and write but she had absorbed a lot of farm survival skills — she cured her own hogs; canned beans, corn, peaches, preserves, jams, and jellies; and made wonderful redeye gravy with bacon grease or ham drippings that her children liked to sop up with biscuits.

Frazier's size — and his nasty temperament — inevitably suggest the consistent references to "the big man" in articles about the Jesse Washington lynching — the big man who climbed over the heads and shoulders of the people in front of him in the courtroom to get at Washington; the big man who may have given Washington his death blow with a large knife to the back of the head right before he was burned; "the 250-pound man" who rode a white horse and dragged Washington's charred torso through the streets of Waco. But the "big man" might also have been the unnamed "driver for the Big Four Ice Company" whom Freeman identifies as the man who led the mob. When the Gildersleeve photographs of the lynching are compared with photographs of William Henry Frazier, it is impossible to positively identify anyone whose face is clearly visible in the lynching pictures as Frazier. It is tempting to speculate about the precise role Frazier may have played in the lynching but unlikely, at this late date, that absolute proof will ever be found.

Toward the end of his life, William Henry Frazier must have known how much his family despised him. "Dad said they had a piano and would play it," said John Frazier, "and Granddad would come into the room where they were playing the piano and everybody would leave the room and leave him alone."

The peculiar fictions of William Henry Frazier's life were maintained even after his death. His obituary identifies his sons Ammon, John, Hubert [Hubbard], and Everett merely as "pallbearers" and lists only his daughters by Ada as his children.[64] He was buried in Waco's Rosemound Cemetery between Zadie and Ada.

But Elisabeth Freeman did not conclude that it was simply mindless race hatred by ignorant southern rednecks that led to the lynching of Jesse Washington. Although she refers to "the disreputable bunch of Waco" as the group that carried out the lynching, she was not satisfied to attribute the lynching to the scum and riffraff and leave it at that. She had a rather different explanation that did not let the "better element" in Waco off the hook: "The whole thing was that they brought the boy back to Waco because a lynching is of political value to the county officials who are running for office. Every man I talked with said that when you solved it down — I talked of it from a race standpoint and from a crime standpoint — that politics was at the bottom of the whole business. All that element who took part in the lynching will vote for the sheriff."[65]

Freeman spoke to Sheriff Sam Fleming and found that he had many ready excuses for what had happened. He was prepared to blame everyone but himself. He said that his responsibility stopped at the courthouse, implying that Guy McNamara, chief of police and brother of County Attorney John McNamara, should have taken over and protected the prisoner during and after the trial.[66] Fleming also blamed Judge Munroe, who might have ordered a change of venue but did not.[67] "Fleming said he had sworn in fifty deputies," reports Freeman. "I asked him where they were. He said, 'O, you want to protect the nigger.' I said, 'No, I want to protect law and order.'"[68]

Barney Goldberg, the deputy who failed to get the word that he was not supposed to defend the prisoner, told Freeman that "Lee Jenkins was the best sheriff, but he is under Fleming . . . 'If Lee Jenkins had had it [Goldberg said], it would never have been, but we are working for the man higher up and must take our orders from him'."[69] Lee Jenkins would have an opportunity just a few years later to demonstrate whether he would handle a similar situation differently, but, as Goldberg pointed out, in 1916, Jenkins was subordinate to Fleming and was not running the show.

When Freeman cornered Judge Munroe, his response was much the same as Fleming's. When Freeman refused to accept his glib excuses — for example, that he could have ordered a change of venue, but the mob would have done the same thing anywhere[70] — when she persisted in her assertions that Munroe could have cleared the courtroom and could have stood up to the mob, a highly irritated Judge Munroe declared, "Do you want to spill innocent blood for a nigger?"[71] In the South of 1916, this kind of remark was supposed to end all further discussion and force persistent questioners to back off instantly.

Judge Munroe was not up for reelection in the summer of 1916, however, and Sam Fleming was in the race of his life. At the time the story of the Waco Horror was developing, Fleming was running campaign ads that did everything but lick the boots of the prospective voter in the hope of getting one more vote: "Mr. Fleming is diseased with a broad philanthropy [says his primary campaign ad]. He believes in the equality of man. He carries with him in the daily walk of his officialdom none of the 'boast of heraldry or the pomp of power.' He is just as courteous, just as obliging, just as accommodating as sheriff as he was when selling buggies and cultivators for the hardware company."[72] It is hard to imagine a modern-day candidate for sheriff in a good-sized municipality who would stress the fact that he used to be not a steely-eyed lawman but a salesman, and that he is known, above all, to be "courteous, . . . obliging and accommodating." But Fleming was attempting, as he had done before, to flatter and fawn his way into another two years in office.

In the meantime, Bob Buchanan's ads, in addition to stressing his fourteen years of experience in law enforcement and the fact that he was a native son, were hammering incessantly at Fleming for breaking his promise and running for a third term.[73] There seems to have been some feeling in those days, when there were no formal term limits in place, that candidates for office should take turns feeding at the public trough. In the case of Fleming versus Buchanan, the slugfest over the issue of Fleming's decision to run for a third term — and the other accusations flying back and forth between the two candidates in the last days of the campaign — reached a pinnacle of absurdity which might serve to remind the modern observer that mudslinging in American political campaigns is not a recent invention.

While Elisabeth Freeman was in Waco, she heard Fleming's accusation that his opponent was illiterate and reported as fact that "the other nominee for sheriff, Buchanan, cannot read or write."[74] To defend himself against these charges, Bob Buchanan asked a former employer to run a paid ad in the newspapers insisting that Buchanan had worked for him eighteen years earlier, for a period of five years, canvassing the city and taking orders, and could certainly read and write.[75]

The charges and countercharges intensified and escalated, ending with mammoth competing advertisements that ran in the *Waco Morning News* on Saturday, July 22, the day of the primary. The final issue in question was whether Sam Fleming, during the campaign of 1912, had promised voters that, if elected, he would serve for only two terms.

It is indisputable that paid ads appeared in the summer of 1912 in which Fleming promised he would not serve for more than two terms. But Fleming produced a letter from a former supporter, a J. B. Woody, in which Woody insists that while Fleming was out of town during the 1912 campaign, *he*, J. B. Woody, in Fleming's name, had written and published the promise not to serve more than two terms. Fleming, he claims, did not approve the commitment and knew nothing about it until afterward. Bob Buchanan then ran a

half-page ad in the *Morning News* and in the *Times Herald* informing voters
that the unfortunate J. B. Woody had been confined to the State Insane Asylum in Terrell for the past six months and was in no condition to write any letter defending Fleming.[76] "The letter signed by Mr. Woody," notes Fleming's
rebuttal ad sarcastically, "was exhibited to Mr. Buchanan, and to *many other
citizens who could read it*, long before Mr. Woody received the blow which
rendered him insane."[77]

As it turned out, Sam Fleming might not have been much of a sheriff, but
his political instincts were second to none. He knew all along that the race
would be close. In fact, it turned out to be the political squeaker of the summer of 1916, just as it was in 1912. This time the results were not known until
three days after the voting. In the end, Sam Fleming defeated Bob Buchanan
by only 53 votes, 4,632 to 4,579. Had Fleming actively opposed the lynch mob,
he almost certainly would have been defeated, and he might have suffered the
ignominious fate of having to return to the buggy and cultivator department at
the McLendon Hardware Store. However he might have rationalized the facts
to himself, however he might have found excuses for his actions and reasons
to place blame elsewhere, Sam Fleming had sold out a mentally deficient
teenager for a mess of pottage: the dubious glories of the office of sheriff of
McLennan County.

Not that Sam Fleming was the only guilty party. There is something especially revolting about rotund, good-natured Mayor Dollins and Police Chief
Guy McNamara, who was reputed to be a fearsome lawman and "the best
peace officer that McLennan County ever had," sitting comfortably in Dollins's
office at City Hall, contemplating with detached interest the burning of Jesse
Washington.[78]

And then there is tiny, implike Fred Gildersleeve, commercial photographer for over forty years, who was notified well in advance that the lynching
would take place, set up his equipment in the mayor's office and returned to
take his memorable pictures as if he were recording any other interesting mile-
stone in Waco's history.[79]

There is also Judge Richard Munroe, who kept a gun in his desk, but made
no attempt to stop the mob. In fairness, there were indications later that even
the hardened Munroe was more disturbed by the lynching of Jesse Washington than he let on at the time.

Emblematic of the "better element" in Waco is a disturbing figure who appears in several of the Gildersleeve lynching photographs. He is not shown actually performing the torture, but is close to the action throughout the lynching.

Unlike the other men who are near the victim, most of whom appear to be workingmen in shirtsleeves, this particular spectator is very well dressed in a dark suit, white shirt, and dark tie with a crisp new boater on his head. The expression on his pleasant face is, if not exultant, then satisfied with the business at hand. He seems quite pleased to be front and center and stands comfortably staring back at the camera. There are others like the well-dressed mystery man in the crowd, nicely attired in summer suits, ties, and boaters. It is clear that, although the better element of Waco may not have participated physically in the dirty work of the lynching, they watched and approved and made no effort to thwart the mob.

By the time Elisabeth Freeman left Waco, boarding the S.S. *San Jacinto* in Galveston on Saturday, May 27,[80] which was scheduled to arrive at Mallory Line Pier 38 in New York City on June 1,[81] she must have felt that she had fallen into a sewer and had to climb out to get clean. The report she wrote for Nash is a disorganized, stream-of-consciousness rambling, concluding with these chilling random observations: "Women and children saw the lynching. One man held up his little boy above the heads of the crowd so that he could see, and a little boy was in the top of the very tree to which the colored boy was hung, where he stayed until the fire became too hot."[82]

But Elisabeth Freeman had given W. E. B. Du Bois everything he needed.

CHAPTER 9

"INJECT LYNCHING INTO THE PUBLIC MIND"

The Follow-up Reaction

By far the most striking achievement by the N.A.A.C.P. during 1916 has been
to inject lynching into the public mind as something like a national problem.

—J. E. Spingarn

D U Bois took Elisabeth Freeman's raw material and photographs and
imposed an organizing principle so that the reader could follow the
story of what he dubbed "the Waco Horror" from start to finish. "The
Waco Horror" was printed as a special eight-page supplement to the July 1916
issue of *The Crisis*. Du Bois begins "The Waco Horror" by offering statistics to
demonstrate the size and prosperity of the community. He then tersely describes the rape and murder of Lucy Fryer, the transfer of Jesse Washington
to jails outside the county, the search of the Waco jail by the mob, and Washington's confession. He concludes this section of the article by saying, "There
was some, but not much doubt of his guilt. The confessions were obtained, of
course, under duress, and were, perhaps, suspiciously clear, and not entirely
in the boy's own words. It seems, however, probable that the boy was guilty of
murder, and possibly of premeditated rape."[1]

Then, quoting an unnamed "investigator," Du Bois explains that politics
was at the root of the lynching. He makes generous use of Elisabeth Freeman's

words in describing Judge Munroe ("a low order of politician and a product of a local machine") and in focusing on Sheriff Fleming's desperate desire to get reelected. Probably under space constraints, Du Bois skips lightly over Washington's trial, but does take the time to tell how Sheriff Fleming abandoned him to the mob.

Du Bois then details at length the slow murder of Jesse Washington, including the castration and extensive mutilation inflicted on him while he was still alive. Du Bois stresses the fact that ten thousand spectators — men, women and children — struggled for vantage points from which to watch, cheered the spectacle, and fought to participate in the torture and killing.

Freeman brought Du Bois conventional photographs of Waco landmarks in addition to photographs of the lynching. The force of the piece was augmented by photographs, and readers paging through the article proceeded from handsome pictures of Baylor University, the "Riggins Hotel" (renamed the Raleigh, where Freeman stayed), the First Baptist Church, the McLennan County Courthouse, and Waco's City Hall to progressively more and more awful pictures of the crowd and the burning of Jesse Washington. *The Crisis* does not spare its readers. The last pictures show the charred, blistered body of the dying boy pulled up against the tree by the chain around his neck, and then the collapsed, burned remains, once the work of the mob was done.

Du Bois's only entirely original contribution to the facts — the only part not derived entirely from Elisabeth Freeman's report — is a quote from a jocular letter sent to him by photographer Fred Gildersleeve: "We have quit selling the mob photos, this step was taken because our 'City dads' objected on the grounds of 'bad publicity,' as we wanted to be boosters and not knockers, we agreed to stop all sale."[2] Gildersleeve's letter betrays the fact that the authorities were waking up at long last to the realization that the lynching they had permitted to take place displayed their little metropolis in a most unfavorable light. But the pressure on Gildersleeve not to sell any more pictures had come much too late.

After describing the lynching in "The Waco Horror," Du Bois discusses the aftermath — the efforts of the newspapers and the more respectable citizens to hush the story up, the complaints of the few Wacoans who wanted to protest, the effort of the NAACP investigator to find a lawyer to "take up the case," the cancellation of a Sunday school convention that was to have taken place in Waco, the declarations of embarrassed Waco businessmen that they would never again register in any hotel that they came from Waco, and the fact (based on Freeman's incomplete information) that, of the city's clergy, only Dr. Caldwell had spoken out.[3]

McLennan County Courthouse, completed ca. 1902, is still standing. *Courtesy* Archives Division of The Texas Collection, Baylor University, Waco, Texas.

Du Bois's article was very powerful as it stood. No one who read "The Waco Horror" and looked at the pictures was likely to forget it. Freeman's most explosive discovery, however, the names of the leaders of the lynch mob, was not revealed. Du Bois's article says only, "The names of five of the leaders of the mob are known to this Association, and can be had on application by responsible parties."[4]

In conclusion, Du Bois presents a tabulation of a total of 2,843 black men lynched in the United States between January 1, 1885, and June 1, 1916, with the figures broken down by year. Then he officially launches the NAACP's Anti-Lynching Campaign with the following final paragraph: "What are we going to do about this record? The civilization of America is at stake. The sincerity of Christianity is challenged. The National Association for the Advancement of Colored People proposes immediately to raise a fund of at least $10,000 to start a crusade against the modern barbarism. Already $2000 is promised, conditional on our raising the whole amount."[5]

There was to be no more helpless bemoaning of lynchings in the pages of *The Crisis*. Now readers were instructed to act. In a full-page ad elsewhere in the July 1916 issue, Du Bois also pushes the call to action: "Read the shame of WACO in this month's supplement . . . Ten thousand dollars is needed before August 1 to back up . . . growing southern sentiment against lynching — trust us to find the way . . . Will you back us with your dollars, or just talk?"[6]

Du Bois told his readers that the NAACP needed thirty thousand new memberships from Crisis readers to fund the Anti-Lynching Campaign. Sustaining members were to pay twenty-five dollars annually; contributing members, two dollars to ten dollars annually; and associate members, one dollar a year. A membership form was attached to the ad, to be filled out and mailed to the NAACP with a check.

The August issue of The Crisis includes another full-page appeal on behalf of the Anti-Lynching Campaign, written by NAACP treasurer Oswald Garrison Villard. "The crime at Waco is a challenge to our American civilization, yes, to every American . . . it is no longer unpopular to speak out against practices which should arouse our holy horror if they were committed by Turks in Armenia or by Mexicans in Sonora."[7] Villard points out that the hands of northerners are not clean either and makes specific reference to the "crimes" of Springfield and Coatesville. He directs his appeal particularly to "the colored people . . . for it is a cause that could be made as moving as most of the phases in the anti-slavery struggle." Villard declares that "the race that suffers most by the crimes" should make the most sacrifices to end lynching and acknowledges that "dollar bills" are coming in, but that the NAACP wants more: "hundred dollar bills" from churches, lodges, societies, and other gatherings to support the antilynching effort.

By September Du Bois was able to announce that $7,260.93 had been raised for the Anti-Lynching Fund and that Philip G. Peabody had graciously written (after a visit to Russia) to say that he would gladly extend the deadline from July 31 to September 15, at which time he would contribute his $1,000 (and Moorfield Storey would add his $1,000) if $8,000 had been raised from other sources.[8] "Colored people of America, we must not fail!" cries Du Bois. "No sacrifice is too great to help in this cause."[9] Du Bois also presents a complete tally of the sources of the contributions so far, listing by name everyone who had sent $25 or more and creating a competition by telling how much each major city had sent to the fund. New York City had contributed the most, $412.32, but amounts of $100 and over had been sent from Detroit, northern California, Columbus, St. Louis, Chicago, Cleveland, Providence, and New Orleans. Someone in faraway Albuquerque, New Mexico, had sent $15.[10]

In the effort to stimulate more donations, Du Bois also published some of the letters he had received from people who had struggled to send in what they could: "deair sir in answer to your appeal of July 6, 1916, for helpe — I am sending you one 1.00 more to helpe fight that hellish Lynching industry in the South . . . May God helpe you for we are dependent uppon you to do Something."[11]

The NAACP's efforts to publicize the story of the Waco Horror and the Anti-Lynching Fund were not confined to sending the special supplement to *Crisis* subscribers alone. Fifty thousand copies were printed — thirty-eight thousand to be sent to subscribers and the remainder to be distributed to a variety of additional potential sources of publicity, funding, and legislative support.[12] "The Waco Horror" was sent to Pres. Woodrow Wilson and his cabinet, to all congressmen and senators, to the "N.A.A.C.P. entire newspaper list," and to practically everyone Elisabeth Freeman had met in Waco, including Judge Munroe and Sheriff Fleming.[13]

For some weeks after her visit to Waco, Freeman continued her quest to find a Texas lawyer (or *any* lawyer) to bring a case against Sheriff Fleming. Among the lawyers suggested to her were several Christian Scientists and a man named Henry Faulk, an Austin lawyer who, according to Freeman's informant, Prof. Lindley M. Keasbey of the University of Texas, mostly represented black people and had left the Democratic Party to run for attorney general on the Socialist ticket.[14] Later Keasbey wrote Elisabeth again, "As for the lawyer you require, — there ain't no sech animal, not in Texa[s] anyway. Every one is holding their precious head down low, as you say, so as not to have it shot off."[15]

In the end, Elisabeth Freeman and Roy Nash gave up the effort to find an attorney to challenge the lynching of Jesse Washington in court. Said Nash to one questioner, by way of explanation, "We have tried our best through several channels to persuade some distinguished Texas lawyer to take up the case against the lynchers of Jesse Washington and not a man could be found with the courage to do so."[16] In fact, the *only* person who was indicted and jailed as a direct result of the lynching of Jesse Washington was A. T. Smith, assistant editor of the *Paul Quinn Weekly*, the journal of Waco's black Paul Quinn College. Smith was indicted for criminal libel because he had reprinted the June 10 *Chicago Defender* story that claimed George Fryer had been arrested for murdering his wife. The editor was arrested in the late summer or early fall of 1916 and jailed until his trial. He was convicted, sentenced to a year at hard labor minus time served, and sent to work on the county road gang.

Waco's only black lawyer at the time, R. D. Evans, did his best to defend Smith, but wrote *The Crisis* that "the college for which he [Smith] worked refused to help and left him to his fate."[17] Evans presented a motion to the court to pay one dollar a day to have Smith relieved of hard labor and put back in jail. He then managed to raise thirty-four dollars from Waco's black community to make the first payment. At the time that Evans wrote to *The Crisis*, Smith had been taken off the county road crew and sent back to jail.[18]

The NAACP had known for some months of Smith's plight. Field organizer Kathryn M. Johnson heard the story from a college friend who lived in Waco and notified Roy Nash during the summer that Smith had been imprisoned and that his wife was sick from shock and destitute.[19] Nash wrote a kind letter to Mrs. Smith inquiring about the circumstances of the case, but finally decided that Smith should have known better than to reprint a story that was patently untrue.[20] Smith was ultimately released from prison and continued in the printing business until his death in 1934 at the age of forty-five.

George Fryer was aggressively pursuing libel judgments against anyone who publicly suggested that he might have had something to do with the murder of his wife. Ironically, Elisabeth Freeman received a letter at her home in New York City from Waco lawyer Tom Hamilton, asking her as "a personal friend" of George Fryer to provide Hamilton with copies of any articles that she saw that might "be libelous in their nature in their reports of the lynching here, and as to what, if anything, he as the husband of the woman murdered had to do with the crime." Hamilton went on to tell Freeman plainly that he expected "to hold any publisher of such articles accountable in a civil action to Mr. Fryer."[21] Apparently, Freeman was so convincing in her sympathetic overtures to George Fryer as part of her effort to gain more information about the lynching that he believed she was a friend who could be relied on. It was undoubtedly Fryer's determination to punish anyone who printed the story that he had somehow been involved in the death of his own wife that caught up with A. T. Smith and caused him to lose a year of his life to the jailhouse and the county road gang.

George Fryer also sued Paul Quinn College, demanding $75,000 in damages (a fabulous sum in those days), on the theory that the college had permitted Smith to print the story against Fryer and was ultimately responsible. Despite an affidavit from Smith in which he acknowledged that the president of Paul Quinn College was his employer and was managing editor of the paper, the jury deadlocked and awarded only $1.00 to George Fryer as a kind of compromise verdict "in order that plaintiff may be relieved of the payment of the costs in said cause."[22]

Enraged perhaps, in his own quiet way, by the very idea that anyone would add to his grief and the grief of his children by accusing him of murdering Lucy, Fryer probably thought he was quashing the rumor forever by making it clear to all that he would take stern action against anyone who publicly libeled him. Instead, the legal actions taken against A. T. Smith and others might have helped spread the story that George Fryer was somehow connected to his wife's death. Smith's fate — when coupled with the hideous nature of Lucy's death and the appalling nature of the death of Jesse Washington — helped give the story that it was actually George Fryer who had killed Lucy Fryer a life of its own. It was, in fact, still being repeated by residents of Robinson more than eighty years after the events of the summer of 1916.

Of course, the shadow of a possibility lingers in the mind of anyone who studies the Waco Horror that George Fryer might have had a guilty secret. Was this the real reason he was so sensitive to any publicly uttered suppositions about his possible role in the crime and so anxious to shut the mouths of those who did the supposing? The notion seems highly unlikely and does not seem to fit with the known history of the Fryers or with George's personality. George Fryer was no William Henry Frazier. But one of the lingering ironies of the whole story of the Waco Horror is that those who were George's nearest neighbors and friends, the people of Robinson, passed on the rumor that George might have gotten away with murder.

Efforts to bring the lynchers to justice in the case of Jesse Washington failed, but the efforts to make his story known far and wide continued with increasing intensity. The NAACP sent the seemingly indefatigable Elisabeth Freeman on a speaking tour "throughout the whole northeast and as far west as St. Louis and Kansas City" to tell the tale of the Waco Horror.[23] Her mission was to publicize the lynching, to raise money for the Anti-Lynching Fund, and to inspire audience members to join the NAACP. There is evidence that Freeman carried her speaking tour even farther than Kansas City — to within shouting distance of Texas. A black citizen of Perry, Oklahoma, W. E. Henderson, wrote to Oswald Garrison Villard in October about the Anti-Lynching Campaign and mentioned that "some weeks ago there went through the country a very able little lady wonderful in the depicting [of] the Waco Lynching." Henderson had heard Freeman speak at Guthrie, a town just north of Oklahoma City.[24] All in all, the efforts of Elisabeth Freeman in Waco cost the NAACP $83.30 in salary and $92.59 in travel expenses; the cost of her later road trip came to a total of $310.00 in salary and $369.77 in travel expenses.[25] It was money well spent.

The *Crisis* supplement had already stimulated the *Chicago Defender* to run another story on Washington's lynching and to announce the campaign to raise $10,000 for the Anti-Lynching Fund.[26] This July 29 article, using the material from Du Bois's story, was far more accurate than the previous *Defender* stories about the Waco Horror. The *Defender* followed up on August 5 with another story about the Anti-Lynching Campaign, mistakenly announcing that Philip Peabody was going to give $20,000 to the Anti-Lynching Fund. But the story does contain the best account available of one of Elisabeth Freeman's speeches on behalf of the NAACP that summer, beginning with this hopeful observation: "Miss Elizabeth Freeman, New York City, who went personally to Waco, Tex., where Jesse Washington was lynched, has stirred 'Old Boston' as did Garrison and Douglas [Douglass] in the days of slavery. The conscience of the old abolitioners has been awakened and they have declared that lynching must be stopped."[27]

The *Defender* story describes Elisabeth Freeman's presentation on the evening of August 4, 1916, at the Michigan Avenue Baptist Church under the auspices of the "National Association for the Protection of Colored People." According to the *Defender* account, Freeman told her audience that those who were enjoying the advantages of living in the North had an obligation to help those who were still oppressed in the South. Freeman, experienced in the art of touching the hearts of her audience, made an emotional and personal appeal: "You must help those who cannot help themselves . . . This is the only national organization working to stop the lynching, working earnestly for the progress of the Race. It is your work . . . You cannot be satisfied with your lot while your brothers are being deprived of their natural rights."

The story depicts Freeman as complaining, during her speech, of the "indignities" that she suffered at the hands of Waco's authorities while conducting her investigation. The article also suggests that Freeman expressed the suspicion that the rape charge was "written into the lad's confession" to add to "his actual crime of murder." Freeman seems to have finally concluded that the rape was either automatically assumed or, worse, made up by the authorities to facilitate Jesse Washington's conviction.

According to the *Defender* article, Freeman "minutely" described every detail of the lynching to her audience and concluded, "Laws won't stop lynching. Enlightened public opinion will. Are you going to help?"[28] It's easy to imagine the impact of the impassioned young orator on an audience of middle-class, church-going black Chicagoans — especially when she could announce the amount of money that two white men, Peabody and Storey, had already pledged to the cause.

All this stir helped foment a number of articles in the liberal journals beyond those that had appeared immediately after the lynching. *The Independent*, inspired by *The Crisis* supplement, ran a longer article on the Waco Horror than the first, this one called "An American Atrocity." After summarizing the story, as absorbed from *The Crisis*, *The Independent* writer says, "Waco is indelibly disgraced. Texas is indelibly disgraced. The United States is indelibly disgraced." The writer goes on to denounce the failure of Waco and Texas authorities to "see to it that punishment is meted out to those who participated in the crime."[29]

In the meantime, the debate over lynching continued in Villard's *Nation*. In the October 5 issue, Villard, in an editor's note following a letter about lynching from a Georgia professor, took the opportunity to doubly condemn Waco, as he had several times before, because "not a single teacher, or preacher, or newspaper, or public official has spoken out against the mob which publicly burned a convicted negro there. We have yet, at this distance, to see a single sign that Waco has a conscience . . . The convictions of a few lynchers in Waco and their punishment would do more to stop the evil than anything we can readily think of."[30]

On October 14, the *New Republic* wholeheartedly joined the battle to raise money for the NAACP's Anti-Lynching Campaign by publishing a hard-hitting article called "The Will-to-Lynch." The will to lynch, says the perceptive author, "is a wandering desire, and will fix upon any torturable object of the despised race that catches its attention. It is the experience and not the end that counts." The writer refers to spectacles such as the Waco lynching as a "social orgy of cruelty, a communal auto-da-fe" celebrating hatred of blacks, Anglo-Saxon dominance, and contempt for law.

It is easy to blame these events on "poor whites," the writer continues, but they are just the nucleus of a mob into which are swept unstable people of all kinds, plus "every person besotted with race-prejudice, possessed with lawless deviltry, or even morbid curiosity." He refers to the pictures of the Waco lynching as displaying "a typical straw-hatted summer crowd gazing gleefully at the hideous crisp of what was once a Negro youth."[31]

There is no law enforcement machinery to suppress the lynch mobs, the writer concludes. The only thing that will stop lynchings is "the rousing of popular anger" and "the pressure of social contempt" against those who lynch. He then vigorously plugs the NAACP campaign to raise money to investigate lynching and marshal public opinion against it.

Perhaps the most interesting of the pieces published on the nature of life in

Waco — and one that casts a stronger light, in retrospect — is a letter about the Jesse Washington lynching that appeared in *The Nation* just before the end of 1916. The letter was written by J. L. Kesler, dean of Baylor University, in an impassioned effort to defend Waco's citizens against the charge that no one there had spoken out to condemn the lynching. Kesler quotes chapter and verse of the actions of the good people of Waco. He first points out that the faculty of Baylor "met and passed resolutions" and that he himself, in the Baylor chapel before an audience of eight hundred students, "condemned it [the lynching] in as strong words as the English language would permit without violating the ten commandments."[32] Kesler goes on to say that the Rev. E. E. Ingram, a Presbyterian, discovered the plot beforehand and got "the leader" to promise that it would not be carried out, "but the leader was not able to control his crowd." Thereafter, says Kesler, Dr. Caldwell of First Presbyterian, Dr. Culver of Austin Street Methodist, and Dr. Groner of Columbus Street Baptist delivered sermons against the mob actions, and "Pastor Dawson of the First Baptist Church, made the strongest possible statement against it." Also, the Seventh and James Street Baptist Church passed resolutions against the lynching, as did the Baptist Pastors Conference. The president of Baylor introduced resolutions against mob violence that were adopted by the Baptist State Convention. The Methodist Conference and other religious groups did much the same. (Many of these actions are confirmed by other sources, as has been seen.)

Kesler quotes the *Semi-Weekly Tribune's* May 20 editorial. He adds that he cannot defend the silence of Waco's public officials, but he insists that they are no worse than most officials in similar circumstances in other towns. "The mob element disgraced Waco, it is true," he says, "but it did not constitute Waco . . . the criminal element takes us unawares and here as elsewhere there is an irresponsible element that misrepresents the community."[33] (Kesler here conveniently ignores the fact that the lynching was premeditated, not spontaneous, which he himself had already acknowledged with his remarks about the efforts of Reverend Ingram to prevent the lynching.)

Kesler ends his letter with a plea for better laws, better law enforcement, and better education so that "humanity shall rise above animality in crises of extraordinary indignation and excitement." He even tries to claim, in a remark that turns logic upside down, that there is something *positive* about the fact that "Waco has shown rare restraint in her just indignation against the mob that disgraced her in its folly and crime," whereas the fact that no action was taken against the mob leaders is, in fact, one of the worst indictments of Waco. "The real Waco with a conscience [in other words, the people *he* knows] is not indifferent." So far so good, says Villard in his editor's note following the letter, "But Waco cannot hold up its head until the criminals are punished."[34]

The strongest commentary on Kesler's defense of his chosen city, however, is the fate of Kesler himself. Pastor Joseph M. Dawson reports in his autobiography that in 1917, he invited a renowned preacher, Dr. James A. Francis of Los Angeles, to come and preach at Baylor Chapel. This event probably occurred less than a year after Kesler wrote to *The Nation* defending Waco and Baylor. Dr. Francis had just made an appearance at Camp MacArthur in Waco. Dean Kesler — whom Dawson calls a fine Christian and excellent teacher — already knew something about Dr. Francis and warned Dawson that Francis was "a hate mongerer."[35] Dawson was only vaguely aware at the time that Baylor had already been criticized for keeping a dean in office, Kesler, who was of German descent, who had been educated at the University of Berlin, and who advocated German educational techniques. Dawson assured Kesler that everything would be all right.

As soon as Francis began to preach, Dawson saw that he had made a major miscalculation. Francis denounced all German people anywhere on earth and ended his sermon by crying out, "May God damn the German Kaiser to hell!" Kesler released an audible groan at this statement. When the Baylor students heard him, they loudly booed their dean.

In no time at all, the local newspapers, consumed by anti-German war fever, began to label Kesler a subversive and the city began to heap abuse on him. Although Pres. S. P. Brooks fought for Kesler, the Baylor Board of Trustees insisted on dismissing him. Says Dawson, "Kesler resigned, a broken-hearted man . . . Dr. Kesler never recovered from those unjust wounds and died with distrust of Baptists."[36] Thus, one of Waco's most energetic and eloquent defenders became a victim of the town's bigotry.

Having engendered enormous amounts of publicity about the Waco Horror, the NAACP reaped some solid benefit for the cause. In his end-of-the-year memorandum to the board of directors, Joel Spingarn was able to report that the NAACP had spent $1,203.73 to publicize the Waco lynching and had succeeded in raising a cash total of $11,869.71 for the Anti-Lynching Fund. On October 16, 1916, Philip Peabody finally sent the NAACP his long-promised check for $1,000.[37]

What was more important, Spingarn announced, "By far the most striking achievement by the N.A.A.C.P. during 1916 has been to inject lynching into the public mind as something like a national problem . . . Lynching has been injected into national consciousness even in the midst of world war, Mexico, and a presidential election, and we enter 1917 equipped to carry on the fight with more vigor than was ever possible before."[38] Said Royal Freeman Nash in a letter to all branch officers, "We have given the story of Waco such publicity as no other lynching has ever received."[39]

Buoyed by the success of publicity efforts, the NAACP also designed and printed 100,000 antilynching circulars to be used in the presidential campaign during the fall of 1916. About 40,000 circulars were distributed through NAACP branches and 60,000 through selected Republican state headquarters with the approval of the Republican National Committee.[40]

Elisabeth Freeman's work for the NAACP in investigating the Waco Horror and making speeches around the country about it was so effective that she was one of five applicants considered during the late summer and early fall of 1916 for the new position of national organizer.[41] In the same letter in which Roy Nash informs Kathryn M. Johnson, who had been a field organizer for two years, that Freeman is a candidate for national organizer, he also fires Johnson, partly because she had unjustifiably accused Freeman of undermining her position with the NAACP. Nash enumerates Johnson's faults and limitations in no uncertain terms to make it perfectly clear to her that she is being dismissed because of her own shortcomings, and not because of any actions taken by Elisabeth Freeman.

Elisabeth Freeman seems periodically to have aroused the envy and resentment of other women in the organizations she chose to support. She occasionally complained about this in the days when she was hawking the *Woman's Journal* in New York.[42] Freeman had an energy, a magnetism, and a persistence that may sometimes have seemed overpowering to others — particularly those who were perhaps more interested in the attention they could gain for themselves than in the goals they were supposed to be trying to achieve. An Edison Kinetoscope, made shortly after the great suffragist march in Washington in March 1913, vividly illustrates why some other suffrage leaders might have resented Freeman. It records some very brief speeches for women's suffrage given by several suffrage leaders. Freeman's appeal is clear — even though the audio portion of the film has been lost. The stolid older women who speak before Freeman appear to be pompous and stiff; Freeman is animated and vivacious and does not hesitate to talk and laugh even while the others are speaking. In her face is a glint of the mischief and wit that is so plain in her letters. She appears to be the perennial skeptic and nonconformist in any crowd, full of amusement and high spirits as well as dedication to the cause. No wonder other, more humorless, reformers were sometimes taken aback and did not quite know what to make of her.[43]

In the end, Elisabeth Freeman was not offered the position of national organizer. The candidate finally appointed to the position was a man who was so superbly well qualified that no one could have questioned his right to the job — James Weldon Johnson, originally of Jacksonville, Florida. Johnson had already achieved success as a lyricist, writer, educator, and diplomat and had written the strong *New York Age* editorials about the Waco Horror.[44]

Before the end of 1916, the NAACP undertook one more activity to underscore the organization's antilynching focus. The leaders of the NAACP decided that the organization would not only publicize horrendous lynchings but also try to attract attention to, and reward, public officials who stood up to mobs and prevented lynchings. In 1916, the chosen hero of the NAACP's antilynching movement was Sheriff Sherman Eley of the small community of Lima, Ohio.

The contrast between the actions of Sheriff Sam Fleming and those of Sheriff Sherman Eley in similar situations is instructive. When a black man named Charlie Daniels was accused of assaulting a Mrs. Barber, the young wife of a prominent farmer, Sheriff Eley had Daniels taken out of Lima and securely stowed in the jail at Ottawa, Ohio, about twenty miles away. While Sheriff Eley was gone, a mob of about three thousand men brutally mishandled Eley's sister as they were breaking into the Lima jail and forced Eley's wife and small daughter to flee from their home. The child was very ill at the time and subsequently died as a result of shock and exposure. When Sheriff Eley returned to town, the mob met him at the edge of town, demanding to know where they could find Charlie Daniels. Eley refused to tell them. The mob stripped off Eley's clothes, dragged him through the streets of town with a noose around his neck, and brutally kicked and beat him, breaking two of his ribs. Finally, the mob threw the other end of the rope over the crossarm of a telephone pole and threatened to hang the nearly unconscious man. Throughout this ordeal, Eley tried to explain to the would-be lynchers that it was his sworn duty to protect any prisoner in his custody, but they refused to listen. At last, the severely injured sheriff broke down and told the mob where Daniels was, but by the time the mob reached Ottawa, Daniels had been moved again.

The NAACP's board of directors voted to award a loving cup to Sheriff Eley, to be engraved with an inscription stating that the cup was presented "for devotion to duty in defending a colored prisoner from lynching, enduring torture and insult, that the majesty of the law might be upheld, at Lima, August 30, 1916."[45] The loving cup was presented to Sheriff Eley by Frank B. Willis, governor of Ohio, in Columbus at the Second Baptist Church, on December 27, 1916. Charles Edward Russell made a speech honoring Eley's achievement.

By publicizing and celebrating the courageous acts of Sherman Eley, the NAACP's leaders — in the hopes of inspiring other public officials to imitate Eley's conduct — intended to present to the world living proof that one brave man, acting alone, could stand up to a lynch mob and protect a prisoner.

CHAPTER 10

"SHERIFF STEGALL
IS PREPARED TO DEFEND THE JAIL"

Change Comes at Last to Waco

Sheriff Stegall is prepared to defend the jail against any sort
of attack and has taken every precaution against a surprise.

—"Mitchell Will Be Kept in Waco," *Waco Times Herald*

I T would be heartening to be able to report that the NAACP's 1916 campaign to shame the nation with the story of the Waco Horror ended the scourge of lynching across the country—or at least ended lynching in Texas, or, at the very least, ended lynching in Waco. Unfortunately, none of these claims would be true. According to one source of lynching statistics, there was a significant drop in the number of lynchings reported in the United States between 1916 and 1917 (from 54 to 38).[1] In 1917, however, the United States went to war, and war was a mighty distraction. The total number of lynchings in the United States rose again in 1918, to 64, a number startlingly higher than the 1916 total. In 1919, the year of the "Red Summer," a time of dislocation and upheaval following the end of World War I, the number of lynchings jumped to 83. The total did not return to near-1916 levels until 1922, and it was not until the 1930s that the number really began to decline, showing that the epidemic was running its course at last.

Nor did Texas' lynching record immediately improve. In 1919, the *San An-*

tonio Express reported that Texas still ranked second only to Georgia in the number of lynchings and set up a fund of $100,000 for rewards for those who were responsible for the conviction and legal punishment of lynchers.[2]

The Anti-Lynching Campaign of 1916 was just the barest beginning of a battle that would last for many years as the NAACP struggled to investigate and publicize lynchings, shame lynching communities, and, at the same time, promote the passage of federal antilynching legislation. Federal legislation was necessary because it was obvious that lynchers would never be convicted in their hometowns, even in communities such as Springfield, Illinois, and Coatesville, Pennsylvania, in which some lynching participants were actually indicted and prosecuted.

Another effort to dramatize the problem of the general mistreatment of America's black citizens was the organizing of the Negro Silent Protest Parade, which marched down Fifth Avenue in New York City on July 28, 1917. The Waco Horror was prominently featured on the signs carried by the marchers. The lynching of Jesse Washington was still on the minds of march organizers more than a year after his death, despite the deaths of at least forty blacks (but possibly many more) just weeks before the parade in riots in East St. Louis.[3] In September 1917, after Du Bois and NAACP staffer Martha Gruening investigated the events in East St. Louis, *The Crisis* published a special twenty-page supplement, following the pattern established in the treatment of the Waco Horror.

In July 1917, James Weldon Johnson, by then national organizer of the NAACP, attended a meeting of the executive committee of the Harlem branch. The primary topic of discussion was possible responses to the East St. Louis pogrom, during which, according to testimony before Congress, the rioting mob went so far as to throw black children into burning buildings. Johnson, remembering an idea that Oswald Garrison Villard had suggested earlier, proposed a silent protest parade to be organized not by the NAACP alone but by "the colored citizens of all Greater New York,"[4] although NAACP members were to hold all the important organizing positions.[5]

The circulars passed around the black churches and fraternal organizations in the weeks preceding the march made it plain that, despite the many lynchings that had taken place between May 1916 and July 1917 and the events in East St. Louis, the sense of the Waco Horror as a watershed atrocity was still vivid in the black community. "We march," reads one circular, "because we want to make impossible a repetition of Waco, Memphis, and East St. Louis, by rousing the conscience of the country and bring the murderers of our brothers, sisters and innocent children to justice."[6] During the march, black Boy Scouts handed out circulars using the same language to spectators along the way.[7] A list of the messages painted on signs carried by the marchers was sent to NAACP branches throughout the country to encourage local chapters to organize similar events. The list began with the legend, "Memphis and Waco — Centers of American Culture?"

At noon on the appointed day, between eight thousand and ten thousand marchers assembled at 59th Street and Fifth Avenue; beginning at 1:00 P.M., they marched south all the way to 23rd Street. First came children, then women wearing white, and, finally, men in dark clothes. They marched to the sound of muffled drums draped in black handkerchiefs.[8] W. E. B. Du Bois was one of the marchers at the head of the parade. Just in front of the marcher carrying the American flag was a banner half the width of the street that read, "Your Hands Are Full of Blood."[9] Other signs read, "Make America Safe for Democracy" (a sarcastic reference to President Wilson's famous phrase about fighting World War I to "make the world safe for democracy"), "Thou Shalt Not Kill," "We have fought for the liberty of white Americans in six wars; our reward is East St. Louis," "So Treat Us That We May Love Our Country," "Mothers, Do Lynchers Go to Heaven?" and "Race Prejudice Is the Offspring of Ignorance and the Mother of Lynching."

The Silent Protest Parade apparently made a powerful impression on the twenty thousand New Yorkers who witnessed it. James Johnson commented that the spectators, many of them black, watched in silence and some had tears in their eyes.[10]

The most important consequence of the parade and the NAACP's overall effort to publicize the East St. Louis riots may have been the fact that Congressman Leonidas C. Dyer (R-Missouri), who had worked to prevent the suppression of the Congressional report on East St. Louis, told Joel Spingarn that he intended to introduce a bill that would make lynching a federal offense.[11]

There is no question that the NAACP had indeed "injected lynching into the public mind" — not as something to gasp at sporadically, but as a great wrong that needed to be stopped. Yet many more lynchings would take place before the holocaust finally ended, including one of the most terrible of all lynchings in the South, one of the very few that rivaled the lynching of Jesse Washington in sheer brutality. Mary Turner of Brooks County, south Georgia, was only nineteen years old and was eight months pregnant in May 1918, when she learned that her husband, Hayes, had been lynched during the rampage that followed the murder of his employer, a white farmer named Hampton Smith.[12] She became so distraught that she openly raged against the murderers of her husband and even threatened to swear out a warrant against them.

Negro Silent Protest Parade on Fifth Avenue in New York City, July 28, 1917.

THE FIRST BLOOD
FOR
AMERICAN
INDEPENDENCE
Was Shed By A Negro
CRISPUS ATTUCKS

Courtesy Library of Congress, Prints and Photographs Division [LC-USZ62-33789].

The mob seized her and carried her off to Folsom's Bridge on the Little River, which divides Brooks and Lowndes counties. The heavily pregnant woman was hanged upside-down from a tree with her ankles tied together. Men in the mob took gasoline and motor oil from their cars and poured the fluids over her and then set her on fire. After her clothes had burned away, one of the men took a large knife — by some accounts, a knife used to split hogs — and cut open the abdomen of the still-living woman. Mary's baby fell to the ground and gave two small cries before it was ground to death under the heel of one of the lynchers. Following this ritual, the mob opened fire and riddled Mary's body with bullets "until it was unrecognizable."[13] Mary and her baby were buried about ten feet from the tree. An empty quart-sized whiskey bottle with a half-smoked cigar stuffed into its mouth was left to mark the grave.

The story of Mary Turner caused a brief national uproar. Walter White visited Georgia governor Hugh Dorsey and handed him in person a complete report on the lynchings along with the names of two ringleaders and fifteen other participants in at least one of the Brooks County lynch mobs. Although Dorsey went through the motion of offering "large rewards" for the apprehension of the lynchers, no one was ever charged, much less prosecuted, for the murder of Mary Turner or her husband.

The NAACP's relentless publicizing of lynchings in the 1910s led directly to the intense campaign of the 1920s, 1930s, and 1940s to force Congress to pass a federal antilynching statute which would provide for fines against counties in which lynchings took place and for both fines and imprisonment for officials who allowed lynchings to occur or failed to prosecute lynchers.[14] On January 26, 1922, only six years after the Waco Horror, Leonidas Dyer's antilynching bill passed in the House of Representatives. Later versions of the bill passed in the House again on April 15, 1937, and on January 10, 1940. Southern senators, however, kept the antilynching bills from ever even coming to a vote in the Senate.[15]

Over time, however, the NAACP plan, voiced by Spingarn in 1916, of "tearing a question open and riddling it with light" achieved its ends. What could not be gained by earnest appeals to a higher morality and the greater good was accomplished by appeals to the homelier human impulses of greed and embarrassment. The "City Dads" of "alert and pushing" southern towns like Waco, hoping to attract northern industry, learned that a grotesque public lynching would not help their cause. Slowly — by inches, it must have seemed to the reformers — the tide of blood receded. But, since the motivation for abolishing the massive-scale spectacle lynching was *not* primarily moral in nature, the end of public lynchings did not mean the end of violence against blacks. Lynchings still occurred, but they took place under cover of night in obscure locations. The perpetrators — in ever-smaller groups — did not seek publicity or newspaper coverage. As time passed and the South was drawn into mainstream American life, lynchers became more and more marginalized. They were the florid-faced men with the vacant grins in newspaper photographs of southern murderers on trial, the bottom feeders who had had a few beers too many and conspired with a small circle of their buddies to bomb a church or gun down a man in his driveway — or to take three civil rights workers out on a rural highway in the dead of night and murder them.

Although even the secret lynching has gradually disappeared as lynchers have been brought to justice — notwithstanding the occasional Jasper, Texas — some would argue that our criminal justice system is nothing but an extension of the tradition of lynching wherein black men are disproportionately charged, convicted, and executed. As of February 2004, of the 450 prisoners on death row in Texas, for example, almost 41 percent were black, the largest percentage of any ethnic group represented. At that time, Texas had executed 317 prisoners since 1982, many more than any other state. Of those executed, almost 33 percent were black — despite the fact that, according to the 2000 census, only 11.6 percent of the population of Texas is black.[16]

If William English Walling, W. E. B. Du Bois, Oswald Garrison Villard, Joel Spingarn, Mary Ovington, and Elisabeth Freeman were alive today, there is not much question that they would still find plenty to criticize, even in our cleaned-up and sanitized ways of putting people to death. They would certainly complain that our society and our criminal justice system are still weighted against black people. Although we have traveled a long road — thanks to the leaders of the NAACP and others like them — they would be unlikely to feel that it was time to close up shop and enjoy a celebratory picnic. They would be far more likely to point out to us how far we still have to go to achieve in full the just society they sought.

But what of Waco? Did the citizens of Waco learn their lesson about the evils attendant on mob violence? One of the best ways to fully understand how lynching was finally stopped is to closely examine what happened in this single lynching town.

Five years passed between the lynching of Jesse Washington and the next lynching in Waco. It would not be strictly accurate, however, to claim that all was, in the immortal words of John Dollins, "harmony and efficiency" in Waco during those years. The revived Ku Klux Klan arrived in Texas in the fall of 1920 and, for a time, was immensely popular, having at its peak perhaps as many as 170,000 Texans as members and possibly many more sympathizers.[17] Waco was one of the areas in Texas where the Klan had the greatest success, although it was also very powerful in Dallas, Houston, Fort Worth, Wichita Falls, and other parts of the state, despite the vigorous opposition of the *Houston Chronicle* and the *Dallas Morning News*, among other newspapers.[18] According to Waco printer and union activist Francis L. Pittillo, "They [the Ku Klux Klan] elected a whole courthouse here in 1922 but it wasn't long [before] they were all out."[19] The Klan was "in" long enough, however, to run grocer Oscar Hessdoerfer's cousin Harry Bahl out of Waco because he was a Catholic — and because his laundry business was competing with a laundry run by a powerful member of the Waco klavern.[20]

In 1921, in a time of increasing Klan-inspired unrest, Wacoans lynched another man, this time a white man. The victim was Curley Hackney, a Fort Worth man between twenty-five and thirty years old, who seems to have been something of a vagrant. Hackney had a crippled hip from a gunshot wound and needed crutches to get around. According to some accounts, he came to town with a traveling circus or carnival.[21] At any rate, Hackney arrived in Waco and ate dinner with a local family on the night of December 13, 1921.

At about seven o'clock in the evening, the mother of the family had to leave the house to mail a letter and left her nine-year-old daughter alone with Hackney. When she returned, the child declared that Hackney had assaulted her.

Hackney was arrested and taken to jail about 8:30 P.M. At 10:30 P.M. a mob of several hundred men showed up at the jail, found Hackney in the "negro cell," put him in a car, and drove him about three miles out of town, where he was hanged from a tree. The stepfather of the child in the story claimed later that Hackney had confessed to the assault.

The fact of Hackney's disability is another vivid illustration of the consistent preference of lynch mobs for victims who could not defend themselves. It seems that if, as in this case, a mob could not victimize a black man, they would do the next best thing and attack someone else who could not fight back.

According to some accounts, perhaps apocryphal, Hackney faced his death bravely and even bantered with the mob with comments like, "No use to argue with a mob, buddy. They hold aces and I hold kings," and "Well, boys, there is one consolation anyway; I'll get to shake hands with several of you in hell," and "I'm going to be awful cold before morning when the cold dew begins to settle on me. I'll bet you're all glad you're not in my place."[22] His gift for repartee did not save him.

This time it appears, however, that the leading citizens of Waco were finally getting fed up. A public announcement was made that the Hackney
lynching would be officially investigated.[23] At a December 17 meeting of the
Waco Bar Association, two judges, James P. Alexander and Richard I. Munroe,
our old friend of the 54th District Court, made angry speeches denouncing
mob violence. Judge Munroe expressed special anger at the common sentiment that lynchings were necessary because the courts were not enforcing the
laws. He presented official figures compiled by County Attorney Frank Tirey
documenting the fact that in Munroe's own court in the previous year, 190
criminal cases had been tried with only 3 acquittals. Munroe declared that he
was going to put the issue of mob action before the grand jury scheduled to
meet in January. The Waco Bar then went on record "condemning lawlessness
and mob violence."[24]

On January 2, 1922, in the process of impaneling a grand jury and charging
them with investigating the lynching of Curley Hackney, Judge Munroe made
another impassioned speech against mob violence, this time explicitly allud-
ing to the lynching of Jesse Washington: "I was born and reared in the South
and I have been used to mob law — or mob outlaw — all my life. The average
citizen will condemn mob law, in a sort of perfunctory manner. Nothing un-
dermines respect for constituted authority so much as mob violence. Every
mob that takes the law into its own hands, whether the person lynched be
guilty or not, is guilty of murder. Unless all good citizens rise up, now, we had
better turn all cases over to the mob to try. Some years ago a negro was taken
from this court room by a mob and lynched: he may have deserved it, but
the mob committed murder when they lynched that negro."[25] Perhaps the 1916
lynching had been keeping the judge up nights, after all.

Munroe followed his opening remarks by giving the grand jury a very
lengthy written charge that reviewed the provisions of the U.S. and Texas con-
stitutions relating to the rights of every accused to a fair trial and the duty of all
citizens to follow the rule of law. The charge specifically required the grand
jury to investigate Hackney's hanging and concluded, "Mob law is no law at
all, but anarchy pure and simple, and it is high time that the question should
be settled finally whether the mob shall rule or whether our constitution and
laws are supreme."[26]

Despite all this sound and fury, when the grand jury concluded its deliberations two and a half weeks later, no indictments were issued in connection
with Curley Hackney's lynching.[27] After lauding themselves for their exhaustive investigation, the members of the grand jury declared in their written re-

port that they were of the opinion that "the men who did the lynching were non-residents of Waco and McLennan county" — a remarkable bit of nonsense which must have much amused the lynchers who read it.[28]

The following July, both Sheriff Bob Buchanan (who had finally defeated Fleming in 1918) and County Attorney Tirey were handily defeated for reelection by Klan-endorsed candidates.[29] Klan-backed candidates won elections in Dallas, Houston, Fort Worth, and Wichita Falls that summer, as well as in Waco. Klan support and financial backing also carried Earle B. Mayfield to the U.S. Senate that same year. One historian has concluded that Klan electoral victories in Texas made the state "the banner Klan state in the nation" in 1922.[30]

Given the social and political climate, it is not surprising that only a few months passed before Waco indulged in another lynching — despite the fact that city authorities were beginning to call in the Texas Rangers to help defend black prisoners when they went on trial for particularly sensational crimes.[31] The trick, if the lynchers could manage it, was to supersede the law and prevent the arrest and trial of the accused altogether.

The events that led up to the killing of yet another black man in 1922 added a new ingredient — hysterical fear — to the usual atmosphere of racism and hairtrigger violence, now intensified by the presence of the Klan. Between February 1922 and January 1923, Waco was plagued by mysterious attacks on courting couples on lonely roads or in isolated spots around the city, along with a handful of other strange and inexplicable murders. On the night of May 25, 1922, the culminating event occurred that led to the lynching — the murder of twenty-seven-year-old Harrell (or Harold) Bolton and the rape of his female companion on the Corsicana road about six miles east of Waco.[32] The girl described her assailant as a "yellow" Negro of medium build wearing a dark coat, light trousers, and a cap and sporting a prominent gold tooth. The gold tooth became the primary mark of identification both for the officers of the law searching for the mystery man and the customary spontaneous "posses estimated at from 1,000 to 2,000" scouring the countryside between Waco and Hillsboro. In that day and time, a black man with a gold tooth was not a rarity; the police careened from one suspect to another like a scattering of billiard balls. Several men were seized and released in rapid succession; three were brought before the young rape victim at her home on South Fourth Street in Waco, but she could not identify them. Nannette Booker Hutchison, who would have been about twelve at the time, described the panic in the black community: "They were looking for a black man with a gold tooth and some knocked their tooth out." It was during this period, Hutchison said, that her parents decided to

Nannette Booker Hutchison, age about nine, standing in front of her father, ca. 1918. By permission of Nannette Booker Hutchison.

send her teenaged brothers to Detroit to live with a friend out of fear for their safety. "I missed growing up with my two older brothers," Hutchison said. "My baby sister never saw her brothers until they were grown."[33]

Two days after the rape and murder, a black man named Jesse Thomas, a service car driver, was walking across the town square in the late afternoon when he was spied by a deputized neighbor of the rape victim's family who thought he resembled the woman's description of the killer. The neighbor craftily told Thomas that he had some "grass that he wanted cut" and ordered Thomas to get in the car so that he could drive him to the field to show him the grass that needed mowing. Instead, the neighbor took Thomas straight to the victim's home. Once there, Thomas was brought before the girl and told to open his mouth.

The traumatized girl spotted Thomas's gold tooth and cried out, "That's him, Papa!" Her father, Sam Harris, grabbed his gun and shot Thomas in the bedroom of their home. Thomas ran through the back hall and into the backyard; Harris ran after him, still shooting, until Thomas fell near the steps and died in a "large pool of blood."

Denied the opportunity to torture and kill a living black man, the mob vented its frustration on the body of a dead one. They seized Thomas's corpse from a city patrol wagon, attached it by a rope to a truck, and dragged it down Franklin Street to the east side of city hall square, where it was ceremonially stripped and burned on a roaring fire before a crowd of about five thousand howling spectators.[34]

The event became a smaller-scale replica of the Washington lynching as people climbed trees, sat in windows, and fought with each other over the chance to get a good view of the burning. "Make way for the ladies!" was a common cry among the crowd as women struggled for a vantage point.

After the body was partially burned, the mob again tied it behind a car and dragged it up and down the main streets of town, including South Fourth Street, where the driver made sure to haul the charred remains past the rape victim's house.[35] When the crowd, except for a few boys, had melted away, Sheriff Leslie Stegall and his deputies finally arrested the boys, took charge of what was left of the body, and delivered it to an undertaker.[36]

It was probably the body of Jesse Thomas that Mildred Richter saw dragged past Goldstein Migel Department Store. Richter also heard a story later that Jesse Thomas's mother died of grief over what happened to her son.[37]

Despite general approval of the identification of the killer and his instant, if informal, execution, the authorities exhibited some uncertainty as to whether the right man had been punished — although no one expressed these doubts publicly. In the context of the times, if an officer of the law had openly questioned whether Jesse Thomas was indeed the killer, he would have seemed to be doubting the word of the victim. On the other hand, the police continued to interview suspects and to exhibit suspects to the first couple who had been attacked.[38]

The by-now predictable general denunciations of the mob followed, but this time the calls for action were more pointed, reflecting again that the power structure in Waco was increasingly embarrassed by the activities of the mob and was on the verge of taking more serious steps to prevent further "exciting events."[39]

This time the Baptist Pastors Association frankly identified mob participants as "men who are themselves dangerous to society, or . . . irresponsible youths who are thus demoralized for all time to come, augmented by the un-reflecting, highly prejudiced or passion-inflamed good citizen." Instead of expatiating at great length on the evil deeds of the lynching victim, this time the Baptist pastors posited the notion that lynch mobs might lead to "the horrible possibility of destroying the innocent" — again suggesting that some white citizens were not convinced of the guilt of Jesse Thomas. The resolution also expresses what must have been increasing disgust with the absence of backbone on the part of law enforcement: "We also call upon our officers to carry out their sworn duties at whatever hazard."[40]

The local American Legion post was even more forceful in its denunciation of the mob. The American Legion's statement called for a plan to be developed so that city, county, and state authorities could work together to suppress mob violence and demanded that the authorities "arrest and prosecute those who incited the riot of May 26."[41]

Despite Jesse Thomas's death, the crime wave continued. On November 20, 1922, a mysterious assailant attacked a couple at Lovers Leap in Cameron Park, killing the man and raping the woman.[42] On January 19, 1923, another couple was attacked, and this time both were murdered. W. Ed Holt, a married forty-six-year-old carpenter, was shot and killed, and his companion, Mrs. Ethel Denecamp, twenty-one, was shot and stabbed to death in a lane off the Springfield road about five miles east of Waco.[43] By this time, the murders had created such general terror that, according to one newspaper story, "for nearly 12 months men were afraid to venture out of the city limits with their families for the accustomed evening automobile ride."[44]

The real murderer may finally have been exposed by the loss of his cap. According to newspaper accounts, a black Wacoan named Jesse Wedlow told Sheriff Leslie Stegall that he thought he recognized a cap that was dropped at the scene of an attempted attack on a couple driving near Rosemound Cemetery, about ten days before the murder of Holt and Denecamp. Wedlow had worked at the Twenty-Twenty service station with a man named Roy Mitchell and thought the cap looked like one that belonged to him.[45]

Stegall had Mitchell brought in for questioning, first telling him he was being arrested for being involved in a dice game.[46] While Mitchell was in Stegall's office, a deputy searched Mitchell's house. According to Stegall, various items were found that belonged to the victims, including Holt's pistol, pocketbook, and fountain pen, and a piece of rope which matched the rope that was tied to Holt's leg when he was found.[47] Some of the evidence, the authorities claimed, had been stuffed up a stove flue in Mitchell's home.

On Monday, January 29, 1923, Stegall arrested Roy Mitchell and had him transported to Hillsboro for safekeeping. Mitchell was described as "a yellow negro with gold filled front teeth, speaks good language." He was already known to the police, according to the newspapers, because of a "shooting scrape" he had been involved in some months earlier.[48]

One might get the impression, reading between the lines of the newspaper stories, that Roy Mitchell, who was bright, literate, articulate, and feisty, had been an irritant to the authorities in Waco for some time. Sheriff Stegall later claimed to have known him for at least ten years.[49] Trial coverage revealed that County Attorney Farmer, in the process of interrogating Mitchell, had told him he might as well confess to his crimes because they had plenty of evidence to hang him, anyway. Mitchell's spunky reply was along the lines of, if you've got so much evidence already, then why do you need my confession?[50]

According to reports of the sheriff's investigations, Roy Mitchell turned out to be a one-man crime wave. In the end, he confessed to at least five murders, four rapes, and three assaults with intent to murder, including the crimes for which Jesse Thomas had been killed and several crimes of which the authorities were unaware until Mitchell confessed. Mitchell's crimes, say the newspaper accounts, were motivated by "robbery and lust." County Attorney Farmer expressed amazement at Mitchell's "ingenuity" and his "careful planning, . . . intimate study of details and execution that seemed well nigh perfection . . . far beyond what one would naturally expect of a negro."[51]

And what of Jesse Thomas, who had already been extralegally executed by Sam Harris and then burned and dragged through the city streets? Some of the newspaper stories refer to his murder and burning in reviewing the history of the crime spree, but nowhere does any journalist or anyone in authority express regret or remorse that an innocent man was killed.[52] The mistake was understandable, readers were told, because, after all, Mitchell and Thomas did look alike.[53]

As another footnote to the bizarre story, one newspaper article reveals that Mitchell was actually an early suspect in the Bolton killing and that two officers were in the process of taking him to the Harris home to see if the rape victim could identify him when they heard the news that Thomas had been identified and killed; they thereupon released Mitchell.[54]

The whole tale is a dramatic exposé of the consequences of summary judgment and mob justice. If the Waco officers had called in the help they needed to control the public following the Bolton killing and the rape of his companion and had handled the entire case more professionally, Mitchell (if indeed he was the culprit) would have been caught much sooner, and some of those who were allegedly murdered by him later would have survived.

Understandably enough, there remains a question in the minds of some Wacoans as to whether Roy Mitchell was in fact responsible for the many crimes of which he was accused. Some have suggested that the "evidence" that convicted him may have been planted in his house to frame him. When Mitchell was tried for murder in five rapid-fire, consecutive judicial proceedings all crammed into the month of March 1923, he recanted his confession.

During his first trial, for the murder of W. E. Holt, Mitchell claimed that he had been tortured in the Hillsboro jail, that his jailers had thrown water in his face, stuck him with pins, jerked his hair out, burned him with matches, kicked him, and beaten him with a club. He was also told, he said, that a mob would get him when he was taken back to Waco. He further claimed that county attorney C. S. Farmer had promised him he would not be hanged if he confessed.[55] Nevertheless, in nine minutes of deliberation, the jury convicted Mitchell of Holt's killing and sentenced him to death.[56]

One of the most poignant observations made by reporters during the extensive coverage of the first trial is the remark that "Mitchell's little girl, about 10 years old, sat in his lap and slept during the proceedings, while the negro's wife sat immediately behind him."[57] Both Mitchell's wife, Minnie, and his daughter, Marguerite, testified that Mitchell had been home on the night of the murder.

The remainder of the trials were rushed to completion in even less time than the first. In each case, the jury required only a handful of minutes to convict Mitchell — a total of twenty-seven minutes of deliberations on five capital charges in five trials.[58] Mitchell was tried a sixth time and convicted of killing a woman named Loula Barker, despite the fact that two other black men had already "confessed" and been convicted for the same crime.[59] One of the men, Cooper Johnson, died at the county prison farm just a few days before Mitchell was hanged.[60] The other, Bennie Young, was not released from prison until a group of grand jurors appealed to Gov. Pat Neff to pardon him.[61]

Questions of Roy Mitchell's guilt or innocence may still tease a modern-day researcher examining the tale of his alleged one-man reign of terror, but it is undeniable that this time Waco's authorities took the necessary steps to make absolutely sure there would be no repeat of the mob violence that had plagued and shamed the town. The actions of the sheriff and the police vividly demonstrated how mob violence could be prevented, even in a profoundly racist environment with the Ku Klux Klan in political ascendancy.

Mayor Ben C. Richards, who was a fish merchant before he became mayor, seems to have been a much stronger character than John Dollins. Richards was involved in Waco politics for twenty-nine years, serving as alderman and commissioner as well as mayor, and was never defeated in any election.[62] The *Times Herald* recorded his sentiments on the subject of mob rule: "The mayor feels very keenly the undesirable reputation the city had gained in the past on account of lawlessness and expressed a determination to demonstrate the ability of the city to protect life and property under any and all circumstances."[63]

This time the mayor had a sheriff and a chief of police who, rather than each trying to pass off the responsibility for a prisoner's safety to the other, took charge and worked together. A key article on the front page of the *Herald* two days after Mitchell was returned to the Waco jail from Hillsboro practically trumpets the intentions of law enforcement to protect Mitchell, no matter what. The very first paragraph of the article reads, "Sheriff Stegall is prepared to defend the jail against any sort of attack and has taken every precaution against a surprise . . . He brought Mitchell back here because this was the place for him and he is determined to protect the negro and his honor as sheriff at any and all cost."

Stegall called all of his deputies together and, like Travis at the Alamo, offered every man the chance to refuse to serve without penalty or disapproval if he felt he could not "help stop a mob." After all the previous years' euphemisms and evasions and efforts to placate all parties, Stegall laid it on the line: "I do not want any man to go there [to the prison] except those who are ready and willing to shoot and shoot to kill if it becomes necessary to stop the mob, if there should be one." No one refused. At the same time that he was serving notice to his men, Stegall was serving notice to the community.

Mayor Richards spoke to the assembled group after Stegall and left no doubt that it was not the pious exhortations of the city's clergy that had effected the radical change in approach. The mayor did not urge everyone to be good for the sake of being good. Waco, he said, had received some "very unwholesome advertising" because of previous mob violence, and "he for one proposed to have no more of it."

Not only did Stegall, with the help of police chief Lee Jenkins, place a well-armed force in the jail (police officers and deputies spelled each other), but he notified Capt. Hugo Martin of the Howitzer Company, 143rd Infantry, to be ready to come and help defend the jail if need be. The Howitzer Company, Wacoans were told, had a machine gun which would make "a formidable defense" if a mob attacked.[64]

Uniformed police and plainclothes officers patrolling the streets of Waco were told to be alert to any rumors that a mob was being planned or organized and to bring these reports to the mayor or chief of police at once. There were to be no more surprise attacks on the jail, as in the case of Sank Majors.

When it came time for Mitchell's first trial, on March 5, 1923, in Judge Munroe's court, Richards, Stegall, and Jenkins continued to exhibit the same careful planning. They had every detail of security under control. The court-room was guarded by Stegall's regular deputies plus twenty special deputies, including officers from other McLennan County towns; former chief of police Hollis Barron; former sheriff — now state fire marshal — George W. Tilley; and the entire headquarters company of the Texas Rangers, led by the renowned Capt. Frank Hamer himself.[65]

Everyone who entered the 54th District courtroom was searched. Once all the seats in the courtroom were filled, no one else was admitted. No one was allowed to stand. The trial reports suggest that even the spectators took pride in their good behavior. They seemed to have attained an awareness that, when the world's eyes were turned on Waco, Wacoans wanted to be seen preserving order. In contrast to the raucous outcries and emotional reactions at the Jesse Washington trial, "only twice during the [first Mitchell] trial was it necessary to quiet the outburst of laughter from the crowd."[66]

Even though the city remained quiet, Stegall never let his guard down. Through all of the subsequent trials he maintained the same tight control. Spectators were admonished not to make any outcry, even when the jury's ver-dict was read at the end of each trial.[67] During the fifth trial, for the killing of Harrell Bolton, there was an eruption in the courtroom, at which point Ranger Wheatley, who was in charge, announced that any further disorder "would bring arrests."[68]

Once Stegall had gotten over the hurdle of the trials, he had to renew his vigilance until the hanging and burial of Roy Mitchell on July 30. The execu-tion was to be the last legal hanging and the last public execution in Texas; the law authorizing the use of the electric chair at Huntsville was to go into effect on August 14.[69]

While Roy Mitchell passed his last days in jail reading magazines, news-papers, and the Bible and composing poetry and songs, Stegall prepared his cadre of deputies once more, to be augmented by a detail of twenty-two local po-licemen.[70] The roster of participating police included, ironically, Joe Dillard, onetime saloonkeeper and purveyor of chili, who had been fingered by Elisa-beth Freeman as one of the leaders of the lynch mob only seven years earlier.[71]

On the morning of Roy Mitchell's execution, the usual immense and ea-ger crowd of spectators assembled, estimated by various sources to be between five thousand and ten thousand.[72] A select one hundred or so—a group including deputies, visiting law enforcement officers from one hundred miles around McLennan County, newspaper correspondents, and friends and relatives of Mitchell's alleged victims—were admitted inside the wall around the jail. Beyond the wall, the jail alley was packed, and spectators leaned out of the courthouse windows and climbed into trees to get a better view.

Mitchell did not leave behind any detailed, written record of his crimes, but Stegall and Farmer claimed that between 9:00 and 10:00 A.M. on the morning of his hanging, Mitchell confessed again to all the crimes of which he had been convicted. The condemned man refused to wear the suit that had been purchased for him and walked out on the gallows in the white shirt and unhemmed blue work pants he had worn throughout his imprisonment. He was barefoot. When he was led out of the jail onto the gallows platform, a great shout went up from the throng. They quieted down and then screamed again as the noose and cap were put over his head.

The last words Mitchell said were, "Goodbye, everyone." Former sheriff John Baker, who had hanged several men, commented that Mitchell was "the coolest man he had ever seen hung."[73]

The hanging took place at 11:02 A.M., but Mitchell was not cut down until 11:26 A.M. because, although his neck was broken, his heart did not stop beating for some time. During the twenty-four minutes he was left to hang, no one left the scene and, even after he was cut down, the crowd lingered to gossip and to try to get a glimpse of the coffin.

Mitchell had told his wife to take the children and go stay with his mother in Bell County until the hanging was over. Neither his wife nor his mother had the money to pay for his funeral.[74] He was immediately placed in a pine box and taken to the cemetery to be buried at county expense. In one final oddity, two white women appeared at the cemetery and asked to see the corpse; the black dentist in charge raised the coffin lid so they could look at Mitchell before he was buried.[75]

Throughout this spectacle the people of Waco, who had been warned over and over about the consequences of any disturbance, behaved themselves admirably. The only action they took that was not in Stegall's script was to pull down the canvas screens that had been placed around the gallows shortly before the execution; thus, Mitchell's death, which was supposed to be partially shielded, occurred in full view of all of the spectators.[76]

Other than that single unauthorized deed, Wacoans demonstrated in the spring and summer of 1923, under the firm leadership of Richards, Stegall, and

Jenkins, that they had learned their lesson and were willing to give up the mob riots and mass public sadism that had given the city such an evil reputation.

The South — the entire country — still had a long road to travel; in those days victories against racism were measured in small increments. But, at least in the case of this one community, the efforts initiated by the NAACP, with the help of Elisabeth Freeman, to end the worst public atrocities of the racist system had finally succeeded.

EPILOGUE

"One of the Best Vote-Getters the County Ever Saw"

Old-timers speak of Fleming as one of the best vote-getters the county ever saw. He was a buggy salesman for the McLennan Hardware Co. when he was elected to office 40 years ago.

—"Former Sheriff Fleming Buried," *Waco Times Herald*

AS the outlook for blacks in America improved by degrees over the decades, time passed for all of the reformers—and for the major players in the Waco portion of this story, as well. Some reached ends that fit the lives they led; others suffered or prospered in ways that do not seem to match the part they played. And some ended in unhappy confusion. One who fits into this last category is William English Walling.

When America entered World War I in 1917, Walling turned against the Socialist Party and began to write impassioned, feverish articles demanding the suppression of all dissent and opposition to the war effort in the United States and condemning old colleagues as treasonous.[1] After the war, his full-time occupation became attacking evidence of American "bolshevism" everywhere he imagined it to be, even in the pages of the "stodgy" *Book Review Digest*.[2] It was a startling transformation for the man whom Charles Edward Russell had once called "the reincarnation of some old exultant crusader."[3]

The magnificent "revolutionary romance" between Walling and his wife was also falling apart.[4] Walling had an affair and he and Anna separated bitterly in 1932. In 1936, Walling died suddenly of pneumonia in Amsterdam at the age of fifty-nine. By then the handsome aristocrat, the impassioned, trailblazing reformer, had become an aging, angry man who had betrayed many of his friends and abandoned his family. But Walling had gone to Amsterdam to meet with underground opponents of Hitler who had been smuggled out of Germany, so perhaps a true desire to make the world better, not just more conformist, still burned within him to the very end.[5]

Moorfield Storey, the elder statesman of the NAACP, died in 1929, as honored in death as he had been in life. Toward the end, in a letter to a friend, Storey expressed in his gentle way his dislike of the modern era and his longing for the world of the nineteenth century. "The world does not seem so good a place as it was in my youth," he wrote, "before the days of automobiles, radios, enormous wealth, and cheap men in power, but perhaps this feeling is only a sign of age."[6] His comments are poignant and express the focus of his entire life. Storey was still motivated by ideals and appalled by those who were inspired only by the struggle for wealth. And he was still self-deprecating — a man who, in his many political struggles, always fought vigorously for the cause at hand, but never believed that his moral exactitude made him either important or infallible.

Oswald Garrison Villard, on the other hand, who never questioned his absolute conviction that he was right, continued to battle fiercely for principle to the end of his life. In 1940, he even abandoned *The Nation* because he remained a pacifist and was convinced that the rest of the editorial staff had capitulated to warmongering as war broke out and intensified once more in Europe. Villard wrote the editor of *The Nation* that she had "prostituted" the journal and that he hoped it would "die very soon or fall into other hands."[7]

Villard, who had fiercely struggled with his colleagues at the young NAACP, declared later in his life that his involvement with the group was one of the activities of which he was proudest. As he got older and reviewed his life, he even had kind words for his old nemesis Du Bois. In his autobiography, Villard says that the NAACP "was one of the movements which I helped to originate as to which I have no regrets, in which I can take unqualified satisfaction."[8] His list of the names of those who were important in building the NAACP is headed by Du Bois, "so many years the editor of our monthly publication *The Crisis*."[9] He has even kinder words for Mary White Ovington. "To the Negroes," he says, "she has given the greater part of her life with an unselfishness, a patience, a sweetness of spirit, and a kindliness hard to describe adequately."[10]

W. E. B. Du Bois had a complicated later life. He left the NAACP in 1934 because he felt that the organization had become an organ for the black middle class and was not doing enough to help the lower classes. He also spoke out in favor of some forms of black nationalism — the development of separate black businesses and cooperatives — which seemed to many members of the NAACP to violate the group's historical struggle against all forms of segregation. Du Bois returned to Atlanta University to teach and write, but then came back to the NAACP from 1944 to 1948. Once again he left, this time amid more philosophical disagreements and quarrels with then-secretary Walter White. As usual, the primary issue was that Du Bois was not allowed to be independent and to express himself as he saw fit, because his frequently controversial comments were viewed by outsiders as being representative of the NAACP.

Through all his long life, Du Bois continued to cling to the United States, despite every wrong and humiliation he and other black Americans suffered, but the anti-Communist hysteria of the 1950s finally convinced him, at age ninety-three, to leave his country. His autobiography conveys the impression that his heart and his faith in America were irretrievably broken at last when he was indicted for the failure of his Peace Information Center to register as "an agent for a foreign government."

Du Bois was acquitted of the charge, but in 1961, he officially joined the Communist Party and moved to Ghana, where he died on August 27, 1963. His death was announced by Roy Wilkins during the March on Washington at which Dr. Martin Luther King Jr. delivered his "I Have a Dream" speech.[11]

Joel Spingarn, Du Bois's "scholar and knight," died much earlier, in 1939, in his early sixties.[12] According to his literary biographer, however, although he retained a role in the NAACP until his death, Spingarn had given up on the notion of influencing the world for the better long before he died.[13] In 1917 he had thrown himself into the war effort. In typical scholarly fashion, he read several books on military tactics and then, despite the fact that he was forty-five and in poor health, he entered an officers' training program and emerged in August 1917 a major — one of only two in his training group to receive this rank. He also fought successfully to have the army establish a training camp for black officers.[14]

After the war, Spingarn joined with two friends to start the Harcourt, Brace and Company publishing house in 1919, but withdrew from active involvement in the project in 1924 because of poor health.[15] He published a small volume of poetry in 1924 and lectured briefly at the New School for Social Research in New York in 1931, but, deeply discouraged about the state of the world and the growing international devotion, throughout the 1930s, to dogmatisms of various kinds, Spingarn devoted most of the last years of his life to — of all things — the writing of articles in horticultural journals about the clematis plant, which he cultivated and studied in his garden at Troutbeck.[16]

One of Joel Spingarn's daughters once said that "becoming involved with black civil rights was the only selfless thing that her father had ever done."[17] Perhaps, however, even if that is true, it was enough. Spingarn's pivotal involvement in the NAACP, his unique capacity to soothe the warring spirits there and lead them to work together, ultimately helped address and change the most flagrant injustice in American society.

Of all of the early founders, however, Mary Ovington stayed most consistently and unswervingly dedicated to the mission she had set for herself. In 1945, near the end of her life, a radio station in Philadelphia broadcast a program called *America's Other Voice* based on Ovington's life and her work to establish the NAACP. The program depicted Ovington as a kind of conscience of America. In July 1946, a columnist for the *St. Louis American* called Ovington "the Guardian Angel of the NAACP" and asked the organization to declare a "Mary White Ovington Day" or to establish a monument for the person "who has done more to make America The Land Of The Free And The Home Of The Brave than any other living soul."[18] In the preface to her autobiography, Walter White says the best description of Mary White Ovington is to call her the "Fighting Saint." "Born of a family of culture and means," White continues, "she might have been secure in conforming to the prejudices and conditions of her society. Instead she threw herself into the most difficult social problem in America — the Negro Question."[19]

In terms of impact on her world, the relatively unsung Mary White Ovington deserves a place in the pantheon of notable American women, alongside such luminaries as Susan B. Anthony, Jane Addams, Margaret Sanger, Ida Tarbell, and others who played a leading role in bringing about great social change. Working always in the shadow of larger-than-life men with colossal egos, Ovington was content to get what she wanted done without the bouquets of public recognition. Perhaps now, at last, the time has come to acknowledge fully her contribution to the betterment of American life.

Sadly, Elisabeth Freeman, the battling suffragist and the investigator who brought the details of the Waco Horror to light, did not fare as well as Mary White Ovington. Freeman seems to have faded from the front ranks of the suffragist battle before victory was achieved in 1920. She was not, for example, where one would have expected her to be, among the ranks of Alice Paul's "militants" of the National Woman's Party, who picketed the White House and went to jail for suffrage in 1917 and 1918. Although the NAACP continued to send its own investigators to determine the facts after each lynching, Elisabeth Freeman never investigated another lynching. Perhaps, after more than ten years at the forefront of the fray, she was finally worn out. There is no question that by the time she was heard from again, her health had begun to suffer.

What little we know of the remaining years of Elisabeth Freeman's life is found in correspondence between Freeman and Rosika Schwimmer, Hungarian suffragist, feminist, diplomat, and peace activist. Freeman and Schwimmer worked together in the cause of pacifism, which apparently succeeded women's suffrage as the focus of Freeman's reformist attention after American women won the vote, at long last, in 1920. The first letter between the two women was written in March 1925, while Freeman was still camping out at the homes of friends. Freeman wrote to Schwimmer from the office or home of Katherine Leckie, a journalist, feminist, labor supporter, and friend of anarchist Emma Goldman. Freeman, who apparently had not yet actually met Schwimmer, offers in the letter to put together a little gathering of pacifists for Schwimmer to meet and also tries to cheer up the Hungarian immigrant. Schwimmer, who had escaped Hungary and fled to the United States in 1921 because of her opposition to the Communist regime of Bela Kun, had been deeply hurt to find herself attacked as both a "German spy" and a "Bolshevist agent" once she arrived in America. "Men are queer birds when you put the lid on their activities," says Freeman, ever the feminist, to Schwimmer, "but to shut up a woman, seems to be one of the joys of their lives."[20]

Many of the most prominent suffragists were apparently unwilling to retire from the political arena after they had won the vote. They were eager to take what they had learned and go on to the next great cause. But achieving world peace in a world recovering from one Great War and preparing for another turned out to be a more difficult, quixotic campaign than the seventy-two-year battle to win the vote for women. Schwimmer, bitterly discouraged by the continuing vilification of her in the American press, comments to Freeman in one of her letters, "Aren't we a bunch of misfits?"[21]

In the next letter of their correspondence, Freeman, who seemed always to be struggling to stay afloat financially, tells Schwimmer that she has become a shopkeeper and has opened "Ye Pilgrim Shoppe" in Provincetown on Cape Cod, where she hopes to sell "antiques (self-collected) and oddments."[22] The "shoppe" does not seem to have been a success. "Just now I am in a very bad way financially," Freeman writes to Schwimmer from Provincetown in June 1930. "I am doing everything myself and cooking all my own food in a very limited space."[23] By October, Freeman is still complaining to Schwimmer of "a very bad season of dull business" and is also suffering from a bad cold, which presages her later illnesses.[24]

Earlier in the same summer, Freeman had endured the sad and strange experience of seeing her dear friend and fellow social activist Katherine Leckie suffer a complete mental and physical collapse brought on by doing work for which she was never paid and by, according to Leckie's brother, "dieting, doctoring and trying to free the entire human race."[25] The task fell to Freeman to listen to Leckie's incoherent ramblings, try to get some food into her, find medical care for her, and finally help her to pack and leave New York for Chicago, where her brother could take care of her.[26] Sadly, shortly after Leckie arrived in Chicago, she died suddenly in her sleep.[27]

Letters between Schwimmer and Freeman also refer to the fact that Freeman's mother, Mary, who had been game enough to help her daughter distribute suffragist literature on Coney Island during the summer of 1913, had died of stomach cancer. This was another devastating loss for Elisabeth.[28]

Seven years passed before the correspondence — or what has been salvaged of it — resumed between Schwimmer and Freeman in 1937. Freeman was by then in her fifties. The exuberant scrawl of her youth had tightened to a pinched, smaller-scale hand. She tells Schwimmer that she has been extremely ill with "flu, pleurisy and toxic posioning [sic]. Any one alone enough to try one's patience."[29] In the same letter of February 3, 1937, Freeman announces that she is moving to California at the end of the month in the hope that the warmer climate will improve her health.

In the last three letters exchanged between Schwimmer and Freeman, who was then living in Altadena on the outskirts of Los Angeles, Freeman complains querulously, without any of her usual spirit and humor, that she has been passed over in a public pacifist tribute to Schwimmer. Earlier in the year, Rosika Schwimmer had been awarded the World Peace Prize, a sum of $8,500, by a small group of friends in various reform movements brought together by Schwimmer's friend Lola Maverick Lloyd. Lloyd organized the awarding of the prize to Schwimmer as a kickoff event to inaugurate a new reform organization called the Campaign for World Government. Freeman expresses great distress because she has discovered that the name of the well-known writer and socialist politician Upton Sinclair was included on the list of the members of the committee awarding the prize to Schwimmer, but Freeman's own name had been left out. "I must say," declares Freeman, "I have supported you ever since I knew you . . . and have had much the same experiences with organizations and individuals that has descended on your life."[30] Upton Sinclair, on the other hand, says Freeman, publicly attacked Schwimmer in a book and never published a retraction. Sinclair lived in Pasadena, next door to Altadena, and Freeman had therefore had an opportunity to confront him about his mistreatment of Schwimmer. "Since this talk with him, he seems to studiously shun me," she says.[31]

Schwimmer declares in response that she had nothing to do with putting together the list of names: "Amongst ourselves, I still consider him [Sinclair] a scoundrel without a grain of ethics or sense of justice and responsibility. Lack of money prevents me from prosecuting him legally as he very well knows."[32] Schwimmer goes on to ask Freeman what she is doing in California besides trying to regain her health.

Thus ends the correspondence. The vivacious, irrepressible suffragist activist and lynching investigator of the 1910s had been reduced to an ailing woman who, though only in her early fifties, was already used up and worn out. Maybe there had been too many treks in the rain and snow for Elisabeth Freeman, too many steamy summer days selling newspapers on the sidewalks of the city, too much picking up and moving from house to house and from friend to friend, trying to find a little quiet, a place to land briefly before going on. Elisabeth Freeman was a restless spirit in a body that had probably always been rather frail — or had become so when the physical demands on her constitution were too much to endure, but the spirit would not give in.

On February 27, 1942, Elisabeth Freeman died of "coronary thrombosis due to coronary sclerosis" in Huntington Memorial Hospital in Pasadena. It is painfully apparent from her death certificate that she died alone, without anyone nearby who knew her well. Her age was recorded as "approx. 55"; she was probably about fifty-seven. Her birth date, birthplace, and the names and birthplaces of her father and mother are all recorded as "unknown."

A brother, one John F. Freeman of 115 Walnut Street in Binghamton, New York — unmentioned in any of Freeman's letters — gave permission to Turner & Stevens, Funeral Directors, for the cremation of her body. (There is no record of any notification having been sent to the sister Freeman was staying with when Katherine Leckie's breakdown occurred during the early summer of 1930.)[33]

John Freeman paid twenty-five dollars, half the cost of the cremation; the remaining twenty-five dollars was provided by a "semi-charity allowance." It appears that John Freeman never actually claimed the ashes of his sister.[34] I have found no obituary of Elisabeth Freeman in Los Angeles, Altadena, New York City, or Binghamton. John Freeman does not seem to have made any effort whatever to memorialize the life of his sister.

And so Elisabeth Freeman sank into darkness and disappeared. Of all her companions along the way, there seems to have been no one left to mourn her. But the work she performed did not disappear. Her efforts in Waco alone survive as a classic exposure of an atrocity that had to be shoved in the face of white Americans so that the lynching of black Americans could be ended.

Turning away from the great reformers of the NAACP and the suffragist investigator Elisabeth Freeman to consider the fate of the Wacoans who played prominent parts in the Waco Horror is a shift from the macrocosm to the microcosm, from the giants to the pygmies. But it is instructive to find out what happened to all the Waco players in the story, and what became of Waco itself.

Waco never became the large city that some of its citizens envisioned in the early part of the last century.[35] The Alico remains the single lonely skyscraper gracing the downtown "skyline." Texas' other major cities had a head start and a faster pace, and maybe, as onetime director of Waco Urban Renewal, Hank Corwin, once said, "[Waco] was the biggest country town in Texas and I still think it is."[36]

Waco's only African American county commissioner at this writing, Lester Gibson, is carrying on the struggle Lawrence Johnson began to wring some sort of apology from the city for the Waco Horror, some kind of official acknowledgment that the lynching of Jesse Washington took place, that it was condoned by the authorities at the time, and that it was wrong.[37]

When workers began restoring the murals in the rotunda of the McLennan County Courthouse in the spring of 2002, they discovered that one of the murals included the enigmatic image of a noose hanging from a tree. A debate ensued in Waco as to the meaning of the noose and whether it should be painted over or al-

Lawrence Johnson, Waco attorney and former city councilman. By permission of Lawrence Johnson.

lowed to remain as an artifact of the times. Commissioner Lester Gibson made a formal presentation to commissioners' court proposing that a plaque be hung on the wall next to the painting of the noose, briefly telling the story of the Waco Horror and, as a "conciliatory atonement," apologizing for the role Waco's authorities played, or refused to play, in the incident. Not one of the four white commissioners would second Gibson's motion or even comment on it during the meeting. When the motion was not seconded, it died and the presiding judge moved on to other business.

The old way of thinking seems to continue in Waco: ignore the ugly past, don't talk about it, refuse to take responsibility for it, and it will go away. This approach has failed to bury the Waco Horror for over eighty years. The editors of the *Waco Tribune Herald* have proposed that the county commissioners and the city council jointly petition the state to place a historical marker on the site where the lynching occurred. As of this writing, however, the issue has still not been resolved.[38]

The story of the Waco Horror remains the story of individuals as well as of a town. As the Roy Mitchell trials and hanging clearly show, it was the individuals in charge who made the difference between what happened in 1916 and what happened in 1923. Far from suffering any lingering or late-developing fall from grace for having witnessed a public lynching from his office window without interfering, Mayor John Dollins was highly praised after his death in 1930. "Waco has never had a citizen who was more universally popular with all classes of people," says his *Times Herald* obituary.[39] "He was kind and good to everyone especially to the children . . . He made Waco a good Mayor during his two years of service," writes the biographer of Waco's early mayors.[40]

Police chief Guy McNamara, who kept Dollins company in his office while the lynching was being carried out, had only just entered the office in 1915 and was to serve until 1921. "He was a very strongwilled, very domineering person," said Guy's nephew John B. McNamara Jr., son of John B. McNamara, the county attorney who prosecuted Jesse Washington. "He dominated his wife and his children. He was everything my daddy wasn't."[41] In the spring of 1933, strong-willed Guy McNamara was appointed deputy U.S. marshal for the Western District of Texas by Pres. Franklin Roosevelt, and served in that position until his death in 1947.[42] At the time of his death, McNamara was described as a colorful throwback to the past, "tall, spare, gray-haired," who still wore dark clothes, a black string tie, and a black hat and "walked with the knee-lifting gait of the old-timer, liked to thrust his fingers into the side pocket of his trousers, with the thumbs outside, as he walked or talked."[43] It is unfortunate

John B. McNamara *(seated)* during his tenure as assistant to county attorney Pat Neff *(standing)*. Neff later became governor of Texas and then president of Baylor University. *Courtesy* Archives Division of The Texas Collection, Baylor University, Waco, Texas.

that the domineering, impressive police chief (and future marshal) did not exercise his powerful personality to try to subdue the crowd that was torturing Jesse Washington to death.

As a young man, John B. McNamara, Guy's brother, "read" law but never obtained a law degree, a practice that was still common in those days. He was the third of five generations of McNamara men to practice law in Waco.[44] John McNamara served as assistant county attorney from 1902 to 1912 under Pat Neff (who was later governor of Texas and then president of Baylor University) and became county attorney himself in 1912. After 1918, when McNamara was defeated by Frank Tirey, he never again served in public office. McNamara's son John Jr. claimed that the women of Waco, newly franchised in Texas primaries in 1918, voted his dad out of office because the county attorney favored the continuation of Waco's red-light district.

After his political defeat, John McNamara practiced criminal law for the rest of his long life. According to his son, McNamara represented many black Wacoans, mostly in minor criminal matters. There were thirteen black families living on the McNamara property near Bosqueville outside Waco, and, said John McNamara Jr., "That's just the way Daddy was. He wasn't going to turn anybody down who needed help." John B. McNamara, according to his son, "was a very gentle person, extremely kind and considerate." McNamara insisted that his father "wouldn't have condoned anything like [the lynching]. It would have been foreign to his personality." The former county attorney was also one of the supporters of the Waco Citizens League, which, in 1922, opposed Klan-sponsored candidates for public office at a time when it was dangerous to take a public stand against the Klan.[45]

There is no record, however, that John B. McNamara ever protested the lynching of Jesse Washington. Perhaps he felt, like W. B. Brazelton, that, as a principal player in Washington's trial, he was in no position to protest. McNamara, like Sam Fleming, was also facing a critical election in July of 1916. If he was disturbed by the lynching, he kept it to himself. Whether intentionally or not, though, McNamara seems to have spent part of the rest of his life making amends to the black community of Waco.

George Fryer, widower of Lucy Fryer, lived very quietly until he died on March 12, 1938, at the age of seventy-eight, and went to join his wife and their small daughter in the cemetery at Lorena. "He lived with us the last few years of his life," said Lucy Wollitz Kirkland, his granddaughter and daughter of Ruby, who had found her mother's body. "He was quiet, just a very nice person," said Lucy, adding that she never knew her grandfather to "show any temper." It was her grandfather, Lucy recalled, who taught her to read.

Lucy said that her grandfather spent a lot of time in his later years playing dominoes at the service station, owned by his son-in-law, at the intersection of Moonlight and Old Robinson Road in the center of the little community of Robinson. In an old photograph taken of him during his days hanging out at the service station, George Fryer sports a bushy moustache, a ten-gallon hat, and a placid expression.

Lucy was only fourteen when her grandfather died, but she remembered that at some point in her childhood, her grandfather told her a little bit about Jesse Washington and the murder of her grandmother. "He said that he [Jesse Washington] was not retarded and had no reason to dislike them," explained Lucy. "He [Jesse] did kill a very innocent woman," she added. "I guess he had to be punished somehow."[46]

The life of Fred Gildersleeve, Waco's commercial photographer for close to fifty years, who took the unforgettable pictures of the Waco lynching through the windows in Mayor Dollins's office, ended rather sadly. Apart from May 15, 1916, Gildersleeve had a magnificent career in Waco. Gildersleeve, or "Gildy,"

Waco photographer Fred Gildersleeve, better known as "Gildy," in 1909. *Courtesy Archives Division of The Texas Collection, Baylor University, Waco, Texas.*

as he was more commonly known, was such a tiny man that in his youth he worked briefly as a professional jockey (he said he had ridden a white mule in a Missouri mule race). But he had a big personality and a flamboyant style that led him to attempt new kinds of photography throughout his career, with Waco as his ongoing subject matter. In order to take his famous nighttime outdoor picture of the 1911 Waco Prosperity Banquet, for instance, Gildersleeve placed synchronized flash powder charges above doorways all along the block and set them off all at once. In 1916, he worked with the Eastman factory to enlarge one of his photographs of Waco's Cotton Palace to the then unheard-of size of ten feet. During World War I he experimented with aerial photography, hanging out of flimsy biplanes to get his pictures.

But in his last years Gildersleeve's life descended into a series of disasters. His wife of thirty years left him and about that time, coincidentally, almost all of his hundreds of acetate negatives disappeared. All he had left were the older glass negatives. Many of these glass plates had been kept for some time in "a moldering little backyard shed, overgrown with trumpet creeper vines."[47] Roger Conger, local Waco historian, who took a special interest in Gildersleeve in his old age, kept pestering Gildersleeve to let him take a look at the negatives in the shed. One day Gildersleeve agreed, but when he opened the door to the shed, he found that the heavy cartons full of glass had pulled the shelves loose and the entire mess had catapulted onto the floor, perhaps many years earlier, leaving about half of the negatives irretrievably shattered. Enough were saved, however, to represent a substantial legacy, a record of fifty years, to the city of Waco.

In Waco the diminutive photographer is still remembered for his classic shots of buildings and notable people — and perhaps more than for any other single picture, for a photograph he took in 1911 of a small biplane circling Waco's pioneering skyscraper. It is the great irony of Gildersleeve's career that, outside of Waco, he is remembered principally for six photographs of a town's populace torturing a black boy to death. The act of taking the pictures, as a routine commercial proposition, was despicable, but the photographs remain as an indelible legacy of the full-blown horror of lynching.

The final postmortem among the Waco characters in the story is the tale of Sam Fleming. What happened to the oversized sheriff who stepped back and allowed a teenaged boy to be burned in order to win an election? Sam Fleming got his wish in the summer of 1916; he was reelected for another two years. But in 1918, the women of Texas weighed in for the first time, and Sam Fleming was embarrassingly defeated by his political nemesis, Bob Buchanan, by a lopsided vote of 9,058 to 4,783.[48] The difference was the 7,990 women who had been added to the roles of McLennan County voters.[49] In contrast to the florid, lengthy ads of his previous campaigns, Fleming ran almost no ads in the newspapers in the days immediately preceding the 1918 election. He probably knew he was done for, despite an appeal in one small advertisement for women and children in particular to come and hear him speak on the courthouse lawn.[50]

Buchanan, on the other hand, whose daughter campaigned with him in 1918, sounds confident in his ads that the women who had finally taken their place alongside the men in Texas primary elections would stand with him against Fleming.[51] "I don't want to neglect to say an especial word about how I appreciate the words of encouragement I have received from so many good women," the ads say, "and with what high resolve in their behalf I will conduct the office, if elected."[52]

From this distance, it is impossible to tell exactly what issues caused the women of McLennan County to support Buchanan over Fleming so over-whelmingly. Perhaps Fleming, like McNamara, was viewed as supportive of the old "reservation" for prostitutes, which had been abolished in 1917. Per-haps Fleming was associated with the political machine and the liquor inter-ests.[53] Whatever the reason, he lost, and the loss was so devastating to him that, soon after, he moved to Dallas, where he spent the remainder of his years. Apparently, he could not, after all, face going back to selling buggies and cul-tivators in Waco, but he pursued a sales career in Dallas, probably because he had no other useful skill.

By 1923, Fleming was already listed in the *Dallas City Directory*; he was still living together with his longtime wife, Flora, and was running the "S. S. Flem-ing Realty Company" in the Melba Theater Building. By 1927, he had a new job, as sales manager of the Radium Ore Revigator Sales Company, and had discarded Flora for a new wife named Tomy.[54] Tomy Vaughn was a beautician, proprietor of the Angelus Beauty Parlor, and almost certainly much younger than Flora, who was approximately the same age as Sam.[55] Flora Fleming moved to Houston, probably to be close to her children who had settled there. It is tempting to conjecture that Fleming's loss of his position as sheriff and his flight to Dallas and return to the sales career he had willingly abandoned led to tension and unhappiness that also destroyed his marriage.

Nevertheless, Sam, Flora, and Sam's new wife, Tomy, were all eventually buried in Oakwood Cemetery in Waco. In death, Fleming returned for good to the scene of his greatest triumph. In his Waco obituaries, old-timers expressed surprise that Fleming's body had been returned to Waco. Leslie Stegall, who was constable when Fleming was sheriff, commented that he had had no idea where Fleming had been all those years. The highest praise the old-timers who were questioned could offer to the *Waco Times Herald* obituary writer was that Fleming was "one of the best vote-getters the county ever saw."[56] That talent got Fleming elected, but it was not enough to enable him to deal with the biggest challenge to his authority during his term in office. In fact, his skill at getting himself elected and his hunger to remain sheriff ran directly counter to his duties as sheriff when a lynching loomed. Fleming lacked the training, the experience, and, above all, the backbone to prevent the Waco Horror. When the critical moment of his life arrived, Sam Fleming disappeared.

Notes

Introduction

1. This claim was made by James Allen, a collector of lynching photographs and postcards, in an interview with Anthea Raymond on National Public Radio's *Morning Edition*, April 4, 2000.

2. Elisabeth Freeman, "Waco Lynching," NAACP Archives, NAACP Administrative File, Subfile under Lynching: Waco, Texas, 1916, Group 1, Box C-370, Library of Congress, 15 (hereafter Freeman, "Waco Lynching").

3. Smith, "Coming to Terms with 1916 'Horror,'" 1A.

4. Interview with Alamo staff, July 14, 2001, San Antonio, Tex.

5. The term "race riot," as used in the late 1800s and the early 1900s, implies a situation in which blacks were rioting against whites. In most cases, however, a so-called race riot was actually a pogrom conducted by whites against blacks.

6. Clarence Darrow, speech, Proceedings of the 1910 Annual Conference of the NAACP, Meetings of the Board of Directors, Records of Annual Conferences, etc., 1909–1950, Group II, Series L, Box 3, Papers of NAACP, Film 17,412, Part 1, Reel 8, University Publications of America, Bethesda, Md.

Chapter 1

1. Information on the history of the founding of Waco is taken from the following references: *Historic Waco*; Conger, *Highlights of Waco History*; and Sleeper and Hutchins, *Waco and McLennan County, Texas*.

2. The 1914 *Texas Almanac* lists the population of Waco, taken from the 1910 census, as 26,425; the 1925 *Texas Almanac* lists the 1920 population as 38,500.

3. "McLennan County Second in Number of Bales Ginned," *Waco Times Herald* (November 11, 1915): 3.

4. "What Chicago Man Thinks of Waco and Her Resources," *Waco Times Herald* (May 26, 1916): 9.

5. W. Du Bois, "The Waco Horror," 1.

6. *Waco City Directory 1916*, 21–24.

7. Ibid., 59; Kelley, *Handbook of Waco and McLennan County, Texas*, 281; Wallace, *A Spirit So Rare*, 72–105.

8. Wallace, *Our Land, Our Lives*, 115.

9. "Waco's Prosperity Toasted at Street Banquet in 1911," *Waco Tribune Herald*, Centennial Special Section (October 30, 1949); Wallace, *Waco, a Sesquicentennial History*, 104.

10. *Waco City Directory 1916*, 21.

11. See, for example, "Commission Held Brief Session Today," *Waco Times Herald* (May 25,

1916): 6. Waco was not the only Texas town to declare itself the "Athens of Texas"; Sherman also claimed that distinction. In 1930, the "Athenians" of Sherman burned down their own court-house in their determination to kill a black prisoner who was in the building. See Raper, *Tragedy of Lynching*, 319–55.

12. "Horror at Waco," 8.

13. Curry, A *History of Early Waco*, 11–12.

14. Conger, A *Pictorial History of Waco*, 170.

15. Coons, "Waco — a Typical Texas City," 66.

16. *Waco City Directory 1916*, 23.

17. Wallace, *Waco, a Sesquicentennial History*, 68.

18. In "Fact and Myth Streets," *Waco Tribune Herald* (July 6, 2000): 8A, Eugene Baker argues convincingly that the nickname Six-Shooter Junction may have been tacked onto Waco's colorful history in modern times by writers who got carried away with their own tales of the many violent episodes in Waco's past. Baker challenges historians to produce an example of Wacoans calling their city Six-Shooter Junction in those days. Other Texas cities were said to have sported the same unsavory nickname; see, for example, F. Bruce, *Lillie of Six-Shooter Junction*, 1, which applies the nickname to the town of Hempstead, Texas. Nevertheless, the legend that Waco was called Six-Shooter Junction has come to have wide currency and even to have fixed itself in the memories of old-timers. Mary Kemendo Sendon, Waco resident, whom I interviewed when she was ninety-nine years old, claimed the city had indeed been nicknamed Six-Shooter Junction and recalled a story that there had once been a sign by the Waco railway depot that said, "Stop 10 minutes and see a killing." Her uncle told her about the sign and also that the city fathers had had it taken down.

19. Getzendaner, "Early Banking Experiences in Texas," 34.

20. R. Brown (*Strain of Violence*, 236–99) provides a good review of the violence in Central Texas in the second half of the nineteenth century, from Civil War–related conflicts to over-reaction to the real or imagined threat of slave revolts to Indian attacks to outlaw bands to violent feuds that sometimes embroiled several counties.

21. Wallace, *Waco: Texas Crossroads*, 34.

22. Wallace, A *Spirit So Rare*, 155.

23. M. Davis, "Harlots and Hymnals."

24. Anna Mae Bell Warner, interview by LaWanda Ball, 93–95.

25. Caldwell, *Historical Sketch*, 96.

26. Webb (*Texas Rangers*, 382) reports that Sam Bass said philosophically, "There's the last piece of '77 gold I have. It hasn't done me the least bit of good, but that is all right. I will get some more in a few days. So let it gush! It all goes in a lifetime."

27. Miller, *Sam Bass & Gang*, 67, 233–34, 241–62; and Veit, "From Waco to Round Rock."

28. Webb, *Texas Rangers*, 319.

29. The story of Judge Gerald is a compilation of material from "G. B. Gerald Renowned as Jurist, Editor, Confederate Hero and Man of Courage," *Waco Tribune Herald*, Centennial special section (October 30, 1949); Conger, "Insults, Innuendos and Invective"; and Carver, *Brann and the Iconoclast*, 48–50, 164–67.

30. Quoted in Duty, "Waco at the Turn of the Century," 2–3.

31. In the end, the girl's baby was born and died. She eventually signed an affidavit exonerating the man she had accused before she returned to Brazil (Carver, *Brann and the Iconoclast*, 59–111).

32. The story of Brann is taken from Carver, *Brann and the Iconoclast*, and from "Brann Won Fame and Wealth in Short Time He Published 'Iconoclast' Here," *Waco Tribune Herald* Centennial special section (October 30, 1949).

33. "Girl Fires 3 Times at Man; Texas Rangers in Courthouse," *Waco Times Herald* (February 24, 1922): 1. Date of February 24, 1921, on microfilmed newspaper is incorrect.

34. Brundage, ed., *Under Sentence of Death*, 4. Brundage's statistics are carefully sourced, but all statistics on lynchings are necessarily tentative. See Tolnay and Beck, *A Festival of Violence*, 259–67, for a detailed discussion of the problems with the classic inventories of lynchings compiled by the NAACP, the *Chicago Tribune*, and Tuskegee University. Some incidents were probably never reported, and those that were reported may have been recorded or detailed inaccurately by original sources or early compilers. In the most cursory examination of lynching accounts, I immediately discovered a lynching reported in Ginzburg's *100 Years of Lynchings* as having taken place in Houston, Texas, that actually took place in Houston, Mississippi. See *Houston Post* (February 9, 1913): 3. The fact that East Texas was practically ground zero for lynchings, however, is indisputable. In the NAACP study of lynchings between 1889 and 1918, only two states, Georgia and Mississippi, experienced more lynchings than Texas. See NAACP, *Thirty Years of Lynching*.

35. Sleeper and Hutchins, *Waco and McLennan County, Texas*, 30; emphasis mine.

36. These headlines are found in the following issues of the Waco papers: *Waco Times Herald* (April 3, 1916: 1; April 5, 1916: 3, 12; April 9, 1916: 7 [two headlines]; April 17, 1916: 1); *Waco Morning News* (April 3, 1916: 2; April 4, 1916: 1; April 6, 1916: 1, 7; April 11, 1916: 2; April 13, 1916: 12).

37. *Waco Morning News* (April 5, 1916): 2.

38. "Paul Quinn College Has Graduation Tomorrow," *Waco Morning News* (April 19, 1916): 5.

39. *Waco Times Herald* (April 1, 1916): 1; *Waco Morning News* (April 26, 1916): 6. See also "Paul Quinn's 35th Commencement Ends Next Thursday," *Waco Times Herald* (April 18, 1916): 3; "Negroes Gather to Preserve Negro Folk Songs," *Waco Times Herald* (April 29, 1916): 2; "Colored Mothers Have Novel Pie Plan," *Waco Morning News* (April 23, 1916): 7; and "Waco Negro Lawyer Admitted to Bar," *Waco Morning News* (April 12, 1916): 3.

40. Carver, *Brann and the Iconoclast*, 43–44.

41. Oscar Emil Hessdoerfer, interviews by Gary W. Hull and Elizabeth Denham Thompson, 91.

42. Sendon interview.

43. Travis, *Madison Cooper*, 101.

44. See, for instance, ibid., 100; and Travis, "Waco Has a Hero."

45. Greene, *The 50+ Best Books on Texas*, 80–81.

46. Travis, *Madison Cooper*, 24–26.

47. Cooper, *Sironia, Texas*, 2: 1484.

48. Henry (or William) Davis was lynched in the town of Robinson, just outside Waco, in 1889 for attempted rape. See "Judge Lynch: A Short but Effective Term of Court," *Waco Weekly Stock and Farm News* (July 19, 1889): 8; NAACP, *Thirty Years of Lynching*, 95.

49. Sank Majors's death certificate lists him as being "about 28," although that may have been based on nothing more than a guess by the coroner. The newspaper accounts describe him as being "not much over 20 years." See "Sank Majors on Trial for His Life in the 19th Judicial District Court," *Waco Times Herald* (August 2, 1905): 8.

50. "Majors Given Death Penalty by the Jury," *Waco Times Herald* (August 3, 1905): 5.

51. "Followed Officer and Gave Him Trouble," *Waco Times Herald* (July 13, 1905): 2.

52. "Majors Denies His Guilt," 2; and "Majors, the Assailant of Mrs. Robert, Captured," *Waco Times Herald* (July 22, 1905): 5.

53. "Major Denies His Guilt."

54. "Sheriff Tilley Sees the Negro," *Waco Times Herald* (July 23, 1905): 2.

55. "Majors Given Death Penalty."

56. "A New Trial Granted Sank Majors," *Waco Times Herald* (August 6, 1905): 16; and "Majors Was Hanged by a Mob," 5.

57. "Unjust Criticism," *Waco Times Herald* (August 7, 1905): 4.

58. The following account of the lynching is taken from "Majors Was Hanged by a Mob."

59. Apparently, this custom of saving portions of the body of lynching victims did not begin with the lynching of blacks in the South. Richard Brown (*Strain of Violence*, 155) describes "the practice of taking trophies from the bodies of vigilante victims" as early as 1799, with the display of the head of a lynched outlaw in Kentucky.

60. Author's interview with Nona Baker, age fifty-four, June 19, 2000.

61. Author's interview with Nona Baker, August 8, 2001, the ninety-sixth anniversary of the lynching.

62. For another version of the same tradition, see Maggie Langham Washington, interviews by Doni Van Ryswyk; and by Marla Luffer, p. 51.

63. "Remains Sent to Gurley," *Waco Times Herald* (August 8, 1905): 2. Gurley was a tiny town in Falls County that has since disappeared. SAP was the San Antonio and Aransas Pass Railway.

64. "Negroes Whipped by Vigilance Committee," *Waco Times Herald* (August 10, 1905): 3.

65. "Reports Have Been Somewhat Exaggerated," *Waco Times Herald* (August 11, 1905): 8; "Officers Keeping Down Incendiary Talk," *Waco Times Herald* (August 12, 1905): 8; and "Another Negro Fined Heavily by Judge Cammack," *Waco Times Herald* (August 10, 1905): 8.

66. Henry Smith, a retarded and also possibly mentally ill black man living in Paris, was accused of raping and murdering a four-year-old girl in an effort to avenge himself on her father. The father, Henry Vance, was a police officer of evil repute who had beaten Smith when he was arrested on a charge of being drunk and disorderly. The details of the murder of the child were apparently highly exaggerated in news reports, and the rape charge was completely fabricated. Smith tried to run away but was captured at Clow, Arkansas, and brought back to Paris on the train; he was viewed along the way by thousands of spectators. A time was appointed in advance for his public torture and execution without any pretense whatever of a trial or other due process. He was carried through the streets from the train on a wagon and then bound on a scaffold and tortured with hot irons by the child's father, brother, and two uncles for an hour before he was burned to death. A cheering crowd of ten thousand watched the entire spectacle and then seized pieces of his clothing and even the charcoal from the fire for souvenirs. See Wells-Barnett, *Southern Horrors*, 91–98.

67. "Negro Saved by County Judge at Paris, Texas," *Waco Times Herald* (August 18, 1905): 3.

68. I have yet to discover an instance in which a determined white man standing up to a lynch mob was killed, although some mobs came close. During the Omaha race riot of 1919, reformist mayor Edward Smith was hanged by a mob but survived. According to some accounts, the riot was orchestrated through inflammatory articles planted in the *Omaha Bee* under the direction of local political boss Tom Dennison. Dennison wanted to discredit the mayor and police commissioner Dean Ringer so that his own candidate, James Dahlman, could be elected. Gen. Leonard Wood, who sent troops to Omaha, accused the Dennison machine of also supplying potential rioters with alcohol and free taxi service to the scene. See Luebke, *Nebraska*, 245–49. In most cases, would-be lynchers did not dare kill a white man for fear they would be prosecuted.

69. "Paris Negro Released, There Being No Bill," *Waco Times Herald* (August 20, 1905): 1.

Chapter 2

1. This brief description of the beginnings of the NAACP is not intended to be an exhaustive analysis of the organization or the protest movements that preceded it, such as the Niagara Movement, but simply a setting of the scene that led to the Waco Horror. For more detail about the beginnings of the NAACP, see, for instance, Kellogg, *NAACP*; Lewis, *W. E. B. Du Bois*; and Wedin, *Inheritors of the Spirit*.

2. This account of the Springfield race riot is taken from Senechal, *Sociogenesis of a Race Riot*.

3. Ibid., 27.

4. W. Walling, "Race War in the North," 530.

5. Senechal, *Sociogenesis of a Race Riot*, 173.

6. Ibid., 165.

7. Ibid., 158–59.

8. *Illinois State Register* (August 15, 1908), quoted in ibid., 42.

9. Senechal, *Sociogenesis of a Race Riot*, 47.

10. Boylan, *Revolutionary Lives*, 51.

11. Ibid., 62–63; A. Walling, ed., *William English Walling*, 13.

12. A. Walling, *William English Walling*, 9.

13. Boylan, *Revolutionary Lives*, 98–102.

14. Ovington, *Walls Came Tumbling Down*, 102.

15. *Illinois State Journal* editorial, quoted in A. Walling, *William English Walling*, 531.

16. W. Walling, "Race War in the North," 531.

17. Vardaman and Tillman were both infamous radically racist politicians. James Kimble-Vardaman (1861–1930) was first governor of Mississippi and then a U.S. senator from Mississippi. "Pitchfork" Ben Tillman (1847–1918) held the positions of governor of South Carolina and later of U.S. senator from that state.

18. W. Walling, "Race War in the North," 534.

19. Ibid.

20. Wedin, *Inheritors of the Spirit*, 106.

21. Boylan, *Revolutionary Lives*, 156.

22. Ibid., 157.

23. Ovington, *Walls Came Tumbling Down*, 106; Boylan, *Revolutionary Lives*, 74–75.

24. Kellogg, *NAACP*, 297–99 (Appendix A).

25. Ibid., 19–21; Wedin, *Inheritors of the Spirit*, 109–111.

26. Clarence Darrow, speech, Proceedings of the 1910 Annual Conference of the NAACP [see introduction, note 6].

27. Nock, "What We All Stand For," 55.

28. Boylan, *Revolutionary Lives*, 172.

29. Ibid., 72–74, 175–80.

30. Hixson, *Moorfield Storey*, 134; Howe, *Portrait of an Independent*, 359.

31. Howe, *Portrait of an Independent*, 22, 39.

32. Ovington, *Walls Came Tumbling Down*, 129.

33. Hixson, *Moorfield Storey*, 111. This information seems to be based on an interview conducted by Storey biographer William Hixson with one of Storey's sons.

34. Ibid., 145, 194–97. Hixson argues in part that Storey applied this model more in fighting for Philippine independence than in fighting for American blacks, but it seems to me that the NAACP revived and made use of many aspects of the abolitionist model very successfully. Storey's personal focus was on leading the legal battles of the NAACP.

35. Moorfield Storey to George Foster Peabody, June 26, 1919 (letterbook copy), Moorfield Storey Papers, Massachusetts Historical Society.

36. Kellogg, *NAACP*, 205–206; Howe, *Portrait of an Independent*, 255–56; Hixson, *Moorfield Storey*, 135–38.

37. Kellogg, *NAACP*, 185–87; Howe, *Portrait of an Independent*, 256–57; Hixson, *Moorfield Storey*, 139–42.

38. Kellogg, *NAACP*, 241–45; Howe, *Portrait of an Independent*, 257.

39. Kirchwey, "Oswald Garrison Villard," 340.

40. Gannett, "Villard and His 'Nation,'" 79.

41. Villard, *Fighting Years*, 45–62. This was not the more renowned driving of the golden spike that completed the first transcontinental railroad at Promontory, Utah, on May 10, 1869.

42. Humes, *Oswald Garrison Villard*, 10–11; Villard, *Fighting Years*, 123.

43. Villard, *Fighting Years*, 123.

44. Humes, *Oswald Garrison Villard*, 9.

45. Oswald Garrison Villard to Fanny Garrison Villard, [April] 1902, Oswald Garrison Villard Papers, bMS Am 1323 (4006), by permission of the Houghton Library, Harvard University (hereafter Villard Papers).

46. Kellogg, NAACP, 14; Wedin, *Inheritors of the Spirit*, 72.

47. Kellogg, NAACP, 13, 18–19.

48. Villard, *Fighting Years*, 194.

49. Lewis, *W. E. B. Du Bois*, 408.

50. Kellogg, NAACP, 97; Lewis, *W. E. B. Du Bois*, 476. The office at 70 Fifth Avenue was twice the cost of the space in the *Post* building, $108 a month.

51. Humes, *Oswald Garrison Villard*, 82–83.

52. Villard, *Fighting Years*, 199.

53. Wedin, *Inheritors of the Spirit*, 112.

54. Humes, *Oswald Garrison Villard*, 3.

55. Lewis, *W. E. B. Du Bois*, 360.

56. Kellogg, NAACP, 33–34.

57. Ovington quoted in ibid., 34.

58. Wedin, *Inheritors of the Spirit*, 137.

59. W. Du Bois, *The Autobiography of W. E. B. Du Bois*, 256–57. See also Oswald Garrison Villard to Paul E. Johnson, May 4, 1908, Villard Papers, bMS Am 1323 (1931), by permission of the Houghton Library, Harvard University. Villard says in the letter to Johnson, "Feeling as you do, like my other southern friends and *like my own wife, for instance* [emphasis mine], I should never think of asking you to sit down at table with a colored person. I should give you absolute liberty of conscience in the matter, and all I should ask in return would be liberty to do as I think right in return."

60. W. Du Bois, *Souls of Black Folk*, 44–45.

61. Russell, *Bare Hands and Stone Walls*, 219.

62. Ibid., 219–20.

63. "The Detective's Report," 1.

64. "Mrs. Alfred Cranford Talks," *Salt Lake City Broad Ax* (June 6, 1899): 1.

65. Ibid.

66. Wells-Barnett, *Lynch Law in Georgia*, 13–18.

67. Quoted in Ginzburg, *100 Years of Lynchings*, 18.

68. "The Detective's Report."

69. Ibid.; Litwack, *Trouble in Mind*, 281. According to Litwack (534), the tale about the piece of Hose's heart intended for Georgia's governor appeared only in a *New York Times* story of April 25, 1899.

70. W. Du Bois, *The Autobiography of W. E. B. Du Bois*, 222.

71. Ibid.

72. W. Du Bois, *Souls of Black Folk*, 230–31; Lewis, *W. E. B. Du Bois*, 228. Another event that probably influenced Du Bois to leave the South was the nearly weeklong Atlanta "race riot" of 1906 in which twenty-five blacks were killed and more than two hundred people, mostly blacks, were injured. See Litwack, *Trouble in Mind*, 315–16; and Crowe, "Racial Massacre in Atlanta," 171–72. In his *Autobiography* Du Bois writes that, as soon as he heard about the riot, he hurried back to

Atlanta from Alabama to protect his wife and six-year-old daughter: "I bought a Winchester double-barreled shotgun and two dozen rounds of shells filled with buckshot. If a white mob had stepped on the campus where I lived I would without hesitation have sprayed their guts over the grass. They did not come. They went to south Atlanta where the police let them steal and kill" (286).

73. W. Du Bois, *The Autobiography of W. E. B. Du Bois*, 223ff.

74. Ovington, *Walls Came Tumbling Down*, 107–108. "Litany at Atlanta," was an impassioned cry to God for help, which Du Bois wrote while traveling from Alabama back to Atlanta after the 1906 race riot began. See Lewis, *W. E. B. Du Bois*, 335–36.

75. Van Deusen, *J. E. Spingarn*, 49; emphasis mine.

76. Ross, *J. E. Spingarn*, 4.

77. Van Deusen, *J. E. Spingarn*, 60.

78. Ross, *J. E. Spingarn*, 5–6; Van Deusen, *J. E. Spingarn*, 76.

79. Ross, *J. E. Spingarn*, 6.

80. See examples of anti-Semitic attacks on Spingarn in Van Deusen, *J. E. Spingarn*, 76–77, 109.

81. Ross, *J. E. Spingarn*, 8–9.

82. Lewis, *W. E. B. Du Bois*, 475–76.

83. Ross, *J. E. Spingarn*, 11–12.

84. Villard, *Fighting Years*, 175.

85. Howe, *Portrait of an Independent*, 126.

86. Ross, *J. E. Spingarn*, 253.

87. Kellogg, *NAACP*, 62–63; Ross, *J. E. Spingarn*, 20–21.

88. Ross, *J. E. Spingarn*, 21.

89. Quoted in ibid., 25.

90. Ibid., 23.

91. Ibid., 29.

92. Ibid., 33.

93. Ibid., 28.

94. Ibid., 69.

95. Lewis, *W. E. B. Du Bois*, 495–96; see also Kellogg, *NAACP*, 103; Wedin, *Inheritors of the Spirit*, 141.

96. W. Du Bois, *Dusk of Dawn*, 255.

97. Ovington, *Walls Came Tumbling Down*, 3–5.

98. Wedin, *Inheritors of the Spirit*, 22.

99. Ovington, *Walls Came Tumbling Down*, 11.

100. Ibid., 12.

101. Ibid.

102. Ibid., 54.

103. Ibid., 79–80.

104. Ibid., 88–99.

105. Wedin, *Inheritors of the Spirit*, 92, 102; Ovington, *Walls Came Tumbling Down*, 48–49.

106. Ovington, *Walls Came Tumbling Down*, 46.

107. Villard, *Fighting Years*, 197.

108. Ovington, *Walls Came Tumbling Down*, 46.

109. Anti-Lynching Campaign, 1912–1955, Group 1, Box C-336, Papers of NAACP, Film 17,412, Part 7, Series A, Reel 1, University Publications of America, Bethesda, Md.; hereafter Anti-Lynching Campaign.

110. Minutes of the Meetings of the Board of Directors, January 3, 1916, p. 21, from Board

Meeting Minutes, 1909–1924, Papers of NAACP, Film 17,412, Part 1, Reel 1, University Publications of America, Bethesda, Md. (hereafter Board Meeting Minutes, 1909–1924).

111. "Lynched on Stage; Shots Came from Pit," *New York Times* (April 21, 1911): 1.

112. Kellogg, *NAACP*, 210–11.

113. "A Lynching of a New Sort," *New York Times* (April 22, 1911): 12.

114. Downey and Hyser, *No Crooked Death*, 32ff; Nock, "What We All Stand For," 53.

115. Downey and Hyser, *No Crooked Death*, 101, 155; Kellogg, *NAACP*, 212–13; Nock, "What We All Stand For," 55–57.

116. Downey and Hyser, *No Crooked Death*, 61, 98, 103–105.

117. Chapin Brinsmade to W. S. Willis of Waco on the lynching of William Williams at Franklin, Texas, April 17, 1914; Chapin Brinsmade to John Slater of El Paso on the Williams lynching, April 3, 1914; both in Anti-Lynching Campaign.

118. "Mob Lynches a Negress," *New York Times* (April 1, 1914): 3.

119. Chapin Brinsmade to Mrs. E. W. Anderson, April 22, 1914, in Anti-Lynching Campaign.

120. James Harold Coleman to MaBelle A. White, May 15, 1914, in ibid.

121. "Mob Rule, Vengeance Led Temple to Public Lynching," *Temple Daily Telegram* (July 29, 1966); "Mysterious Murder Is Puzzle to Authorities," *Temple Daily Telegram* (July 30, 1915); "The Beast Is Abroad," *Temple Daily Telegram* (July 30, 1915).

122. From the *Temple Daily Telegram*: "Negro Suspect Is Caught at Rogers" (July 31, 1915); "Brutal Black Murderer Is Burned at the Stake" (July 31, 1915).

123. "The Late Unpleasantness," *Temple Daily Telegram* (August 4, 1915).

124. "The Burden," *The Crisis* (January 1916): 145.

125. The Will Stanley lynching photograph appears in Allen, ed., *Without Sanctuary*, nos. 25 and 26. The victim is misidentified as Jesse Washington, who was the victim of the Waco Horror about a year later.

126. Minutes of the Meetings of the Board of Directors, January 3, 1916, p. 2, Board Meeting Minutes, 1909–1924.

127. Ibid., 25.

128. When Peabody died in 1934, the *New York Times* memorialized him by dwelling on the 145 trips he had made across the Atlantic Ocean. Peabody had gotten into the habit of crossing the Atlantic both ways three times a year—not, he said, because he particularly enjoyed ocean voyaging, but because "he disliked a sedentary life" ("P. G. Peabody Dies; Good Will 'Envoy,'" *New York Times* [February 26, 1934], Sec. L+, 17). Also see T. W. Herringshaw, *Herringshaw's National Library of American Biography*, #110, 1909–1914. Peabody meant well but had little understanding of anyone outside his own race and class. In the early 1920s, he wrote a series of letters to the NAACP complaining bitterly that he had urged his friends and relations to hire black people as servants in order to help the race, and that most of his friends had thereafter complained that the black servants they hired at his urging were uniformly disappointing—lazy and insubordinate instead of grateful and obsequious. See Correspondence, 1910–1939, Group 1, Series C, Box 71, 0402 Peabody, Philip; Papers of NAACP, Film 17,412, Part 7, Series A, Reel 20, University Publications of America, Bethesda, Md. (hereafter Correspondence, 1910–1939).

129. Philip G. Peabody to Moorfield Storey, February 14, 1916, Correspondence, 1910–1939.

130. Philip G. Peabody to Roy Nash Esq., March 2, 1914, Correspondence, 1910–1939; original emphasis.

131. Ibid.

132. Kellogg, *NAACP*, 217.

133. Anti-Lynching Campaign, "Memorandum for Mr. Philip G. Peabody on Lynch-Law and the Practicability of a Successful Attack Thereon," by Roy Nash, May 22, 1916, pp. 22–23.

134. Ibid., 34.

135. Kellogg, *NAACP*, 217–18.

Chapter 3

1. Wherever Elisabeth Freeman's name appears in print in documents of the time, her first name is spelled "Elizabeth," but in most of her own correspondence, she signed her name "Elisabeth." I use her spelling throughout this book. I determined Freeman's age from the records of the White Star Line's steamship *Baltic*, which arrived in New York on September 15, 1911.

2. The term *suffragette* was first applied to the activists of Emmeline Pankhurst's Women's Social and Political Union (WSPU) by the *Daily Mail* in January 1906. These women were also sometimes called "martyrettes" because of their hunger strikes in prison. Since the word *suffragette* was often used derisively, however, serious American students of the women's suffrage movement usually prefer to call suffrage activists "suffragists." See Harrison, *Connecting Links*, 48, and Morrell, *"Black Friday,"* 18, for the origin of the word *suffragette*. I use the term "suffragette" here to refer specifically to Parkhurst's WSPU militants, as opposed to other suffrage activists.

3. "Elizabeth Freeman: Lecturer on Woman Suffrage," unpublished pamphlet, National American Woman Suffrage Association Records (hereafter NAWSA Records), General Correspondence, 1839–1961, Freeman, Elisabeth, Containers 11 and 12, Reels 7 and 8, Library of Congress. Quotations from *Buffalo Courier* (September 30, 1911), and *Buffalo Express* (September 30, 1911).

4. Elisabeth Freeman to Agnes Ryan, July 28, 1913. The letters cited in this book between Ryan and Freeman are all from NAWSA Records, General Correspondence, 1839–1961, Freeman, Elisabeth, Containers 11 and 12, Reels 7 and 8, Library of Congress. Please note that both women sometimes wrote more than one letter to each other on the same day.

5. "Letter from Rev. A. H. Shaw," 142.

6. Ibid.

7. Harrison, *Connecting Links*, 137.

8. Morrell, *"Black Friday,"* 11.

9. Ibid., 13.

10. Ibid.; and Pankhurst, *My Own Story*, 28–31.

11. Morrell, *"Black Friday,"* 21.

12. Ibid., 20.

13. Ibid., 21.

14. "Elizabeth Freeman: Lecturer on Woman Suffrage."

15. WSPU pamphlet in the Fawcett Library in London.

16. Harrison, *Connecting Links*, 125.

17. Harrison, *Connecting Links*, 143; Morrell, *"Black Friday,"* 32ff.

18. "Letter from an American," *Woman's Journal* (January 7, 1911): 4.

19. Luscomb, "American Girls Abroad," June 10, 1911, 178–79.

20. Luscomb, "American Girls Abroad," June 24, 1911, 195.

21. Morrell, *"Black Friday,"* 56.

22. Harrison, *Connecting Links*, 190.

23. Davison's story is told in Pankhurst, *My Own Story*, 313–15.

24. Luscomb, "American Girls Abroad," June 10, 1911, 178.

25. "She Defends London Window Smashing," *New York Times* (March 12, 1912): 1.

26. Rosalie Jones was a fascinating character in her own right, a Long Island socialite who found her identity and heart's work in the suffrage movement. See George DeWan, "A Pioneer for Female Power," Long Island: Our Past; http://www.lihistory.com/histpast/past1215.htm.

27. "The Hike to Washington," *Woman Voter and the Newsletter* (March 1913): 10.

28. "Wearied Hikers Plod On in the Dark," *New York Times* (February 14, 1913): 3.

29. Ibid. The irony of this remark is, of course, that there was an element of racism within the suffragist movement. Some American suffragist leaders knew that southerners opposed women's suffrage because of fear that black women would vote; therefore, these suffragists discouraged the participation of black women in the movement and sometimes made statements implying that there would be ways of keeping black women from voting, even if women's suffrage passed. See, for instance, Weatherford, *A History of the American Suffragist Movement*, 177. In the October 1911 *Crisis*, Du Bois quotes Anna Howard Shaw, president of NAWSA, as saying, "Do not touch the Negro problem. It will offend the South" (Lewis, *W. E. B. Du Bois*, 417).

30. "Suffrage Hikers Send Wilson a Flag," *New York Times* (February 27, 1913): 6; "Message to Wilson Taken from Hikers," *New York Times* (February 28, 1913): 3.

31. "Gen. Jones Dodges the Color Question," *New York Times* (February 20, 1913): 6.

32. "Cardinal Gets Flag and Praises Hikers," *New York Times* (February 26, 1913): 10.

33. Emphasis mine.

34. "Message to Wilson Taken from Hikers"; and "Why Message Was Taken," *New York Times* (February 28, 1913): 3.

35. "Parade Struggles to Victory Despite Disgraceful Scenes," 73.

36. Ibid.

37. Sheridan Harvey, "Marching for the Vote," 2.

38. Elisabeth Freeman to Agnes Ryan, July 12, 1913.

39. Ibid.

40. Elisabeth Freeman to Agnes Ryan, July 28, 1913.

41. Agnes E. Ryan to Elisabeth Freeman, June 10, 1913.

42. Agnes E. Ryan to Elisabeth Freeman, June 13, 1913.

43. Elisabeth Freeman to Agnes Ryan, June 30, 1913.

44. Elisabeth Freeman to Agnes Ryan, July 12, 1913.

45. Elisabeth Freeman to Agnes Ryan, June 30, 1913.

46. Agnes Ryan to Elisabeth Freeman, July 17, 1913.

47. Elisabeth Freeman to Agnes Ryan, July 18, 1913.

48. Lewis, *W. E. B. Du Bois*, 417-19.

49. *New York Evening Post* (January 24, 1914).

50. Elisabeth Freeman to Caroline Lexow Babcock, July 9, 1915, Babcock-Hurlburt Papers, Schlesinger Library, Radcliffe Institute for Advanced Study, Harvard University.

51. E. DuBois, *Harriot Stanton Blatch*, 173-81.

52. Annette Finnegan to Mary Sumner Boyd, August 31, 1916, Annette Finnegan Collection, Mss. 158c, Woman's Collection, Texas Woman's University Library.

53. "'Suffrage First,'" 8.

54. "Women Suffrage Workers Have Their Petition," *Waco Morning News* (April 2, 1916): 19.

55. "Officers Chosen by Texas Suffragists," *Dallas Morning News* (May 13,1916): 8. Freeman's name is third on a long list of women contributing five dollars each to the "Joseph Weldon Bailey Monument Fund" to be spent on the suffrage campaign, in ironic tribute to a speech made by former Texas senator Bailey in which he compared women before voting to a clear goblet of water and, after voting, to the same water blackened with ink.

56. "State Equal Suffrage Meeting Opens May 10," *Dallas Morning News* (May 7, 1916): 18.

57. "'Suffrage First.'"

58. "Women Pledge $5,800 for Equal Suffrage," *Dallas Morning News* (May 12, 1916): 4.

Chapter 4

1. "John Dollins Dies," 1.

2. "Slogan Is Harmony and Efficiency," *Waco Morning News* (April 13, 1916): 8.

3. "Weevil Destined to Infest Entire Cotton Section," *Waco Times Herald* (April 14, 1916): 1.

4. "Boll Weevils Taking Cotton," *Waco Semi-Weekly Tribune* (June 21, 1916): 7.

5. "Cotton Culture," Handbook of Texas Online; http://www.tsha.utexas.edu/handbook/online/articles/view/CC/afc3.html.

6. Waco, like most southern cities, had already enthusiastically greeted productions of Thomas Dixon's play *The Clansman*, first produced in Norfolk, Virginia, on September 22, 1905; *The Birth of a Nation* is based on this play. *The Clansman* played in Waco on December 15, 1905, at the auditorium to great acclaim. The review in the *Waco Times Herald*, quoting a Confederate veteran who had seen the play, begins, "This is as near real as can be, and is not exaggerated in the least . . . I speak from observation, for I lived in the days when the events pictured tonight were real." See "At the Auditorium: The Clansman," *Waco Times Herald* (December 16, 1905): 4.

7. "Mighty Spectacle Is Birth of a Nation," *Waco Times Herald* (November 12, 1915): 4.

8. "Address Is Issued against Mob Law," *Waco Morning News* (November 7, 1915): 5.

9. "Gen. Pershing Knows Where Bandit Villa Is," *Waco Times Herald* (May 7, 1916): 1. Pershing's troops never found Villa.

10. "Texas Border Raided Again," *Waco Morning News* (May 8, 1916): 1.

11. "Militia of Texas, Arizona, and New Mexico Ordered to Report to General Funston for Duty on the Mexican Border," *Waco Times Herald* (May 9, 1916): 1; "President Wilson Calls for the Mobilization of the Texas National Guard," *Waco Morning News* (May 10, 1916): 1.

12. "Great Ovation Is Given Waco Soldier Boys as They Start for Service," *Waco Morning News* (May 11, 1916): 1.

13. "Company K Ordered to Report for Duty on Mexican Border," *Waco Times Herald* (May 9, 1916): 5.

14. "Germans Make More Gains in Offensive at Verdun," *Waco Morning News* (May 8, 1916): 1.

15. "Reply to Germany Gives Assurance That While the Submarines Follow Instructions There Will Be No Break," *Waco Times Herald* (May 8, 1916): 1.

16. "Sheriff's Parents Return to Old Home," *Waco Times Herald* (April 19, 1914); "Death Last Night of Sheriff Fleming's Mother," *Waco Times Herald* (March 24, 1915): 4.

17. "S. S. Fleming for Sheriff," 8. Also, "Sam Fleming Is Running on Record," 11.

18. "S. S. Fleming for Sheriff," 5.

19. "Why Not Vote for Bob Buchanan for Sheriff?" *Waco Times Herald* (July 21, 1912): 3.

20. "Former Sheriff Fleming Buried," 14.

21. William Robert "Bob" Poage, interviews by Thomas L. Charlton, Robert T. Miller, and Phillip A. Thompson, 122–27.

22. "S. S. Fleming for Sheriff," 5.

23. "M'Lennan County in Colquitt Column by Majority of 49: Surratt Loses by 37 Votes, Fleming Wins by Margin of 21," *Waco Times Herald* (July 31, 1912): 1.

24. "Final Words from Bob Buchanan," 10.

25. "Influential Citizens Endorse Bob Buchanan for Sheriff McLennan County," *Waco Times Herald* (July 14, 1918): 26. Buchanan's brother Coke was also a policeman. Coke Buchanan was killed on the job in Borger, Texas, in 1927 by a "bandit" named Whitey Walker (see "Illness Ends Fatally for Bob Buchanan," *Waco Times Herald* [December 4, 1929]: 1).

26. W. Du Bois, "The Waco Horror," 3.

27. "Attacking Negro Killed by Officer Bob Buchanan," *Waco Morning News* (November 9, 1915): 6.

28. *Waco Morning News* (May 8, 1916): 1.

Chapter 5

1. Details vary in newspaper coverage of the Waco Horror. Even official court documents are not entirely reliable. Robinson is sometimes called Robinsonville, the town's original name. The Fryers' neighbor, "Chris Simon," is referred to in a variety of ways. In one news story, Ruby Fryer is called "Lucy" Fryer, and the Fryer name is frequently misspelled as "Fryar." I have tried to use correct spellings and verify details wherever possible. Ruby Fryer was born on November 8, 1894; George Fryer Jr. was born on September 3, 1901, according to my interview with Lucy Wollitz Kirkland, age seventy-six, July 4, 2000. "Lucy Bee," as Lucy Wollitz Kirkland is known, is the granddaughter of the Lucy Fryer who was killed on May 8, 1916, in Robinson, and the daughter of Ruby Fryer Wollitz. The "Bee" stands for Beatrice. Lucy Bee was named after her grandmother and the aunt who died at the age of nine.

2. Freeman, "Waco Lynching," 7; "Negro Confesses to Terrible Crime at Robinsonville," *Waco Times Herald* (May 9, 1916): 5.

3. Freeman, "Waco Lynching," 8; "Statement of Facts" (transcript of trial testimony), testimony of Leslie Stegall, *State of Texas v. Jesse Washington*, No. 4141, 54th District Court, McLennan County, March Term A.D. 1916, 7, from NAACP Archives, NAACP Administrative File, Subfile under Lynching: Waco, Texas, 1916, Group 1, Box C-370, Library of Congress (hereafter "Statement of Facts").

4. "Negro Confesses to Terrible Crime at Robinsonville," 1.

5. Author's interview with Lucy Wollitz Kirkland, June 23, 2000.

6. McLennan County, Texas, Marriage Records, vol. 2 (January 1871–July 1892): 125.

7. Gravestone of Beatrice Pearl Fryer, Lorena, Texas, cemetery.

8. "Negro Confesses to Terrible Crime at Robinsonville," 5.

9. "Murder of Robinson Woman Breaks McLennan Records for Fiendish Brutality," *Waco Morning News* (May 9, 1916): 1.

10. "Statement of Facts," testimony of Dr. J. H. Maynard, 1–2.

11. "Lee Jenkins' Vivid Career Comes to End," *Waco Times Herald* (June 10, 1929): 1.

12. "Ex-Sheriff Leslie Stegall Dies in Waco," *Waco News Tribune* (October 12, 1953): 1.

13. "Statement of Facts," testimony of Criss [*sic*] Simon, 6.

14. "Negro Confesses to Terrible Crime at Robinsonville," 5.

15. Freeman, "Waco Lynching," 7.

16. Ibid., 10.

17. Author's interview with Thomas Hague, age sixty-nine. Hague told me that Robinson or Robinsonville was originally a settlement of primarily German immigrants, established only three years after Waco was founded. The Germans of Robinson tended to stick together, and English immigrants like the Fryers and the Hagues also tended to stick together. Lucy Fryer, according to Hague's father, was "an extremely beautiful woman." Judging from available photos of Lucy, she may well have been a beauty as a young woman. But a photo taken of her in middle age records the image of a rather ordinary looking, roly-poly little person, her early loveliness dimmed perhaps by years of hard farm work and the pain of losing a beloved child at a tender age.

18. Hall, *Revolt against Chivalry*, 207.

19. Wells, *Southern Horrors*, 96. For an abridged version of the story of the lynching of Henry Smith, see chapter 1, note 66.

20. Hall, *Revolt against Chivalry*, 129.

21. Freeman, "Waco Lynching," 7.

22. Ibid., 8.

23. Ibid., 17–18. Washington was probably "driving" a buggy or wagon.

24. "Negro Confesses to Terrible Crime at Robinsonville," 5.

25. Ibid.

26. Freeman, "Waco Lynching," 8.

27. "Statement of Facts," testimony of Lee Jenkins, 5.

28. "Statement of Facts," testimony of Leslie Stegall, 7.

29. "Negro Confesses to Terrible Crime at Robinsonville," 5.

30. Ibid.

31. Freeman, "Waco Lynching," 10.

32. "Statement of Facts," testimony of Sam Fleming and Lee Jenkins, 4–5.

33. "Sheriff's Alertness Saves Negro's Life," 7; "Sworn Confession by Jesse Washington," 4; "Grand Jury Indicts Slayer of Mrs. Fryar," 5.

34. "Sheriff's Alertness Saves Negro's Life."

35. Ibid.

36. "Farmers from Robinson Form Mob and Search Jail for Black Brute," 1.

37. Ibid.

38. "Sheriff's Alertness Saves Negro's Life"; "Special Session of Grand Jury Called to Consider Robinson Murder Case," 5.

39. "[Illegible] Body on a Robinson Farm," *Waco Semi-Weekly Tribune* (May 10, 1916): 5.

40. Hall, *Revolt against Chivalry*, 150. "The myth of the black rapist reached pathological proportions at the turn of the century, in part because of its congruence with the exaggerated sexual tensions of a dying Victorianism," says Hall (148).

41. The misspelling "Fryar" appears often in the newspaper accounts of the crime. In the court transcription of the confession, the name is also consistently misspelled, but as "Frier."

42. Several phrases that don't appear in the actual transcribed confession were added to the newspaper version: "I then" was added at this point to make sense of the edited sentence. The phrase "and went about forty steps south of the planter" was added in the next paragraph, and the word "woods," which appears a little later in the same sentence is a substitution for "weeds," which appeared in the transcribed confession.

43. Transcript of confession says "twist."

44. Original confession appears in "Statement of Facts," 8–9. The published confession appears in "Sworn Confession by Jesse Washington"; "Special Session of Grand Jury Called to Consider Robinson Murder Case"; and "Murderer of Mrs. Lucy Fryer to Be Tried Next Monday," *Waco Semi-Weekly Tribune* (May 13, 1916): 2.

45. See Elisabeth Freeman to Royal Freeman Nash in [undated] series of letters. The letters and wires exchanged between Nash and Freeman about her investigation in Waco are found in the NAACP Archives, NAACP Administrative File, Subfile under Lynching: Waco, Texas, 1916, Group 1, Box C-370, Library of Congress (hereafter Freeman/Nash Letters).

46. See chapter 9. Freeman implied during her NAACP-sponsored speaking tour to publicize the story of the lynching of Jesse Washington that she believed that the rape "was written into the lad's confession" ("Phillip Peabody Gives $20,000 to Fight Lynching," *Chicago Defender* [August 5, 1916]).

47. Freeman, "Waco Lynching," 11.

48. Nona Baker, letter to editor of *Waco Tribune Herald*, undated [summer 1998].

49. Freeman, "Waco Lynching," 4.

50. Author's interviews with Bill Wuebker, age seventy-three, and with Martha Frosch Kettler, age ninety.

51. "[Illegible] White Man for Crime Which Boy Was Lynched," 7.

52. On his death certificate, A. T. Smith's birthday is listed as January 24, 1888, which would have made him twenty-eight when Jesse Washington was lynched. But A. T. Smith describes himself in an interrogatory in one of the libel suits related to his publication of the *Chicago Defender* story as age twenty-seven. The interrogation was probably completed during the fall of 1916.

53. Nash memorandum to J. E. Spingarn, August 11, 1916, Anti-Lynching Campaign. There is a longer discussion of the fate of A. T. Smith and of George Fryer's lawsuits for libel in chapter 9.

54. Freeman, "Waco Lynching," 6, 11.

55. Ibid., 11–12.

56. Kettler interview. Kettler told me that after the lynching of Jesse Washington, black children in Robinson made up a rhyme that went, "I never did and I never will/Pick cotton for Old Man Fryer in Robinsonville."

57. "Grand Jury Indicts Slayer of Mrs. Fryar."

58. "Colorful Career of Noted Jurist Closed by Death," 1.

59. Ibid.

60. Freeman, "Waco Lynching," 4, 17.

61. "J. W. Taylor Jr., Veteran Lawyer of Waco, Is Dead," *Waco News Tribune* (August 28, 1947): 1; "J. W. Taylor Is Dead; Funeral Service Today," *Waco Times Herald* (August 28, 1947): 1; "Society of Yesterday," *Waco Tribune Herald*, centennial special section (October 30, 1949). Death certificate of Joe Willis Taylor.

62. "Frank M. Fitzpatrick Sr. Dies; Longtime Lawyer," *Waco News Tribune* (January 31, 1973): 8B; "Rites Thursday for Longtime Waco Attorney," *Waco Times Herald* (January 31, 1973): 1A; death certificate for Frank Minnock Fitzpatrick Sr.; "Deserved Compliment for Frank Fitzpatrick," *Waco Times Herald* (April 12, 1916): 12.

63. "Frank Fitzpatrick to Make Race for Floater," *Waco Times Herald* (June 11, 1916): 6; "Frank Fitzpatrick," *Waco Semi-Weekly Tribune* (June 14, 1916): 12.

64. "C. H. Machen, Lawyer and Veteran, Dies," *Dallas Morning News* (February 19, 1943): 2–4.

65. "Kyle Vick's Last Rites Here Today," *Waco News Tribune* (October 17, 1956): 18; "Veteran Waco Attorney Dies Early Today," *Waco Times Herald* (October 16, 1956): 1; death certificate of Kyle Vick Sr.

66. "Bowden Hays, Jr., Dies from Injuries in Auto Accident," *Waco News Tribune* (August 7, 1922): 1; "Injuries Fatal for Bowden Hays," *Waco Times Herald* (August 7, 1922): 3; "Attendants Announced for the Hays-Campbell Wedding," *Waco Times Herald* (December 25, 1921): 3.

67. Walters, "Great War in Waco, Texas," 63.

68. The story of the incident is told in the following *Waco Times Herald* articles: "Wife Rescues Man from 5 Masked Men" (June 7, 1921): 1; "Alleged Whitecappers Placed under Bond; Cummings Is Tarred" (July 9, 1921): 1; "Man Tarred and Feathered Says He'll Leave Waco" (July 10, 1921): 3; "Whitecapping Cases Will Come Up Wednesday" (July 12, 1921): 3; "One Dismissed in Whitecap Cases, $1000 Bond for Three; Make Rush to Sign Bonds," (July 13, 1921): 1. Also see Walters, "Great War in Waco," 62–64. I am much indebted to Katherine Walters for sharing information on this subject and also providing me with copies of court documents relating to George Fryer's libel lawsuits over the article published in the *Paul Quinn Weekly*, reprinted from the *Chicago Defender*, that announced Fryer's "arrest" for the murder of his wife.

69. "Grand Jury Indicts Slayer of Mrs. Fryar"; "Negro Indicted for Murder of Robinson Woman: Trial Monday," *Waco Morning News* (May 12, 1916): 8; "Murderer of Mrs. Lucy Fryer to Be Tried Next Monday," *Waco Semi-Weekly Tribune* (May 13, 1916): 2.

70. "Robinson Gives Assurance Will Not Molest Murderer," *Waco Morning News* (May 13, 1916): 6.

71. "Swift Vengeance Wreaked on Negro," 5.

72. "Will Permit Law to Take Its Course in Negro Boy's Trial," *Waco Times Herald* (May 13, 1916): 3.

73. "Robinson Gives Assurance Will Not Molest Murderer."

74. [No headline], *Waco Times Herald* (May 12, 1916): 8.

75. "Swift Vengeance Wreaked on Negro," 5.

76. Ibid., 1.

77. Ibid., 5.

78. "Mob Takes Negro from Court House," 1.

79. "Swift Vengeance Wreaked on Negro," 1.

80. Ibid., 5.

81. Freeman, "Waco Lynching," 7.

82. "Swift Vengeance Wreaked on Negro," 5.

83. "Mob Takes Negro from Court House," 1.

84. "Swift Vengeance Wreaked on Negro," 1.

85. "Mob Takes Negro from Court House," 1.

86. Ibid.

87. "Swift Vengeance Wreaked on Negro," 1.

88. Ibid.

89. See "Three Outstanding Waco Business Men Claimed by Death," *Waco Tribune Herald* (June 17, 1934): 1. W. B. Brazelton was the grandfather of noted pediatrician Dr. T. Berry Brazelton, the "Dr. Spock" of America in the 1980s, author of numerous books on child development, and host of the TV show *What Every Baby Knows*. Dr. Brazelton, who was born in 1920, has vivid and unpleasant memories of his early childhood in Waco. Every Friday night the Ku Klux Klan burned a cross on the hill above his parents' home, and his father would leave the house and hide out somewhere. (Brazelton's father was considered a liberal and was, therefore, a Klan target.) Dr. Brazelton told me that while his father was gone, he, his brother, his mother, and a black woman who worked for the family hid under the bed (author's interview with Dr. T. Berry Brazelton).

90. "Swift Vengeance Wreaked on Negro," 5.

91. "Mob Takes Negro from Court House," 1, 5; "Statement of Facts," testimony of S. S. Fleming and Lee Jenkins, 4–6.

92. "Statement of Facts," testimony of Jesse Washington, 10.

93. "Swift Vengeance Wreaked on Negro," 5.

94. Ibid.

95. "Negro Burned to a Stake," 7.

96. "Court's Entry Not Finished," 5.

97. "Negro Burned to a Stake."

98. Ibid.

99. "As to Barney Goldberg," *Waco Semi-Weekly Tribune* (May 17, 1916): 7; "No Part Taken in Guarding Negro by Barney Goldberg," *Waco Morning News* (May 16, 1916): 2; Freeman, "Waco Lynching," 12.

100. "Mob Takes Negro from Court House," 1; "Swift Vengeance Wreaked on Negro," 1.

101. "Negro Burned to a Stake."

102. "Swift Vengeance Wreaked on Negro," 1.

103. Freeman, "Waco Lynching," 13.

104. "Swift Vengeance Wreaked on Negro," 1.

105. "Mob Takes Negro from Court House," 1.

106. "Swift Vengeance Wreaked on Negro," 5.

107. See page XXX and note 40 in this chapter.

108. "Negro Burned to a Stake."

109. "Mob Takes Negro from Court House," 1; emphasis mine.

110. Freeman, "Waco Lynching," 14.

111. "Mob Takes Negro from Court House," 1.

112. Freeman, "Waco Lynching," 14. When I first read Faulkner's *Light in August*, I thought the castration of the dying Joe Christmas by army captain Percy Grimm was a stunning example of overripe southern gothic melodrama. As it turns out, Faulkner's account of a lynching and castration is mild compared to the lynchings that were actually occurring in the South during the period the novel covers.

113. Hague interview.

114. Baker interview, June 19, 2000.

115. Sandra Harvey, "Going Up Bell's Hill," 70. Harvey obtained this information from a 1994 interview with Helen Geltemeyer, an elderly Waco resident.

116. "Negro Burned to a Stake."

117. "Mob Takes Negro from Court House," 1.

118. Freeman, "Waco Lynching," 15.

119. "Mob Takes Negro from Court House," 1.

120. Freeman, "Waco Lynching," 16.

121. "Swift Vengeance Wreaked on Negro," 1.

122. "Mob Takes Negro from Court House," 1.

123. "Negro Burned to a Stake."

124. Freeman, "Waco Lynching," 24.

125. Freeman, "Waco Lynching," 15. Freeman's syntax is confusing at this point. The "rake-off" to which she refers may simply mean that she felt she personally was overcharged for the photographs. She says the Gildersleeve pictures were going for ten cents apiece to the general public, but she had to pay fifty cents each.

126. "Negro Burned to a Stake."

127. "Swift Vengeance Wreaked on Negro," 1.

128. Freeman, "Waco Lynching," 16.

129. "Negro Burned to a Stake."

130. Freeman, "Waco Lynching," 16.

131. "Court's Entry Not Finished."

132. "Swift Vengeance Wreaked on Negro," 5.

133. Ibid.

134. Ibid.

135. E. G. Senter, "Vengeance Is Mine, Saith the Lord," *Waco Morning News* (May 16, 1916): 4.

136. "New Editor of News Is Speaker," *Waco Morning News* (April 5, 1916): 6.

137. Harlon Morse Fentress, interview by Thomas L. Charlton, 24–25. The Waco newspapers acquired by Marsh and Fentress became the headquarters of a chain headquartered in Waco that owned thirteen daily newspapers at its peak.

138. "Artemas R. Roberts Sells His Holdings in Morning News," *Waco Morning News* (June 4, 1916): 2.

139. Freeman, "Waco Lynching," 20.

140. Ibid., 6

141. "Funeral Today 4:30 P.M. Editor A. R. McCollum," *Waco Times Herald* (November 10, 1918): 7.

142. Freeman, "Waco Lynching," 6.

143. "Statements by Senator A. R. M'Collum," *Waco Semi-Weekly Tribune* (June 17, 1916): 6.

144. "The Mob," *Waco Semi-Weekly Tribune* (May 17, 1916): 6.

145. "The Work of the Mob," *Waco Semi-Weekly Tribune* (May 17, 1916): 6.

146. "E. M. Ainsworth's Death Ends Long Newsman Career," *Waco News Tribune* (November 26, 1940): 1.

147. Freeman, "Waco Lynching," 18.

148. "Court's Entry Not Finished."

Chapter 6

1. Litwack's *Trouble in Mind* offers detailed examinations of the hardships, indignities, and dangers of growing up black and living black in the South in the early part of the twentieth century.

2. Dollard, *Caste and Class*, 359.

3. George Moses Fadal, interview by Gary W. Hull, 21.

4. "Mob Lynches Man Held for Attack Here," *Waco Times Herald* (December 14, 1921): 1.

5. Fadal interview, 24.

6. Waco is not, in fact, west of the Pecos River, which meanders through one of the emptiest parts of West Texas.

7. Francis Lollie Pittillo, interviews by Thomas L. Charlton and Gary W. Hull, 207–209.

8. Joseph M. Dawson, interviewed March 12, 1971, by Rogers Melton Smith ("Waco Lynching," 113–14). Smith wrote his thesis on the Jesse Washington lynching despite the opposition of his advisers and was able to interview several persons who were living in Waco at the time of the lynching. Smith had always been curious about the lynching; his father had witnessed it at age five. Smith's aunt, Mrs. Ike Ashburn, also interviewed for Smith's thesis, was about sixteen at the time of the lynching (author's interview with Rogers Melton Smith).

9. Smith, "Waco Lynching," 112–13. Smith interviewed Jenkins on June 1, 1971.

10. Ibid., 112. Smith interviewed Naman on May 12, 1971.

11. The lynchings of Curley Hackney in 1921 and Jesse Thomas in 1922 will be discussed in detail in chapter 10.

12. Author's interview with Mildred Richter.

13. Smith, "Waco Lynching," 114. Smith interviewed Mrs. Ashburn on May 30, 1971.

14. Harold Lester Goodman, interview by Gary W. Hull, 28, 31–32.

15. Ibid., 28.

16. Ibid., 32.

17. Ibid., 29.

18. Ibid., 24.

19. Leo Frank, a Jew and a northerner, was manager of the National Pencil Factory in Atlanta. On April 26, 1913, a young girl named Mary Phagan was found brutally murdered in the factory. Frank was convicted of the crime and condemned to death, but, in June 1915, Georgia governor John Slaton, just before he left office, commuted Frank's sentence to life in prison. On August 17, 1915, Frank was taken out of his prison cell by a mob, driven to Cobb County (Mary Phagan's home), and lynched near a place called Frey's Mill.

20. Goodman interview, 34. Goodman defended his community, but it is easy to see from his earlier remarks that the Waco area was not free of anti-Semitism, though there may have been no violence directly related to it. Farther on in the interview, Goodman admits that, during the 1920s, when the Ku Klux Klan was active in Waco, "if there was a choice of doing business with a Catholic or a Protestant, a lot of people would boycott the Catholics or the Jews" (ibid., 37).

21. Author's interview with Nannette Booker Hutchison, age ninety.

Chapter 7

1. Allen Brooks was accused of assaulting a three-year-old white child. He was seized at the courthouse as his trial was about to begin on March 3, 1910, and hanged before a mob of five thousand to six thousand. Not a single police officer on the scene tried to save him, and all claimed later that they had not recognized anyone in the mob. See Shapiro, *White Violence and Black Response*, 113–14.

2. "Shocking Exhibition of Mob Rage," *Houston Post* (May 17, 1916): 6.

3. Ibid.

4. "Horror at Waco," 8.

5. Ibid.

6. On June 25, 1906, Harry K. Thaw, a deranged millionaire, shot and killed noted architect Stanford White at Madison Square Garden's rooftop theater because he believed White had raped and deflowered his wife, Evelyn Nesbit, when she was only sixteen. After two "trials of the century," Thaw was acquitted.

7. "Horror at Waco."

8. "Monstrous and Abominable."

9. Ibid.

10. "Punished a Horror Horribly," 10.

11. Ibid.

12. "The Background of Lynching," *San Francisco Bulletin* (May 16, 1916), from clipping file, NAACP Archives, NAACP Administrative File, Subfile under Lynching: Waco, Texas, 1916, Group 1, Box C-370, Library of Congress (hereafter Clippings, NAACP Lynching File).

13. "Judge Lynch At His Worst" [the name of the publication summarizing various newspaper stories on the lynching is illegible] (May 20, 1916), from Clippings, NAACP Lynching File.

14. Ibid.

15. Ibid.

16. "Imperial and Foreign News Items," *Times of London* (May 17, 1916): 7.

17. "Waco Holocaust," from Clippings, NAACP Lynching File.

18. Ibid.

19. I. Ford, "An Open Letter."

20. Ibid.

21. James W. Johnson, "Chance for Humanity," *New York Age* (May 25, 1916).

22. "More Than Hundred Guardsmen Refuse to Serve Uncle Sam," *Waco Morning News* (May 23, 1916): 1.

23. "Many Guardsmen Faint," *Waco Morning News* (May 26, 1916): 2.

24. "Alleged Coercion in National Guard Is Popular Subject," *Waco Morning News* (June 3, 1916): 3.

25. "Texas Guardsmen Must Face Trial by Court Martial," *Waco Morning News* (May 26, 1916): 1; "Very Few of Texas Guard to Be Tried by Court Martial," *Waco Morning News* (May 28, 1916): 3; "Militia Slackers Expected to Take the Muster Oath," *Waco Times Herald* (May 28, 1916): 1.

26. J. Johnson, "Those Valiant Texans."

27. "American negro troops faced almost certain death at Carrizal with smiles in their eyes and slang on their lips and they burst into song once or twice as they fought their grim fight against odds" ("Singing as They Fight, Negroes Met Death Bravely at Carrizal, Says Morey," *Waco Morning News* [June 27, 1916]: 1).

28. J. Johnson, "Those Valiant Texans."

29. The newspaper would eventually earn a fortune for its founder, Robert S. Abbott (Ottley, *The Lonely Warrior*, 138–39).

30. H. Walker, "Southern White Gentlemen Burn Race Boy at Stake," 1.

31. Ibid.

32. Ottley, *Lonely Warrior*, 107.

33. "Mob's Victim Buried in Potter's Field," *Chicago Defender* (June 3, 1916): 1.

34. "[Illegible] White Man for Crime Which Boy Was Lynched," 7.

35. "White State Troopers in Trouble: Texas National Guardsmen Refused to Join Colors When Called, Yet Can Find Time to Lynch Black Men," *Chicago Defender* (June 10, 1916).

36. "A Terrible Crime in Texas," 325.

37. "Editorial Notes," 102.

38. Another oblique reference to the Leo Frank lynching of the year before.

39. "The Week," 530–31.

40. Winston, "Lynching Defended," 671.

41. L. P. Chamberlayne, "Correspondence: Lynching," *The Nation* (July 13, 1916): 34–35.

42. "J. M. S.," in *The Nation* (July 13, 1916): 35.

43. Oscar Woodward Zeigler, "White Man and Negro," *The Nation* (July 27, 1916): 82.

Chapter 8

1. Lewis, *W. E. B. Du Bois*, 500.

2. Royal Freeman Nash to Elisabeth Freeman, telegram, May 16, 1916, Freeman/Nash Letters. References in this chapter to the correspondence between Freeman and Nash are from this source. See chapter 5, note 45.

3. Royal Freeman Nash to Elisabeth Freeman, May 16, 1916.

4. Royal Freeman Nash, "The Cherokee Fires," *The Crisis* (March 1916): 268. Nash reports the tale of the rape and beating (and the girl's subsequent death of pneumonia) matter-of-factly and does not delve into the truth of the story or the identity of the perpetrators. His point is that the incident set off a rash of killings of blacks which escalated into a concerted effort to drive all black people out of the county.

5. Elisabeth Freeman to Royal Freeman Nash, "Thursday" [May 18, 1916].

6. Elisabeth Freeman to Royal Freeman Nash, undated.

7. Elisabeth Freeman to Royal Freeman Nash, May 18, 1916. These are the Gildersleeve photographs.

8. Freeman, "Waco Lynching," 21.

9. Elisabeth Freeman to Royal Freeman Nash, undated.

10. Freeman, "Waco Lynching," 3, 5.

11. Elisabeth Freeman to Royal Freeman Nash, undated [stamped "May 27, 1916," upon receipt].

12. Judge Pickle was apparently a distant relative of former congressman Jake J. Pickle of Austin, who served in the U.S. House of Representatives from 1963 to 1995.

13. NAACP, *Mobbing of John R. Shillady*; "White Secretary Negro Society Chased Out of City," *Austin Statesman* (August 22, 1919): 1.

14. White, *A Man Called White*, 46–47.

15. Ibid., 50–51. White could easily have chosen to "pass" as white all of his life, but decided instead to openly identify himself as a black man and to fight for the rights of other blacks. In his autobiography, he explains how his experience of the Atlanta race riot of 1906, which took place when he was thirteen years old, confirmed in him a determination to maintain his black identity: "I was glad I was not one of those who hated. I was glad I was not one of those whose story is in the history of the world, a record of bloodshed, rapine, and pillage" (12).

16. Freeman, "Waco Lynching," 3.

17. Ibid.

18. Ibid., 4.

19. Ibid., 7.

20. Ibid., 20.

21. "Letters Decrying Mobbing Flood In," *Waco Morning News* (May 24, 1916): 10.

22. "Who Will Cast the First Stone," 4.

23. Ibid.

24. "The Fruitage of Mob Rule."

25. Ibid.; emphasis mine.

26. Freeman, "Waco Lynching," 14.

27. Ibid., 14–15.

28. Elisabeth Freeman to Royal Freeman Nash, undated.

29. Freeman, "Waco Lynching," 1.

30. Ibid.

31. *History of New Hope Baptist Church*, 13.

32. Freeman, "Waco Lynching," 17.

33. Ibid.

34. "Death Takes Dr. G. S. Conner," *Waco Messenger* (February 17, 1939), George S. and Jeffie O. A. Conner Papers, The Texas Collection, Baylor University, Waco, Texas; *Waco City Directory 1916*, 189.

35. Freeman, "Waco Lynching," 2–3.

36. Ibid., 19. Freeman's spelling of names is extremely sloppy throughout her report. Other details, however, where I could confirm them in other sources, seem to be substantially correct.

37. "Southern Baptists Oppose Mob Violence and Support National Prohibition," *Waco Morning News* (May 23, 1916): 2.

38. Emphasis mine. The phrase "the few" does not seem accurately to describe half the population of a town of thirty thousand.

39. "Waco Pastors Will Take a Stand Denouncing Lynching," *Waco Morning News* (May 29, 1916): 3.

40. "Baptist Pastors of Waco Denounce the Mob Spirit," *Waco Morning News* (May 31, 1916): 10; emphasis mine.

41. "Condemn Action of Mob," *Waco Semi-Weekly Tribune* (May 31, 1916): 5.

42. "The Baylor Expression on [illegible]," *Waco Semi-Weekly Tribune* (May 31, 1916): 4.

43. Caldwell, *Historical Sketch*, 91.

44. J. Dawson, *A Thousand Months to Remember*, 165.

45. Waco's mayors from 1849 to 1934 are listed and briefly described in Sleeper, *A Brief History*.

46. Freeman, "Waco Lynching," 18–19.

47. Elisabeth Freeman to Royal Freeman Nash, undated [stamped "May 27, 1916," upon receipt].

48. Elisabeth Freeman to Royal Freeman Nash, undated.

49. Elisabeth Freeman to Royal Freeman Nash, Sunday [May 21, 1916].

50. Elisabeth Freeman to Royal Freeman Nash, Friday [May 26, 1916; stamped "May 29, 1916," upon receipt].

51. Freeman, "Waco Lynching," 22.

52. Ibid., 13.

53. Ibid., 22.

54. Ibid., 13.

55. It is interesting to note that, by the time James T. Hancock Sr. died in Houston in 1936

at the age of seventy, his Waco history had been thoroughly sanitized. His obituary describes him as a resident of Waco for forty years, "a retired chemical soap manufacturer [who] was formerly in the loan business in Waco." At the time of his death, most of Hancock's sons, including Edgar, Leamon, and James T. Jr., were living in Corpus Christi. See obituary for James Thomas Hancock, *Houston Chronicle* (July 21, 1936): 19.

56. "There Never Was Any Chili."

57. Ibid.

58. "Dillard Services Scheduled Today," *Waco News Tribune* (August 2, 1947): 12.

59. "There Never Was Any Chili."

60. "C. C. Sparks Funeral Set," *Waco News Tribune* (November 9, 1954): 3.

61. Information about William Henry Frazier is derived largely from my interviews with Kenneth Frazier, sixty-three, and John Frazier, fifty-nine, grandsons of William Henry Frazier; from genealogical materials supplied by John Frazier; and from obituaries and census records.

62. In the 1910 *Waco City Directory*, Zadie is even identified as "Mrs. *Charles* Frazier." Ada is first formally listed as William Henry's wife in the 1917–18 *Waco City Directory*, but wives' names are frequently absent in earlier directories.

63. These spellings are taken from the 1920 census. The 1920 census listings for the Fraziers are an intriguing treasure trove of information and misinformation. They are depicted, at this point, as two separate farming families living side by side in the small community of Downsville, south of Robinson. "Henry" Frazier headed one family, "Sadie Frazier," the other. The census taker recorded all of Ada's children as having been born in Texas and all of Zadie's children as having been born in Tennessee — which was highly unlikely, if Evert and Evoline were born in 1912 or thereabouts. The oddest aspect of the census record, however, is that almost every member of the two families except the youngest children is described as being younger than he or she actually was. It seems that the adult Fraziers told so many different stories about who they were and their relationships to each other and to their children that the historical record is an indecipherable tangle of truths, half-truths, and outright lies.

64. Obituary of William H. Frazier, *Waco News Tribune* (July 23, 1936): 2.

65. Freeman, "Waco Lynching," 5.

66. Ibid., 12.

67. Ibid., 4–5.

68. Ibid., 12.

69. Ibid., 23.

70. Ibid., 5.

71. Ibid., 11.

72. "Sam Fleming Is Running on Record," 11.

73. "Bob Buchanan for Sheriff of McLennan County," *Waco Morning News* (May 25, 1916): 11.

74. Freeman, "Waco Lynching," 23.

75. "The Real Buchanan," *Waco Morning News* (July 18, 1916): 6.

76. "To the Voters of McLennan County," *Waco Morning News* (July 22, 1916): 5.

77. "Affidavits Explained: Fleming Made No Such Statement," *Waco Morning News* (July 22, 1916): 6; emphasis mine.

78. Torrance, "Eighty Years on Horseback," 22.

79. "Famed Waco Photographer Dies at 77," 1.

80. Elisabeth Freeman to Royal Freeman Nash, Sunday [May 21, 1916].

81. Elisabeth Freeman to Royal Freeman Nash, Friday [May 26, 1916; stamped May 29, 1916, upon receipt].

82. Freeman, "Waco Lynching," 24.

Chapter 9

1. W. Du Bois, "The Waco Horror," 2–3.

2. Ibid., 6.

3. This assertion was based on Freeman's limited knowledge at the time. See chapter 8 and the letter to *The Nation* from J. L. Kesler, "In Justice to Waco."

4. W. Du Bois, "The Waco Horror," 5.

5. Ibid., 8.

6. "National Association for the Advancement of Colored People Anti-Lynching Fund," *The Crisis* (July 1916): 149.

7. Oswald Garrison Villard, "Harken!" *The Crisis* (August 1916): 168.

8. W. Du Bois, "Anti-Lynching Fund," unnumbered page, 219. The $7,260.93 includes the anticipated pledges from Peabody and Storey.

9. Ibid., no page.

10. Ibid., 219.

11. Ibid., 220.

12. J. E. Spingarn, Memorandum from the Chairman of the Board, December 24, 1916, Anti-Lynching Campaign, 2; hereafter Memorandum from the Chairman of the Board.

13. List of Mailings, NAACP Archives, NAACP Administrative File, Subfile under Lynching: Waco, Texas, 1916, Group 1, Box C-370, Library of Congress (hereafter, NAACP Waco Lynching Archives).

14. Lindley M. Keasbey to Elisabeth Freeman, May 30, 1916, NAACP Waco Lynching Archives. For more on the remarkable Professor Keasbey, see "Lindley Miller Keasbey," Department of Geology, College of Liberal Arts, University of Texas at Austin, http://www.utexas.edu/depts/grg/knapp/faculty/faculty/keasbey.html; and "Lindley Miller Keasbey," Handbook of Texas Online, http://www.tsha.utexas.edu/handbook/online/articles/view/KK/fke46.html. Austin lawyer Henry Faulk was the father of Texas humorist, writer, and politician John Henry Faulk, who was blacklisted as a Communist in 1957. The blacklisting ended his successful career as a radio entertainer. Faulk sued the organization responsible for getting him blacklisted and, in 1962, won the largest libel judgment in history up to that point. See John Henry Faulk (1913–1990), Handbook of Texas Online, http://www.tsha.utexas.edu/handbook/online/articles/view/FF/ffa36.html.

15. Lindley Keasbey to Elisabeth Freeman, June 16, 1916, NAACP Waco Lynching Archives.

16. Royal Freeman Nash to Rev. T. S. Williams, October 9, 1916, NAACP Waco Lynching Archives.

17. R. D. Evans began practicing law in Waco in 1914; he may have been the first black attorney in the city. Acknowledged even by the white newspapers as "one of the most brilliant Afro-American attorneys in the state," Evans earned his law degree at Howard University and in 1916, was admitted to practice before the U.S. Supreme Court. Evans was killed in a car-train collision in 1938 at the age of sixty. He was about thirty-eight when he defended A. T. Smith. See "Waco Negro Lawyer Admitted to Bar," 3; "Three Perish in Local Accidents," *Waco News Tribune* (June 27, 1938): 1. One unconfirmed story still being told in Waco is that, in the very early days of his practice, Evans was not allowed to enter a courtroom during a trial; the person he was defending had to leave the courtroom to consult with Evans and then return to the courtroom (author's interview with Lawrence Johnson).

18. R. D. Evans, letter to *The Crisis*, January 1917, 122–23.

19. Kathryn M. Johnson to Roy Nash (telegram, undated), Anti-Lynching Campaign.

20. Royal Freeman Nash to Mrs. A. T. Smith, July 27, 1916, Anti-Lynching Campaign.

21. Tom M. Hamilton to Elisabeth Freeman, July 1, 1916, NAACP Waco Lynching Archives.

22. *George Fryer v. Paul Quinn College*, No. 1194, 74th District Court, McLennan County, January Term A.D. 1917. See chapter 5, note 68.

23. J. E. Spingarn, Memorandum from the Chairman of the Board, 2.

24. W. E. Henderson to Oswald Garrison Villard, October 11, 1916, Anti-Lynching Campaign.

25. Board Meeting Minutes, October 9, 1916, from Board Meeting Minutes, 1909–1924.

26. "Waco Horror Stirs Race to Action," *Chicago Defender* (July 29, 1916): 2.

27. "Old Boston" seems to be a figure of speech referring perhaps to the old abolitionist spirit. The speech the *Defender* describes was apparently delivered in Chicago ("Phillip Peabody Gives $20,000 to Fight Lynching").

28. Ibid.

29. "An American Atrocity," *The Independent* (July 31, 1916): 146.

30. "A Southern Professor on Lynching," editor's response to letter from R. P. Brooks, *The Nation* (October 5, 1916): 321.

31. "The Will-to-Lynch," *New Republic* (October 14, 1916): 261.

32. Kesler, "In Justice to Waco," 609.

33. Ibid.

34. Ibid.

35. Dawson, *A Thousand Months to Remember*, 163.

36. Ibid.

37. Philip G. Peabody to J. E. Spingarn, October 16, 1916, Correspondence, 1910–1939.

38. Spingarn, Memorandum from the Chairman of the Board, 1, 3.

39. Royal Freeman Nash to All Branch Officers, July 1, 1916, Yale Collection of American Literature, Beinecke Rare Book and Manuscript Library.

40. Board Meeting Minutes, November 13, 1916, from Board Meeting Minutes, 1909–1924.

41. Roy Nash to Kathryn M. Johnson, August 16, 1916, Correspondence, 1910–1939.

42. Freeman reported to Agnes Ryan that "from all sides comes [*sic*] complaints and fault-finding from the N.Y. suffragists cause of my girls and the selling of the *Journal* . . . It is a good thing one has a funny bone as well as a wishbone and a backbone. It's most necessary in this movement . . . I sometimes wonder if they are really out for the vote or to scrap with each other" (Elisabeth Freeman to Agnes Ryan, July 23, 1913, NAWSA Records, General Correspondence, 1839–1961, Freeman, Elisabeth, Containers 11 and 12, Reels 7 and 8, Library of Congress).

43. "Votes for Women," Edison Kinetoscope, 1913; Library of Congress Film Archives, FEA 9595. This Kinetoscope was apparently part of an experiment to produce short films with sound called "talkers," which would be played in movie theaters. The reaction to the "Votes for Women" film, however, was so negative that the whole scheme was brought to a halt. Male theatergoers hooted, jeered, hissed, and threatened to "break up the show," according to a story in *Variety*: "The Last of 'The Talkers' with This Week's Series," *Variety* (April 11, 1913). The *Variety* article pronounces the "death" of the "talking picture" after the violent reaction to the suffrage film.

44. Kellogg, *NAACP*, 133.

45. The account of Eley's deeds is taken from "Ohio Mob Nearly Lynches Sheriff," *Chicago Defender* (September 9, 1916): 1; "Ohio Lynchers Noose Sheriff," *New York Times* (August 31, 1916): 1; and an NAACP news release dated December 24, 1916, in Anti-Lynching Campaign.

Chapter 10

1. Raper, *Tragedy of Lynching*, 481. Lynching figures are only estimates. There are many inaccuracies in the old data tables, and there were also, probably, lynchings that were never reported (see chapter 1, note 34). Year-to-year figures are useful for purposes of comparison, however.

2. "Lynching," *Chicago Plaindealer* (January 25[?], 1919); "Texas Movement," *Hartford Courant* (February 12, 1919), both in Anti-Lynching Campaign.

3. Rudwick, *Race Riot,* 50. The true number of dead in East St. Louis will probably never be known for reasons that Rudwick explains.

4. J. Johnson, *Along This Way,* 320.

5. Board Meeting Minutes, September 17, 1917, from Board Meeting Minutes, 1909–1924.

6. NAACP Administrative File: Lectures, Etc., Silent March, Aug.–Oct. 1917, NAACP Archives, Library of Congress. "Memphis" refers to the sadistic lynching of a black man named Ell Persons in that city in late May 1917. *The Crisis* published a four-page supplement on the Memphis lynching in the June 1917 issue.

7. J. Johnson, *Along This Way,* 321.

8. Rudwick, *Race Riot,* 135.

9. J. Johnson, *Along This Way,* 321.

10. Ibid.

11. Kellogg, *NAACP,* 226–27.

12. This account is a compilation of details from White, *Rope and Faggot,* 27–29; Anti-Lynching Campaign; and Armstrong, "The Infamous Story of Mary Turner." Armstrong discusses various literary and artistic works based on Mary Turner's death that have been produced by black artists.

13. NAACP news release dated August 1, 1918, Anti-Lynching Campaign.

14. Zangrando, *NAACP Crusade,* 43.

15. Ibid., 64, 143, 162, 212. The excuse given for not passing the antilynching bill was that it was unconstitutional because it violated states' rights. But around the same time that the anti-lynching bill failed in 1922, Congress passed other laws such as the Mann Act, the White Slave Traffic Act, and the Harrison Narcotics Act, which encroached on the rights of states to exercise complete control over criminal matters. See Holden-Smith, "Lynching."

16. The Texas Department of Criminal Justice provides detailed, regularly updated statistics on death row at http://www.tdcj.state.tx.us/stat/deathrow.htm. For differing views on the subject of the disproportionate punishment of minorities and the poor in our judicial system, see, for instance, Blume, Eisenberg, and Wells, "Explaining Death Row's Population"; Cole, *No Equal Justice;* Kennedy, *Race, Crime and the Law;* Walker, Spohn, and DeLone, *The Color of Justice.* Also see Amnesty International, "United States of America. Death by Discrimination: The Continuing Role of Race in Capital Cases," April 24, 2003, http://web.amnesty.org/library/index/engamr510462003. For population statistics, see Texas State Data Center: http://txsdc.tamu.edu/tpepp/presskit/.

17. N. Brown, *Hood, Bonnet and Little Brown Jug,* 51, 160, 211, 404.

18. Ibid., 75.

19. Pittillo interview, 54.

20. Hessdoerfer interview, 92–93. All through this period there were many articles in the newspapers that alternated between associating the Klan with violence ("Dare Klan in Hearing of 20 for Shooting," *Waco Times Herald* [December 19, 1921]: 1) and recounting virtuous acts performed by the Klan, as in the following stories from the *Waco Times Herald:* "Ku Klux Klan Sends Groceries to Widow" (December 15, 1921): 8; "Groceries Sent by Ku Klux with Xmas. Greetings"(December 19, 1921): 5; "Ku Klux Sends Caps to Orphans" (December 21, 1921): 3; "Ku Klux Present Big Flag to Scouts"(March 18, 1922): 3; "Klansmen Give $75 for Relief Preacher Ill with Pneumonia" (July 23, 1922): 2. The Methodist Orphanage, however, returned the caps donated to the boys by the KKK: "Board of Control Methodist Orphanage Declines Ku Klux Gifts," *Waco Times Herald* (December 22, 1921): 5.

21. Fadal interview, 21; Curry, *History of Early Waco,* 90.

22. Curry, *History of Early Waco,* 90–91.

23. "Probe Lynching 'Curly' Hackney," *Waco Times Herald* (December 15, 1921): 8.
24. "Judges Stamp Disapproval on Mob Activity," *Waco Times Herald* (December 18, 1921): 1.
25. "Mob Rule Is Blot on State," 1.
26. Ibid.
27. "Sheriff Billed for Crow Death," *Waco Times Herald* (January 20, 1922): 1.
28. "Grand Jury Files Written Report," *Waco Times Herald* (January 28, 1922): 5.
29. "C. S. Farmer Wins Attorney Race; Stegall Sheriff," *Waco Times Herald* (July 23, 1922): 1.
30. N. Brown, *Hood, Bonnet, and Little Brown Jug*, 124–28.
31. See, for example, "Rangers Will Be Here Next Week during Negroes' Trial," *Waco Times Herald* (January 10, 1922): 2; "Rangers with Machine Guns Ordered Here," *Waco Times Herald* (March 13, 1922): 1.
32. "Mob Menaces Jail with Negro's Capture," *Waco Times Herald* (May 26, 1922): 1.
33. Hutchison interview.
34. "Harris Goes to Stegall and Surrenders," 1, 3.
35. Ibid.
36. "Negro's Murder Story," 10.
37. Richter interview. See chapter 6 for her description of what she saw.
38. "Negro Taken before Couple Shot in Park," *Waco Times Herald* (May 29, 1922): 1.
39. "Officers Link Road Tragedy with Cameron Park Shooting," *Waco Times Herald* (May 28, 1922): 1.
40. "Baptist Pastors Condemn Mobs," *Waco Times Herald* (May 29, 1922): 5.
41. "Resolutions of Censure for Mobs," *Waco Times Herald* (May 30, 1922): 5.
42. "New Charge Filed against Mitchell; Boucher Trio Free," *Waco Times Herald* (January 31, 1923): 1; "Negro's Murder Story," 10.
43. "Three Grilled in Double Murder Mystery," *Waco Times Herald* (January 22, 1923): 1, 8.
44. "Mitchell Admits All Crimes," 3.
45. "Negroes Arrested in Murders," 1, 8; "Fourth Murder Officially Charged to Mitchell," 1.
46. "Roy Mitchell on Stand," 1; "Mitchell Admits All Crimes," 3.
47. "Fourth Murder Officially Charged to Mitchell," 1.
48. "Negroes Arrested in Murders," 1. According to Curry's *History of Early Waco* (91–92), Mitchell had been hunting rabbits with a man named Dink White when they stopped at a grocery store to get some tobacco and fell into an argument with the owner over heavyweight boxing champion Jack Johnson, among other things. Mitchell and White ran away, but then decided to return to the store and kill the owner. White was given a fifteen-year sentence for the murder; Mitchell was given a two-year suspended sentence.
49. "Roy Mitchell on Stand," 8.
50. Ibid., 1.
51. "Negro's Murder Story," 1.
52. See "Negroes Arrested in Murders," and "Negro's Murder Story," for instance.
53. "Last Legal Texas Hanging Recalled"; "Mitchell Admits All Crimes," 3.
54. "Negro's Murder Story," 10.
55. "Roy Mitchell on Stand," 1.
56. "Jury Gives Mitchell Death Penalty," 1
57. "Five Men Are Chosen for Roy Mitchell Jury," *Waco Times Herald* (March 15, 1923): 1.
58. "Mitchell Given Fifth Sentence in Bolton Case," *Waco Times Herald* (March 31, 1923): 8.
59. "Mitchell in Good Spirits," 1.
60. "Mitchell Admits All Crimes," 3.
61. "Last Legal Texas Hanging Recalled."

62. Sleeper, *A Brief History*, 4–5.

63. "Mitchell in Good Spirits," 1.

64. "Negro's Murder Story," 1.

65. Hamer was one of Texas' most famous lawmen, known primarily for his service as a Texas Ranger, as marshal of Navasota County, and as special investigator for the Texas prison system. He battled bandits, outlaws, bootleggers, arms smugglers, and official and financial corruption. He was criticized at times for excessive use of force, especially along the border and in the ambush and killing of Bonnie Parker and Clyde Barrow on May 23, 1934. In 1968, Hamer's widow and son sued the producers of *Bonnie and Clyde* for Hamer's portrayal in the movie; the case was settled out of court in 1971. See Handbook of Texas Online: http://www.tsha.utexas.edu/handbook/online/articles/view/HH/fha32.html.

66. "Jury Gives Mitchell Death Penalty," 4.

67. "Mitchell Given Fourth Penalty," *Waco Times Herald* (March 29, 1923): 7.

68. "Evidence Being Given in Roy Mitchell's 5th Murder Case," *Waco Times Herald* (March 30, 1923): 1.

69. "Roy Mitchell to Hang Tomorrow Forenoon," 7. See note 76, this chapter; Mitchell's execution was not the last public hanging in Texas, after all.

70. "Preparations for Execution Roy Mitchell," 5. One newspaper account reports that Mitchell avoided the eating of pork for scriptural reasons. This "dislike for pork" was accounted "very unusual for a negro." See "Roy Mitchell to Hang Tomorrow Forenoon," 7.

71. "Roy Mitchell to Hang Tomorrow Forenoon," 1.

72. "Mitchell Admits All Crimes," 1; Curry, *History of Early Waco*, 94.

73. "Mitchell Admits All Crimes," 1.

74. "Preparations for Execution Roy Mitchell," 5; "Roy Mitchell to Hang Tomorrow Forenoon," 1.

75. "Mitchell Admits All Crimes," 1.

76. According to one story, a Western Union boy was bribed to cut the rope holding the tarp up. See Biffle, "No Noose Good News for Senator." The Mitchell hanging was widely reported, then and later, to be the last legal hanging and the last public execution in Texas, but there was a later, much less sensational, hanging of a man named Nathan Lee in Angleton on August 31, 1923. See idem, "Rewriting History," and "Waco's Claim to Last Hanging."

Epilogue

1. Boylan, *Revolutionary Lives*, 237.

2. Ibid., 262.

3. A. Walling, *William English Walling*, 75.

4. Boylan, *Revolutionary Lives*, 265.

5. Ibid., 267.

6. Letter written October 31, 1926, quoted in Howe, *Portrait of an Independent*, 358.

7. Gannett, "Villard and His 'Nation,'" 81.

8. Villard, *Fighting Years*, 194.

9. Ibid.

10. Ibid., 192.

11. This account of Du Bois's later years is taken from *The Autobiography of W. E. B. Du Bois*, Encyclopedia Britannica Guide to Black History Web site: http://blackhistory.eb.com/micro/179/2.html; and Lewis, *W. E. B. Du Bois*.

12. Dedication in W. Du Bois's *Dusk of Dawn*.

13. Van Deusen, *J. E. Spingarn*, 70–72.

14. Ibid., 62–63; Lewis, *W. E. B. Du Bois,* 528–43.

15. Van Deusen, *J. E. Spingarn,* 67–68.

16. Ibid., 70–73; Mumford, "Introduction to *Politics and the Poet,*" 74.

17. Wedin, *Inheritors of the Spirit,* 204.

18. Ibid., 293–94.

19. Ovington, *Walls Came Tumbling Down,* vii.

20. Elisabeth Freeman to Rosika Schwimmer, March 10, 1925. All the correspondence cited in this chapter related to Freeman can be found in the Rosika Schwimmer Papers, 1914–1948, Schwimmer-Lloyd Collection, Manuscripts and Archives Division, New York Public Library, Astor, Lenox, and Tilden Foundations.

21. Rosika Schwimmer to Elisabeth Freeman, June 8, 1925.

22. Elisabeth Freeman to Rosika Schwimmer, June 14, 1925.

23. Elisabeth Freeman to Rosika Schwimmer, June 18, 1930.

24. Elisabeth Freeman to Rosika Schwimmer, October 6, 1930.

25. William H. Leckie to Elisabeth Freeman, June 21, 1930, enclosed in a letter from Elisabeth Freeman to Rosika Schwimmer, June 23, 1930. Although Freeman's letters suggest that Leckie was not eating because she had no money (Freeman had lent her some money, but had little to give), William Leckie's reference to "dieting" raises the question of whether Katherine Leckie could have been an early victim of anorexia. See also Elisabeth Freeman to Rosika Schwimmer, June 18, 1930.

26. Elisabeth Freeman to William H. Leckie, June 16, 1930.

27. Elisabeth Freeman to Rosika Schwimmer, July 22, 1930; Rosika Schwimmer to Elisabeth Freeman, July 25, 1930.

28. Rosika Schwimmer to Elisabeth Freeman, October 31, 1927; Elisabeth Freeman to Rosika Schwimmer, November 6, 1927.

29. Elisabeth Freeman to Rosika Schwimmer, February 3, 1937.

30. Elisabeth Freeman to Rosika Schwimmer, June 17, 1937.

31. Ibid.

32. Rosika Schwimmer to Elisabeth Freeman, June 30, 1937.

33. Elisabeth Freeman refers several times to her "sister" in her letter to William H. Leckie about Katherine Leckie's condition, written on June 16, 1930. Apparently, Freeman's sister helped her take care of Leckie before Leckie was safely put on the train to Chicago. In the letter, Freeman's sister is not named, but the *Baltic* ship manifest of 1911 indicates that Freeman, returning from her years in England, was going to stay at the home of her sister, Clara Freeman, who lived at 1110 Carnegie Hall in New York City. At the time the Carnegie Hall complex included 150 studios that were rented at very reasonable rates primarily to actors, dancers, musicians, and artists, many of whom lived as well as worked in their studios. See Francesoni, "The Carnegie Hall Studios."

34. From file documents from 1942 provided by Mountain View Cemetery-Mortuary-Crematory of Altadena, California, a successor to Turner & Stevens Co.

35. See http://txsdc.utsa.edu/tpepp/presskit/prstab-09t.txt online site of the Texas State Data Center: Total Population and Population by Race/Ethnicity in 2000 and Projected Population and Percent Population Change, 2000–2040. The population in the last census for the Waco metropolitan area was about 200,000.

36. Henry Lloyd "Hank" Corwin interviews by Thomas T. Charlton and Rebecca S. Jimenez, 95.

37. In 2000, Lawrence Johnson was defeated for reelection to City Council after ten years in office.

38. For a review of the debate over "the hanging tree," see the following: Kendra Willeby,

"Saving Reflections of the Past: County to Vote on Funds to Restore Murals of Waco History," *Waco Tribune Herald* (April 7, 2002); Tommy Witherspoon, "County OKs Restoration of Murals: 'Hanging Tree' Painting Held Back, May Be Altered," *Waco Tribune Herald* (April 10, 2002); Mike Anderson, "Hanging Tree Stays in Mural," *Waco Tribune Herald* (May 1, 2002): 1A; Tommy Witherspoon, "County Rejects Expression of 'Atonement' for Lynching," *Waco Tribune Herald* (May 8, 2002): 1A; Letter, Christopher D. Montez, "The Silent Four," *Waco Tribune Herald* (May 8, 2002): 10A; Editorial, "Why Silence?" *Waco Tribune Herald* (May 9, 2002); Editorial, "We're Ones Left Hanging: Commissioners Love to Talk, Just Not While We're Listening," *Waco Tribune Herald* (May 12, 2002): 12A; "No Apology from County" [letters from readers], *Waco Tribune Herald* (May 15, 2002). E-mails from county commissioner Lester Gibson, Waco, December 3, 2003, confirmed that the issue still had not been resolved.

39. "John Dollins Dies," 1.

40. Sleeper, *A Brief History*, 4.

41. Author's interview with John B. McNamara Jr., eighty-five. John B. McNamara III, the county attorney's grandson, was practicing law in Waco at the time of this interview. The wife of John McNamara III, LaNelle McNamara, also an attorney, served as mayor of Waco from 1986 to 1987.

42. Kelley, *Handbook of Waco and McLennan County, Texas*, 176.

43. "Guy McNamara, U.S. Marshall for 13 Years, Is Dead," *Waco News Tribune* (January 25, 1947): 1.

44. McNamara interview.

45. "Citizens' League Plans Last Meeting Tuesday," *Waco News Tribune* (July 18, 1922): 9.

46. Kirkland interview, June 23, 2000.

47. Conger, "Photographs Tell the Story." See also "Famed Waco Photographer Dies at 77," *Waco Times Herald* (February 26, 1958): 1; and Turner, "Photographs by Gildersleeve, Waco," 15–17ff.

48. "McLennan's Total Vote Gives Hobby Majority in this County of 3600," *Waco Times Herald* (July 31, 1918): 3.

49. "7990 Women Registered as Voters — Voting Strength of County Will Be 18,604," *Waco Times Herald* (July 13, 1918): 3.

50. "Sheriff S. S. Fleming to Speak Tomorrow Night on Court House Lawn," *Waco Times Herald* (July 22, 1918): 10.

51. "Bob Buchanan Addresses the Voters," *Waco Times Herald* (July 14, 1918): 22.

52 . "Final Words from Bob Buchanan," 10.

53. "McLennan County to Soon Have First Woman Treasurer," *Waco Times Herald* (August 25, 1918): 1.

54. The Radium Ore Revigator was a patent medicine–like scheme, a water jar containing some low-grade radioactive ore that was supposed to reinvigorate "tired or wilted" drinking water. See an article on the Revigator from the *Journal of the American Medical Association*, November 21, 1925, posted at http://www.mtn.org/quack/devices/revig.htm.

55. Fleming died in Dallas at the age of eighty-two in February 1952, just a couple of months after his first wife, who died in Houston in December 1951 at the age of eighty-three (*Waco Times Herald* [December 17, 1951]: 2). Tomy (sometimes spelled "Tommie") Vaughn Fleming did not die until March 1973. See funeral notice in *Dallas Morning News* (March 21, 1973): 4D. Her age at death is not given. There is no record in Dallas County of Flora's divorce from Sam or of Sam's marriage to Tomy, but Flora could have gone elsewhere to get a divorce, and Sam and Tomy could have gone elsewhere to be married.

56. "Former Sheriff Fleming Buried," 14; "S. S. Fleming Dies in Dallas," *Waco News Tribune* (February 20, 1952): 1.

BIBLIOGRAPHY

Interviews by the Author

Baker, Nona, June 19, 2000, and subsequent sessions, Waco, Tex.
Brazelton, Dr. T. Berry, by telephone.
Frazier, John, July 4, 2001, Elk, Tex.
Frazier, Kenneth, July 4, 2001, Waco, Tex.
Hague, Thomas, June 21, 2000, Robinson, Tex.
Hutchison, Nannette Booker, June 21, 2000, Waco, Tex.
Kettler, Martha Frosch, June 22, 2000, Robinson, Tex.
Kirkland, Lucy Wollitz, June 23 and July 4, 2000, Robinson, Tex.
Johnson, Lawrence, June 22, 2000, Waco, Tex.
McNamara, John B., Jr., August 23, 2000, Waco, Tex.
Richter, Mildred, June 21, 2000, Waco, Tex.
Sendon, Mary Kemendo, August 27, 2000, Waco, Tex.
Smith, Rogers Melton, September 4, 2000, Houston, Tex.
Wuebker, Bill, June 21, 2000, Robinson, Tex.

Archives and Collections

Baylor University Institute for Oral History. Archives Division of The Texas Collection, Baylor
    University, Waco, Texas. Transcribed memoirs of the following:
    Baldwin, Miriam Helen Pool. Interview by Blakie Le Crone, September 27, 29, 30, 1976
    Clemons, Kneeland Hilburn. Interview by Vivienne Malone Mayes, October 21, 1988
    Corwin, Henry Lloyd "Hank." Interviews by Thomas L. Charlton and Rebecca S. Jiménez,
        June 30, 1981–June 30, 1983
    Fadal, George Moses. Interview by Gary W. Hull, July 23, 1977
    Fentress, Harlon Morse. Interview by Thomas L. Charlton, June 18–July 19, 1974
    Goodman, Harold Lester. Interview by Gary W. Hull, June 23, July 11, July 14, 1977
    Hessdoerfer, Oscar Emil. Interviews by Gary W. Hull and Elizabeth Denham Thompson,
        September 22, October 1, 1982
    Pittillo, Francis Lollie. Interviews by Thomas L. Charlton and Gary W. Hull, August 6–August 26, 1974
    Poage, William Robert "Bob". Interviews by Thomas L. Charlton, Robert T. Miller, and
        Phillip A. Thompson, August 28, 1971–December 22, 1983
    Smith, Harriett Caufield. Interview by Thomas L. Charlton, November 22, 1977
    Warner, Anna Mae Bell. Interview by LaWanda Ball, February 13, 16, 1976
    Washington, Maggie Langham. Interviews by Doni Van Ryswyk, March 10, April 18, May
        19, 1988; by Marla Luffer, March 7, 9, 13, 1989

Babcock-Hurlburt Papers. Schlesinger Library, Radcliffe Institute for Advanced Study, Harvard University.

Finnegan, Annette, Collection. Woman's Collection, Texas Woman's University Library, Denton.

McLennan County, Texas, Marriage Records. Waco: Central Texas Genealogical Society, 1982.

National Association for the Advancement of Colored People (NAACP) Archives. Library of Congress. Available on microfilm.

National American Woman Suffrage Association (NAWSA). Records. Library of Congress. Available on microfilm.

Schwimmer, Rosika. Papers, 1914–1948. Schwimmer-Lloyd Collection, Manuscripts and Archives Division, New York Public Library, Astor, Lenox, and Tilden Foundations.

Storey, Moorfield. Papers. Massachusetts Historical Society.

Villard, Oswald Garrison. Papers. Houghton Library, Harvard University.

"Votes for Women." Edison Kinetoscope, 1913. Library of Congress Film Archives, FEA 9595.

Yale Collection of American Literature, Beinecke Rare Book and Manuscript Library. New Haven, Conn.

Books and Articles

Allen, James, editor. *Without Sanctuary: Lynching Photography in America*. Santa Fe, N.M.: Twin Palms, 2000.

"An American Atrocity." *The Independent* (July 31, 1916): 145–46.

Ayers, Edward L. *Vengeance and Justice: Crime and Punishment in the 19th Century American South*. New York: Oxford University Press, 1984.

Baker, Louise (as told to Roger Conger and K. R. Hamorszky). "It's a Winding Road to One Hundred Years: The Oral Memoirs of Louise Baker." *Waco Heritage and History* 13:2 [*sic*] (Summer 1982): 1–16.

Baker, Ray Stannard. "Following the Color Line." *American Magazine* (April 1907): 563–79.

———. *Following the Color Line: American Negro Citizenship in the Progressive Era*. New York: Harper & Row, 1964. First published 1908 by Doubleday, Page.

———. "What Is a Lynching: A Study of Mob Justice, South and North." *McClure's Magazine* (January 1905): 299–314; (February 1905): 422–30.

Barrow, Elliott G. "On Lynching." *The Nation* (July 6, 1916): 11.

Beck, E. M., and Stewart E. Tolnay. "The Killing Fields of the Deep South: The Market for Cotton and the Lynching of Blacks, 1882–1930." *American Sociological Review* 55 (August 1990): 526–39.

Biffle, Kent. "No Noose Good News for Senator." *Dallas Morning News* (May 13, 2001).

———. "Rewriting History: Author Sorts through Texas' Past to Find Real Site of State's Last Public Execution." *Dallas Morning News* (July 5, 1987).

———. "Waco's Claim to Last Hanging Stretches Truth." *Dallas Morning News* (February 15, 1998).

Blalock, H. M. "Percent Black and Lynchings Revisited." *Social Forces* 67:3 (March 1989): 631–33.

Blume, John; Theodore Eisenberg; and Martin T. Wells. "Explaining Death Row's Population and Racial Composition." *Journal of Empirical Legal Studies* 1, no. 1 (March 2004): 165–207.

Boylan, James. *Revolutionary Lives: Anna Strunsky and William English Walling*. Amherst: University of Massachusetts Press, 1998.

Brooks, R. P. "A Southern Professor on Lynching." *The Nation* (October 5, 1916): 321–22.

Brown, Norman D. *Hood, Bonnet and Little Brown Jug: Texas Politics, 1921–1928*. College Station: Texas A&M University Press, 1984.

Brown, Richard Maxwell. *Strain of Violence: Historical Studies of American Violence and Vigilantism*. New York: Oxford University Press, 1975.

Bruce, Florence Guild. *Lillie of Six-Shooter Junction: The Amazing Story of Lillie Drennan and Hempstead, Texas*. San Antonio: Naylor, 1946.

Bruce, Philip A. *The Plantation Negro as a Freeman: Observations on His Character, Condition and Prospects in Virginia*. Williamstown, Va.: Corner House Publishers, 1970. First published 1889 by G. P. Putnam's Sons.

Brundage, W. Fitzhugh. *Lynching in the New South: Georgia and Virginia, 1880–1930*. Urbana: University of Illinois Press, 1993.

———, editor. *Under Sentence of Death: Lynching in the South*. Chapel Hill: University of North Carolina Press, 1997.

Caldwell, C. T. *Historical Sketch of the First Presbyterian Church, Waco, Texas*. Waco, Tex.: Methodist Home Press.

Carver, Charles. *Brann and the Iconoclast*. Austin: University of Texas Press, 1957.

Cole, David. *No Equal Justice: Race and Class in the American Criminal Justice System*. New York: New Press, 1999.

"Colorful Career of Noted Jurist Closed by Death." *Waco News Tribune* (February 6, 1942): 5.

Conger, Roger Norman. *Highlights of Waco History*. Waco, Tex.: Hill Printing and Stationery Company, 1945.

———. "Insults, Innuendos and Invective: Waco in 1897." *Waco Heritage and History* 9, no. 3 (Fall 1978): 21–32.

———. "Photographs Tell the Story. Gildersleeve/Waco. Gildy Remembered." *Waco Heritage and History* 7, no. 4 (Winter 1976), 10 pages [unnumbered].

———. *A Pictorial History of Waco with a Reprint of Highlights of Waco History*. 2d ed. Waco, Tex.: Texian Press, 1998.

Cook, Raymond A. *Fire from the Flint: The Amazing Careers of Thomas Dixon*. Winston-Salem, N.C.: John F. Blair, 1968.

———. *Thomas Dixon*. New York: Twayne Publishers, 1974.

Coons, C. Wilbur. "Waco—a Typical Texas City: Her Past, Her Present, Her Future." *Texas Magazine* (April 1910): 66–68.

Cooper, Madison. *Sironia, Texas*. 2 vols. Boston: Houghton Mifflin, 1952.

"Correspondence: Lynching." *The Nation* (July 13, 1916): 34–35.

"Court's Entry Not Finished When Mob Secured Negro." *Waco Times Herald* (May 16, 1916): 1.

Courtwright, David T. *Violent Land: Single Men and Social Disorder from the Frontier to the Inner City*. Cambridge, Mass.: Harvard University Press, 1996.

Creech, James C., Jay Corzine, and Lin Huff-Corzine. "Theory Testing and Lynching: Another Look at the Power Threat Hypothesis." *Social Forces* 67:3 (March 1989): 626–30.

Crouch, Barry. "A Spirit of Lawlessness: White Violence; Texas Blacks, 1865–1868." *Journal of Social History* 18 (Winter 1984): 217–32.

Crowe, Charles. "Racial Massacre in Atlanta: September 22, 1906." *Journal of Negro History* 54:2 (April 1969): 150–73.

Curry, William H. *A History of Early Waco with Allusions to Six-Shooter Junction*. Waco, Tex.: Texian Press, 1968.

Davis, Horace B. "A Substitute for Lynching." *The Nation* (January 1, 1930): 12–14.

Davis, Margaret. "Harlots and Hymnals: An Historic Confrontation of Vice and Virtue in Waco, Texas." *Waco Heritage and History* 9:3 (Fall 1978): 1–20.

Dawson, Carol. "Cooper's Town." *Texas Monthly* (November 2000): 70–76.

Dawson, Joseph M. *A Thousand Months to Remember*. Waco, Tex.: Baylor University Press, 1964.

"The Detective's Report." *Richmond Planet* (October 14, 1899): 1.

Dodge, Bertha S. *Cotton: The Plant That Would Be King*. Austin: University of Texas Press, 1984.

Dollard, John. *Caste and Class in a Southern Town*. 3d ed. Garden City, N.Y.: Doubleday Anchor Books, 1957. First published 1937 by Yale University Press.

Downey, Dennis B. and Raymond M. Hyser. *No Crooked Death: Coatesville, Pennsylvania, and the Lynching of Zachariah Walker*. Urbana: University of Illinois Press, 1991.

Dray, Philip. *At the Hands of Persons Unknown: The Lynching of Black America*. New York: Random House, 2002.

Dubois, Ellen Carol. *Harriot Stanton Blatch and the Winning of Woman Suffrage*. New Haven, Conn.: Yale University Press, 1997.

Du Bois, W. E. B. "The Anti-Lynching Fund." *The Crisis* (September 1916): [unnumbered page], 219–20.

———. *The Autobiography of W. E. B. Du Bois: A Soliloquy on Viewing My Life from the Last Decade of Its First Century*. New York: International Publishers, 1968.

———. *Black Reconstruction in America: An Essay toward a History of the Part Which Black Folk Played in the Attempt to Reconstruct Democracy in America, 1860–1880*. New York: Free Press, 1998. First published 1935 by Harcourt Brace.

———. *The Correspondence of W. E. B. Du Bois*. Edited by Herbert Aptheker. Vol. 1, 1877–1934. Amherst: University of Massachusetts Press, 1973.

———. *Dusk of Dawn: An Essay toward an Autobiography of a Race Concept*. New Brunswick, N.J.: Transaction Publishers, 1984. First published 1940 by Harcourt, Brace & World.

———. "The Shape of Fear." *North American Review* 223:2 (June–July–August 1926): 291–305.

———. *The Souls of Black Folk*. New York: Penguin Books, 1995. First published 1903 by A. C. McClurg.

———. "The Waco Horror." *The Crisis*, supplement to July 1916 issue.

Duty, Tony. "Waco at the Turn of the Century." *Waco Heritage and History* 3:2 (Summer 1972): 1–18.

"Editorial Notes." *New Republic* (June 3, 1916): 102.

"Famed Waco Photographer Dies at 77." *Waco Times Herald* (February 26, 1958): 1–2.

"Farmers from Robinson Form Mob and Search Jail for Black Brute" *Waco Morning News* (May 10, 1916): 1.

"Final Words from Bob Buchanan, 'I Want to Be Your Next Sheriff.'" *Waco Times Herald* (July 26, 1918): 10.

Fischer, David Hackett. *Albion's Seed: Four British Folkways in America*. New York: Oxford University Press, 1989.

Foner, Eric. *A Short History of Reconstruction*. New York: Harper & Row, 1990.

Ford, I. Gustavus R. "An Open Letter." *Washington Bee* (May 27, 1916).

Ford, Linda. *Iron-Jawed Angels: The Suffrage Militancy of the National Woman's Party, 1912–1920*. Lanham, Md.: University Press of America, 1991.

"Former Sheriff Fleming Buried." *Waco Times Herald* (February 20, 1952): 14.

"Fourth Murder Officially Charged to Mitchell." *Waco Times Herald* (February 1, 1923): 1.

Franklin, John Hope. *The Militant South, 1800–1861*. Cambridge, Mass.: Harvard University Press, 1970. First published 1956 by President and Fellows of Harvard College.

Fredrickson, George M. *The Black Image in the White Mind: The Debate on Afro-American Character and Destiny, 1817–1914*. Hanover, N.H.: Weslayan University Press, 1987. First published 1971 by Harper & Row.

Freeman, Elizabeth. "A Day at an English Bye-Election." *American Suffragette* 1:8 (February 1910): 24ff.

"The Fruitage of Mob Rule." *Waco Semi-Weekly Tribune* (May 20, 1916).

Gannett, Lewis. "Villard and His 'Nation.'" *The Nation* (July 22, 1950): 79–82.

Gerber, David A. "Lynching and Law and Order: Origin and Passage of the Ohio Anti-Lynching Law of 1896." *Ohio History* 83 (Winter 1974): 33–50.

Getzendaner, W.H. "Early Banking Experiences in Texas." *Texas Magazine* (October 1909): 33–35.

Gilje, Paul A. *Rioting in America*. Bloomington: Indiana University Press, 1996.

Ginzburg, Ralph. *100 Years of Lynchings*. Baltimore, Md.: Black Classic Press, 1962.

Graham, Stephen. *Children of the Slaves*. New York: Johnson Reprint Company, 1970. First published 1920 by Macmillan and Co.

"Grand Jury Indicts Slayer of Mrs. Fryar." *Waco Times Herald* (May 11, 1916): 5.

Grant, Donald L. *The Way It Was in the South: The Black Experience in Georgia*. Edited by Jonathan Grant. Athens: University of Georgia Press, 1993.

Greene, A. C. *The 50+ Best Books on Texas*. Denton: University of North Texas Press, 1998.

Hale, Grace Elizabeth. *Making Whiteness: The Culture of Segregation in the South, 1890–1940*. New York: Vintage Books, 1998.

Hall, Jacquelyn Dowd. *Revolt against Chivalry: Jessie Daniel Ames and the Women's Campaign against Lynching*. Rev. ed. New York: Columbia University Press, 1993.

Harlan, Louis R., and Raymond W. Smock, eds. *The Booker T. Washington Papers*. Urbana: University of Illinois Press, 1981.

"Harris Goes to Stegall and Surrenders." *Waco Times Herald* (May 27, 1922): 1, 3.

Harrison, Patricia Greenwood. *Connecting Links: The British and American Woman Suffrage Movements, 1900–1914*. Westport, Conn.: Greenwood Press, 2000.

Harvey, Sheridan. "Marching for the Vote: Remembering the Woman Suffrage Parade of 1913." *Library of Congress Information Bulletin* 57:3 (March 1998).

Haynes, Robert V. *A Night of Violence: The Houston Riot of 1917*. Baton Rouge: Louisiana State University Press, 1976.

Historic Waco. Waco, Tex.: Historic Waco Foundation, 1970.

History of New Hope Baptist Church, 1866–1976. Pamphlet, Waco–McLennan County Library.

Hixson, William B., Jr. *Moorfield Storey and the Abolitionist Tradition*. New York: Oxford University Press, 1972.

Holden-Smith, Barbara. "Lynching, Federalism, and the Intersection of Race and Gender in the Progressive Era." *Yale Journal of Law and Feminism* 8, no. 31 (1996): 31–78.

Holmes, William F. *The White Chief: James Kimble Vardaman*. Baton Rouge: Louisiana State University Press, 1970.

"The Horror at Waco." *Houston Chronicle* (May 16, 1916): 8.

Howe, M. A. DeWolfe. *Portrait of an Independent: Moorfield Storey, 1845–1929*. Boston: Houghton Mifflin, 1932.

Humès, D. Joy. *Oswald Garrison Villard: Liberal of the 1920s*. Syracuse, N.Y.: Syracuse University Press, 1960.

"John Dollins Dies 11:55 A.M. Saturday." *Waco Times Herald* (May 3, 1930): 1.

Johnson, Charles S. *Growing Up in the Black Belt: Negro Youth in the Rural South*. New York: Schocken Books, 1970. First published 1941 by American Council on Education.

Johnson, James Weldon. *Along This Way: The Autobiography of James Weldon Johnson*. New York: Da Capo Press, 1973. First published 1933 by Viking Press.

———. "Chance for Humanity." *New York Age* (May 25, 1916).

———. "Those Valiant Texans." *New York Age* (June 1, 1916).

"Judge Lynch At His Worst." [Illegible] (May 20, 1916). Clipping file, NAACP Archives, NAACP Administrative File, Sub file under Lynching: Waco, Texas, 1916, Library of Congress.

"Jury Gives Mitchell Death Penalty." *Waco Times Herald* (March 18, 1923): 1, 4.

Kelley, Dayton, editor. *The Handbook of Waco and McLennan County, Texas*. Waco, Tex.: Texian Press, 1972.

Kellogg, Charles Flint. *NAACP: A History of the National Association for the Advancement of Colored People*. Baltimore, Md.: Johns Hopkins University Press, 1967.

Kennedy, Randall. *Race, Crime and the Law*. New York: Pantheon Books, 1997.

Kesler, J. L. "In Justice to Waco." *The Nation* (December 28, 1916): 609.

Kirchwey, Freda. "Oswald Garrison Villard." *The Nation* (October 8, 1949): 340.

"Last Legal Texas Hanging Recalled." *Dallas Morning News* (November 8, 1953).

"Letter from Rev. A. H. Shaw." *Woman's Journal* (August 27, 1910): 142.

Lewis, David Levering. *W. E. B. Du Bois*. Vol. 1: *Biography of a Race, 1868–1919*. New York: Henry Holt, 1993.

Litwack, Leon. *Trouble in Mind: Black Southerners in the Age of Jim Crow*. New York: Vintage, 1999.

Logan, Rayford W. *The Betrayal of the Negro from Rutherford B. Hayes to Woodrow Wilson*. New York: Da Capo Press, 1995. First published 1965 by Collier Books.

Luebke, Frederick. *Nebraska: An Illustrated History*. Lincoln: University of Nebraska Press, 1995.

Luscomb, Florence H. "American Girls Abroad." *Woman's Journal* (June 10, 1911): 178–79; (June 24, 1911): 195.

Maier, Pauline. *From Resistance to Revolution: Colonial Radicals and the Development of American Opposition to Britain, 1765–1776*. New York: W. W. Norton, 1991. First published 1972 by Alfred A. Knopf.

"Majors Denies His Guilt in Austin Jail." *Waco Times Herald* (July 22, 1905): 2.

"Majors Given Death Penalty by the Jury." *Waco Times Herald* (August 3, 1905): 5.

"Majors Was Hanged by a Mob." *Waco Times Herald* (August 8, 1905): 5.

McSwain, Betty Ann McCartney, editor. *The Bench and Bar of Waco and McLennan County, 1849–1976, including Reprint of Waco Bar and Incidents of Waco History, by William M. Sleeper and Allan D. Sanford*. Waco, Tex.: Texian Press, 1976.

McWhiney, Grady. *Cracker Culture: Celtic Ways in the Old South*. Tuscaloosa: University of Alabama Press, 1988.

Meier, August, and John H. Bracey Jr. "The NAACP as a Reform Movement, 1909–1965: 'To Reach the Conscience of America.'" *Journal of Southern History* 59:1 (February 1993): 3–30.

Meier, August, and Elliott Rudwick. *Along the Color Line: Explorations in the Black Experience*. Urbana: University of Illinois Press, 1976.

"Message to Wilson Taken from Hikers." *New York Times* (February 28, 1913): 3.

Miller, Rick. *Sam Bass and Gang*. Austin, Tex.: State House Press, 1999.

"Mitchell Admits All Crimes and Hangs Monday with Smile." *Waco Times Herald* (July 30, 1923): 1, 3.

"Mitchell in Good Spirits." *Waco Times Herald* (February 10, 1923): 1.

"Mob Rule Is Blot on State, Munroe Says." *Waco Times Herald* (January 3, 1922): 1, 3.

"Mob Takes Negro from Court House, Burns Him at Stake." *Waco Times Herald* (May 15, 1916): 1, 5.

Monroe, Andy. "The Man Who Built the Raleigh Hotel." *Waco Heritage and History* 14:2 (Winter 1983): 1–18.

"Monstrous and Abominable." *Austin American* (May 17, 1916).

Morrell, Caroline. *"Black Friday" and Violence against Women in the Suffragette Movement*. London: Women's Research and Resources Centre Publications, 1981.

"Moving against Lynching." *The Nation* (August 3, 1916): 101–102.

Mumford, Lewis. "Introduction to *Politics and the Poet*, a Prophecy by J. E. Spingarn." *Atlantic Monthly* (November 1942): 73–74.

National Association for the Advancement of Colored People (NAACP). *Mobbing of John R. Shillady, Secretary of the National Association for the Advancement of Colored People at Austin, Texas, August 22, 1919.* New York: NAACP, 1919.

———. *Thirty Years of Lynching in the United States, 1889–1918.* New York: Arno Press/New York Times, 1969. First published 1919 by the NAACP.

"Negro Burned to a Stake in the Yard of the City Hall." *Waco Semi-Weekly Tribune* (May 17, 1916): 7.

"Negro Confesses to Terrible Crime at Robinsonville." *Waco Times Herald* (May 9, 1916): 1, 5.

"Negroes Arrested in Murders." *Waco Times Herald* (January 30, 1923): 1, 8.

"A Negro's March with Muffled Drums." *Survey* (August 4, 1917): 405–406.

"Negro's Murder Story." *Waco Times Herald* (February 9, 1923): 1, 10.

Nock, Albert Jay. "What We All Stand for." *American Magazine* (February 1913): 53–57.

Ottley, Roi. *The Lonely Warrior: The Life and Times of Robert S. Abbott.* Chicago: Henry Regnery, 1955.

Ovington, Mary White. *The Walls Came Tumbling Down.* New York: Harcourt, Brace, 1947.

Pankhurst, Emmeline. *My Own Story.* Westport, Conn.: Greenwood Press, 1985. First published 1914 by Hearst's International Library Co.

"Parade Struggles to Victory Despite Disgraceful Scenes." *Woman's Journal* (March 8, 1913): 73, 78.

Patterson, Orlando. *Rituals of Blood.* New York: Basic Civitas, 1998.

"Phillip Peabody Gives $20,000 to Fight Lynching." *Chicago Defender* (August 5, 1916).

"Preparations for Execution Roy Mitchell." *Waco Times Herald* (July 22, 1923): 1, 5.

"Punished a Horror Horribly." *New York Times* (May 17, 1916): 10.

Raper, Arthur. *The Tragedy of Lynching.* New York: Arno Press/New York Times, 1969. First published 1933 by the University of North Carolina Press.

Reed, John Shelton. "Comment on Tolnay, Beck and Massey." *Social Forces* 67:3 (March 1989): 624–25.

"Robinson Gives Assurance Will Not Molest Murderer." *Waco Morning News* (May 13, 1916): 6.

Rosenbaum, H. Jon, and Peter C. Sederberg, editors. *Vigilante Politics.* Philadelphia: University of Pennsylvania Press, 1976.

Rosenbaum, Ron. *Explaining Hitler: The Search for the Origins of His Evil.* New York: Random House, 1998.

Ross, B. Joyce. *J. E. Spingarn and the Rise of the NAACP, 1911–1939.* New York: Atheneum, 1972.

"Roy Mitchell on Stand." *Waco Times Herald* (March 17, 1923): 1, 8.

"Roy Mitchell to Hang Tomorrow Forenoon." *Waco Times Herald* (July 29, 1923): 1, 7.

Rudwick, Elliott. *Race Riot at East St. Louis, July 2, 1917.* Urbana: University of Illinois Press, 1982. First published 1964 by Southern Illinois University Press.

Russell, Charles Edward. *Bare Hands and Stone Walls: Some Recollections of a Side-Line Reformer.* New York: Scribners, 1933.

St. James, Warren D. *The National Association for the Advancement of Colored People: A Case Study in Pressure Groups.* New York: Exposition Press, 1958.

"Sam Fleming Is Running on Record for Re-Election." *Waco Morning News* (May 25, 1916): 11.

Senechal, Roberta. *The Sociogenesis of a Race Riot: Springfield, Illinois, in 1908.* Urbana: University of Illinois Press, 1990.

Shapiro, Herbert. *White Violence and Black Response: From Reconstruction to Montgomery.* Amherst: University of Massachusetts Press, 1988.

"Sheriff's Alertness Saves Negro's Life." *Waco Times Herald* (May 10, 1916): 7.

"Shocking Exhibition of Mob Rage." *Houston Post* (May 17, 1916): 6.

Short, James F., and Marvin Wolfgang. *Collective Violence*. Chicago: Aldine-Atherton, 1972.

Sleeper, John. *A Brief History of the Mayors of the City of Waco, Texas, 1849–1934*. Prepared for the Historical Society of Waco and McLennan County, Texas, Waco, 1934.

———, and J. C. Hutchins. *Waco and McLennan County, Texas, Containing a City Directory of Waco, Historical Sketches of the City and County, Biographical Sketches and Notices of a Few Prominent Citizens*. Waco, Tex.: Texian Press, 1966. First published 1876 by J. W. Golledge.

Smith, J. B. "Coming to Terms with 1916 'Horror.'" *Waco Tribune Herald* (May 31, 1998): 1A, 6A, 7A.

SoRelle, James. "The 'Waco Horror': The Lynching of Jesse Washington." *Southern Historical Quarterly* 86:4 (April 1983): 517–37.

"Special Session of Grand Jury Called To Consider Robinson Murder Case." *Waco Morning News* (May 11, 1916): 5.

Stevens, Doris. *Jailed for Freedom: American Women Win the Vote*. Edited by Carol O'Hare. Troutdale, Ore.: NewSage Press, 1995. First published 1920 by Boni & Liveright.

Storey, Moorfield. *Problems of Today*. Boston: Houghton Mifflin, 1920.

"'Suffrage First' T.W.S.A. 1916 Slogan." *Dallas Morning News* (May 8, 1916): 8.

"Swift Vengeance Wreaked on Negro after Jury Brings in Death Penalty." *Waco Morning News* (May 16, 1916): 1, 5.

"Sworn Confession by Jesse Washington." *Waco Times Herald* (May 10, 1916): 4.

Taylor, A. Elizabeth. *Citizens at Last: The Woman Suffrage Movement in Texas*. Austin, Tex.: Ellen C. Temple, 1987.

"A Terrible Crime in Texas." *The Independent* (May 29, 1916): 325.

"There Never Was Any Chili Anywhere Else Like Dillard's." *Waco Tribune Herald*, centennial special section (October 30, 1949).

Tolnay, Stewart E., and E. M. Beck. *A Festival of Violence: An Analysis of Southern Lynchings, 1882–1930*. Chicago: University of Chicago Press, 1995.

———, and James L. Massey. "Black Lynchings: The Power Threat Hypothesis Revisited." *Social Forces* 67:3 (March 1989): 605–23.

———. "The Power Threat Hypothesis and Black Lynching: 'Wither' the Evidence?" *Social Forces* 67:3 (March 1989): 634–40.

Tolson, Mike. "A Deadly Distinction: Between Life and Death Borderline Capital Cases Raise Questions of Justice." *Houston Chronicle* (February 5, 2001): 1ff.

"To Lynch or Not to Lynch." *Outlook* (January 24, 1917): 137–38.

Toomer, Jean. *Cane*. New York: Norton, 1988. First published 1923 by Boni & Liveright.

Torrance, J. R. "Eighty Years on Horseback." Collected and compiled by Roger Conger. *Waco Heritage and History* 13:2 (Spring 1982): 1–33.

Travis, Marion. *Madison Cooper*. Waco, Tex.: Word Books, 1971.

———. "Waco Has a Hero." *Waco Heritage and History* 11:3 (Fall 1980): 1–11.

Turner, Terry J. "Photographs by Gildersleeve, Waco." *Waco Heritage and History* 1:2 (Summer 1970): 15–27.

Van Deusen, Marshall. *J. E. Spingarn*. New York: Twayne Publishers, 1971.

Veit, Richard J. "From Waco to Round Rock: The Last Days of Sam Bass." *Waco Heritage and History* 19:1 (September 1989): 44–54.

Villard, Oswald Garrison. *Fighting Years: Memoirs of a Liberal Editor*. New York: Harcourt, Brace, 1939.

Waco City Directory, various years. Houston, Tex.: Morrison & Fourmy Directory Co.

"The Waco Holocaust." *Dallas Express* (May 20, 1916).

"Waco Negro Lawyer Admitted to Bar of Supreme Court." *Waco Morning News* (April 12, 1916): 3.

Waldrep, Christopher. *The Many Faces of Judge Lynch: Extralegal Violence and Punishment in America*. New York: Palgrave Macmillan, 2002.

Walker, Henry. "Southern White Gentlemen Burn Race Boy at Stake." *Chicago Defender* (May 20, 1916): 1.

Walker, Samuel, Cassia Spohn, and Miriam Delone. *The Color of Justice: Race, Ethnicity and Crime in America*. 2d ed. Belmont, Calif.: Wadsworth, 2000.

Wallace, Patricia Ward. *Our Land, Our Lives: A Pictorial History of McLennan County*. Norfolk, Va.: Donning Company, 1986.

———. *A Spirit So Rare: A History of the Women of Waco*. Austin, Tex.: Nortex Press, 1984.

———. *Waco, a Sesquicentennial History*. Virginia Beach, Va.: Donning Company, 1999.

———. *Waco: Texas Crossroads*. Woodland Hills, Calif.: Windsor Publications, 1983.

Walling, Anna Strunsky, editor. *William English Walling: A Symposium*. New York: Stackpole Sons, 1938.

Walling, William English. "The Race War in the North." *The Independent* (September 3, 1908): 529–34.

Weatherford, Doris. *A History of the American Suffragist Movement*. Santa Barbara, Calif.: ABC-CLIO, 1998.

Webb, Walter Prescott. *The Texas Rangers: A Century of Frontier Defense*. 2d ed. Austin: University of Texas Press, 1980. First published in 1935 by Houghton Mifflin.

Wedin, Carolyn. *Inheritors of the Spirit: Mary White Ovington and the Founding of the NAACP*. New York: John Wiley & Sons, 1998.

"The Week." *The Nation* (May 18, 1916): 530–31.

Wells-Barnett, Ida B. *Lynch Law in Georgia: A Six-Weeks' Record in the Center of Southern Civilization, as Faithfully Chronicled by the "Atlanta Journal" and the "Atlanta Constitution."* Chicago: Chicago Colored Citizens, 1899.

———. *Southern Horrors and Other Writings: The Anti-lynching Campaign of Ida B. Wells, 1892–1900*. Edited by Jacqueline Jones Royster. Boston: Bedford/St. Martins, 1997.

White, Walter F. *A Man Called White: The Autobiography of Walter White*. Bloomington: Indiana University Press, 1948.

———. *Rope and Faggot: A Biography of Judge Lynch*. Manchester, N.H.: Ayer Company, 1992. First published in 1929 by Knopf.

"[Illegible] White Man for Crime Which Boy Was Lynched: Police Jail Husband of Dead Woman," *Chicago Defender* (June 10, 1916): 7.

"Who Will Cast the First Stone." *Waco Morning News* (May 24, 1916): 4.

Williamson, Joel. *The Crucible of Race: Black-White Relations in the American South since Emancipation*. New York: Oxford University Press, 1984.

"The Will-to-Lynch." *New Republic* (October 14, 1916): 261–62.

Winston, J. T. "Lynching Defended." *The Nation* (June 22, 1916): 671.

Zangrando, Robert L. *The NAACP Crusade against Lynching, 1909–1950*. Philadelphia: Temple University Press, 1980.

Zeigler, Oscar Woodward. "White Man and Negro." *The Nation* (July 27, 1916): 82.

Papers, Theses, and Dissertations

Armstrong, Julie Buckner. "The Infamous Story of Mary Turner: Neglected but Not Forgotten." Paper presented February 28, 2001, at Valdosta State University.

Ellis, Mary Louise. "'Rain Down Fire:' The Lynching of Sam Hose." PhD diss., Florida State University, 1992.

Findley, James Lee, Jr. "Lynching and the Texas Anti-Lynch Law of 1897." Master's thesis, Baylor University, 1974.

Francesoni, Gino. "The Carnegie Hall Studios." Paper by the director of the Carnegie Hall Archives. N.d.

Gordon, John Ramsay. "The Negro in McLennan County, Texas." Master's thesis, Baylor University, 1932.

Harvey, Sandra Denise. "Going Up Bell's Hill: A Social History of a Diverse, Waco, Texas, Community in the Industrial New South, 1885–1955." Master's thesis, Baylor University, 1995.

Smith, Rogers Melton. "The Waco Lynching of 1916: Perspective and Analysis." Master's thesis, Baylor University, 1971.

Walters, Katherine Kennis Kuehler. "The Great War in Waco, Texas: African Americans, Race Relations, and the White Primary, 1916–1922." Master's thesis, Southwest Texas State University, 2000.

Internet Sources

Handbook of Texas Online: http://www.tsha.utexas.edu/handbook/online.

INDEX

Photos are indicated with *italic* typeface.